A Bee in the Mouth

A Bee in the Mouth

Anger in America Now

PETER WOOD

ENCOUNTER BOOKS
NEW YORK

First edition published in 2006 by Encounter Books, an activity of Encounter for Culture and Education, Inc., a nonprofit, tax exempt corporation.

Encounter Books website address: www.encounterbooks.com

Manufactured in the United States and printed on acid-free paper.

The paper used in this publication meets the minimum requirements of ANSI/NISO Z39.48-1992 (R 1997)(*Permanence of Paper*).

FIRST EDITION

Library of Congress Cataloging-in-Publication Data

Wood, Peter
    A bee in the mouth: anger in America today/Peter Wood
        p. cm.
        ISBN 1-59403-053-7

1. United States—Social conditions—21st century. 2. Anger—Social aspects—United States. 3. Social psychology—United States. 4. Popular culture—United States—Psychological aspects. 5. National characteristics, American. I. Title.

HN59.2.W683 2006
303.60973'090511-dc22
2006013255

10 9 8 7 6 5 4 3 2 1

CONTENTS

To Ingrid Wood

PREFACE

"A bee in the mouth is always bad." I was walking down Bay State Road in Boston in summer 2004 when I heard a workman say this to his partner. He was gripping one end of a blue Plexiglas shower stall that they had hauled out of a townhouse. Having lugged their wobbly load down the steps only to discover that their truck was gone, they were understandably angry. But when his partner began to curse the absentee driver, the older of the two offered his bee-in-the-mouth observation. I have never succeeded in tracing this seeming proverb. Maybe he made it up. Or maybe he had once accidentally inhaled a yellow jacket and knew whereof he spoke.

"A bee in the mouth" was an apt phrase for the stinging language coming from the shower de-installer, but that fellow is certainly not alone in having venomous things to say and no compunction about saying them. The bee in the mouth of that particular workman has whole hives of cousins angrily buzzing in the mouths of politicians, pundits, and professors. Some of America's most popular music today consists of rhymed vituperation, as though the singers had swallowed a nest of hornets. Our sports are filled with trash talking; the Internet swells with bee-mad bloggers stinging the press and each other; and talk radio offers a diet of all-umbrage-all-the-time.

A lot of Americans have noticed the excesses of anger in our midst, but we are having a hard time deciding why it has suddenly swarmed around us. Is it the consequence of two bitterly fought presidential elections? Are the news media to blame? Have we endured a slow erosion in civility that has finally exposed the raw feelings underneath? Have we developed a hair-trigger intolerance for one another?

Some scholars assure us that this profusion of anger isn't really new. Americans, say these scholars, were always angry. We had an uncivil Boston Tea Party and an eight-year Revolution. We had a presidential election in 1800—Adams vs. Jefferson—at least as nasty as Bush vs. Gore or Bush vs. Kerry. We fought a bloody Civil War with over a million casualties. And we can't forget the 1960s, replete with protests, riots, teargas, and more protests.

Some scholars also argue that the angry "culture war" of recent years ("red states" vs. "blue states"; NASCAR fans vs. Volvo drivers; Sunday-morning-go-to-church vs. Friday night at the vegan Dean rally) is mainly an illusion. We are, they say, mostly in agreement on the important matters, and it is the political elites and the controversy-hungry media that conjure up the so-called "culture war."

I think these views are mistaken. The anger we see and hear around us differs in character from the anger of previous epochs, and it is no illusion. The anger of the present is, among other things, more flamboyant, more self-righteous, and more theatrical than anger at other times in our history. It often has the look-at-me character of performance art.

For instance, in mid-July 2004, Ben Cohen, the cofounder of Ben & Jerry's Ice Cream, launched his Pants on Fire Tour in Spokane, Washington. Cohen planned to tour the country, as an Associated Press writer put it, "towing a 12-foot tall effigy of President Bush with fake flames shooting out of the pants."[1] This was presumably a not-so-subtle subtle allusion to the children's rhyme, "Liar, liar,/Pants on fire."

The anger in America now also differs from earlier epochs in that many people seem proud of their anger. It has become a badge of authenticity, and holding back or repressing anger is often depicted as a weakness or failure of self-assertion rather than a worthy form of self-control. We have elaborated this view into several popular theories that encourage the expression of anger as a way for members of ethnic groups, women, political parties, children, or people in general to "empower" themselves. This is new. However angry Americans were in 1776, 1800, 1860, or 1963, they were not congratulating themselves for getting angry.

The people and situations that evoke our anger today also differ in some interesting ways from angers past. Today we don't pick too many fights over family honor; and we don't seem to get especially worked up by people who defy our authority. We can be calm in the face of insults that not so long ago would have led to armed duels. But then we flare into livid fury for reasons that would have baffled our ancestors.

What was the nineteenth-century equivalent of road rage on the Los Angeles freeways? Something has happened to us that allows hugely disproportionate responses to what are, after all, small provocations. We also can get furious if we feel disrespect aimed at our self-definition. "Take me seriously" is the message of much of our anger, where, in another time and place, a self-reliant American would have shrugged and walked away. Some of the contemporary rhetoric of anger is based on claims that our *rights* have been violated. Rights-based grievances are old, but our sense of what those rights are has ballooned beyond anything Jefferson, Lincoln, W. E. B. Du Bois, or even Justice Earl Warren might have imagined. And our anger is especially sharp at those who pretend to be one thing and really are another. A characteristic anger of our times enunciates outrage at the phony, the hypocrite, the liar, and the fake—so much so that we often reframe anger caused by something else into an accusation of phoniness, hypocrisy, lying, and fakery. They are the trump cards in our anger deck.

The performance-art aspect of anger; its merit-badge "I'm angry, therefore I'm real" quality; and road-rage-respect-me-rights-based-you're-a-liar fury are not the only

characteristics of what I call the New Anger. They will do for
a start, but a principal aim of this book is to provide an
overview of the new emotional terrain in which anger has
achieved prestige and a kind of celebrity. We have become,
without really noticing it, a culture that celebrates anger.
Beyond tracing the beelines through various departments of
America, from everyday life through politics, music, feminism, the counterculture, sports, and the media, I offer an
explanation of *why* we have found not just one but many
bees in our mouth.

Early in 2006, a small political ruckus broke out over a
remark by Ken Mehlman, chairman of the Republican
National Committee. Speaking on ABC's *This Week* (February 5), he said that Senator Clinton "seems to have a lot of
anger," and added, "voters do not send angry candidates to
the White House."[2] Within a few days, Democrats and left-
leaning pundits responded by attacking the Republicans for
running an "anger strategy." They countered the depiction of
Hillary with the claim that it is the Republicans, including
Mehlman, who really are angry. George Lakoff, a University
of California at Berkeley linguistics professor who frequently
advises Democrats about how issues are rhetorically framed,
accused Mehlman of deploying a sexist stereotype, "the
crone—angry, nasty, but powerful."[3]

Whether Hillary Clinton's public persona and temperament will remain topics of political "I'm rubber, you're glue"
remains to be seen, but the episode did, once and for all,
bring the peculiar dynamic of contemporary political anger
out in the open. We now know that, although many millions
of Americans regard their own anger as empowering, in the
national political arena an angry temperament is still seen
as a defect. We also know that Hillary Clinton's political
ambitions are bound to incite a great many repetitions of
the feminist cliché that men are honored for their anger
while women are castigated for theirs. The truth is considerably more complicated, but the reminder that men and
women get angry in different ways and often about different things is worth bearing in mind.

As to the bee-in-the-mouth phrase, having missed my opportunity to ask the workman where he got it, I have since tried without much success to find it elsewhere. The *Guinness Book of World Records* says that a man has held 109 honeybees in his closed mouth for ten seconds. In August 1997, Mr. David Skorupa in Glasgow, Scotland, died of anaphylactic shock after being stung by a bee in the mouth. A passenger on a bus in Laurie Fox's novel *My Sister from the Black Lagoon* (1999) explains that "Certain people scream because of what's inside them. Like, you know, having bees in the mouth." The horror film *Candyman 2* features a sequence in which a character has live bees in his mouth. The "bee wrangler" who managed that special effect had to vacuum them out afterward.[4]

These little discoveries suggested some reasons why having a bee in the mouth might make a person anxious, but didn't cast much light on the workman's calm philosophy. Because I thought his accent Middle Eastern, I asked around, but found no sources in Arabic, Persian, Armenian, or Turkish. I tried further afield: Albanian, Uzbeck, and Urdu. No luck.

There are many reasons why someone might not enjoy the company of a fellow with a bee in his mouth, but the phrase also suggests that the danger is posed as much or more to the owner of the mouth than to his companions. Of course, to tell an angry person, in effect, "You are only hurting yourself" is sanctimonious and might well escalate the anger.

A story is told of both Plato and St. Ambrose that when they were infants, a swarm of bees flew in and out of their mouths, presaging their future eloquence. (A bee in the mouth, apparently, isn't *always* bad.) Ambrose, as it happened, grew up to have special wisdom about anger, counseling his followers that when confronted by anger, they should keep their mouths shut:

> When we find ourselves in company with quarrelsome, eccentric individuals, people who openly and unblushingly

say the most shocking things, difficult to put up with, we should take refuge in silence, and the wisest plan is not to reply to people whose behavior is so preposterous. Those who insult us and treat us contumeliously are anxious for a spiteful and sarcastic reply: the silence we then affect disheartens them.... Leave them to chew the cud of their hasty anger.[5]

St. Ambrose became the patron saint of beekeepers. One legend, however, says that near the end of his life, the bees returned and stung Ambrose on the mouth, rendering him mute.[6]

Perhaps this was a warning against being too free with advice. *This* book, however, is not a self-help manual. The excessively angry have legions of anger management therapists to turn to and bookstore shelves devoted to helping the choleric personality find his or her inner Gandhi.

Actually, some therapists and self-help manuals seem to be aimed more at helping the milquetoast personality find his inner Rasputin. For example, while many counselors have warned that chronic anger is a cause of heart disease and other ailments, such counsel doesn't sit well with some *furiosos*. When a recent study at the University of California at San Francisco purported to show that *women* with high levels of anger are at no increased risk of heart disease compared to women with sunnier dispositions, the Women's Bioethics Project heralded the news: "Feeling Angry? Good for You!"[7]

Well, maybe. My aim is neither to cure anger nor to enhance its undoubted pleasures. Rather, I want to describe our New Anger in contrast to our older habits of emotional restraint and then to explain how it became so widespread and so intense in American life.

Let's take our antivenom serum with us and find out what has caused all this angry buzzing.

ONE

ANGRI-CULTURE

December 2, 1983, a postal worker named James Brooks opened fire on his manager, the postmaster of Anniston, Alabama, killing him and wounding another supervisor. Mr. Brooks started a trend of sorts. In the following decade, ten other post office shootings around the nation left thirty-five people dead, and inspired the term "going postal" for that boil of frustration that results in murderous rage.[1]

Anger that triggers a man (it's almost always a man) to pack a gun to work and shoot people is rare and, of course, not culturally sanctioned. It does, however, occupy a place in our collective imagination. Most of the time, when we use the phrase "going postal," we don't mean a murderous rampage. We mean, instead, a noisy, dramatic outburst against someone—usually a bureaucrat—who has exhausted someone's patience. The *metaphor* of going postal, not Mr. Brooks and his flesh-and-blood imitators, says something about the sardonic, darkly self-pleased way in which many Americans regard expressions of anger.

The symbolic representation of anger has, in fact, become ubiquitous in American life, and like other stuff we see every day, has ceased to be especially noticeable. By way of experiment, one day, notebook in hand, I took a fifteen-minute walk through Boston's Kenmore Square, in the shadow of Fenway Park. My goal was to press the question:

how many symbolic expressions of anger would I find in those few minutes?

Naturally, I started at the post office. "I see dumb people," read a bumper sticker on a car parked in front, declaring the driver's notional contempt for whatever portion of humanity crossed his path. The smalltime misanthrope was apparently inside dealing with the clerks. "I see dumb people" plays off the catchphrase for the movie *The Sixth Sense* (1999), in which the psychic child, Cole Sear, says, "I see dead people." The twist in the movie is that the dead people didn't know they were dead. The bumper sticker thus coyly abuses other drivers who presumably don't realize their own lack of mental agility. The bumper sticker thus presents the owner's hauteur and offers a general insult to fellow drivers. But is it angry?

A young man swaggered past in baggy jeans and a black sweatshirt, the hood—fringed with silver spikes, a corona of malice—thrown back, taunting passersby. Nearby a young red-toenailed woman sits on some steps lapping an ice cream, unperturbed for the moment by whatever demon of self-loathing caused her to sew her own face and leave the needles in. Perhaps both the boy and the girl are better understood as making fashion statements. But then the question becomes, why the popularity of fashions that represent hostility and self-loathing?

I don't judge either the boy or the girl to have been angry when I saw them—not angry as physiologists describe the state. Their pulses didn't drag; their temperatures weren't rising or falling. They weren't scowling; they didn't glare. They neither flushed red nor turned pale. They weren't twitching; they didn't clench their fists. They looked relaxed, rather than tensed. They weren't sweating. If I had sent drops of their blood to a laboratory, I would have expected to find that neither had been secreting noradrenaline, the chemical trigger to the bodily signs of anger. No, they were just two people mindful of a fine afternoon.[2]

But while neither of them was literally angry, both were adorned with the insignia of anger. And to some extent, that harmonized with their environment. Like the bumper sticker, the boy's baggy jeans and hood with silver spikes and the girl's face mutilated with an assortment of needles and pins were not direct expressions of emotion, but they summed up an emotional stance that an individual chose to convey as his general attitude. Moreover, these were not just private, wholly individual statements, however much the individuals themselves might have liked to believe so. Rather, they were personal appropriations from the wardrobe and accessories of American culture. The bumper sticker played on a tag line from a mass-market movie. The baggy jeans, spikes, and pins were the easily read insignia of easily recognized precincts of popular style. The baggy jeans announced identification with hip-hop, and along with the hooded sweatshirt, they suggested a young man who took his bearings from gangsta rap. The girl's self-mutilations announced that she saw herself in the post-punk scene. The driver, the boy, and the girl all sported an implied message, "Don't mess with me."

The New Anger is not a set of isolated events: a swollen-faced speech by Al Gore here, a rant by Dennis Miller there; a protest against globalization and the WTO this week, a march against gay marriage next week. The New Anger may seem at times to flare up suddenly like a sunspot to fry our satellites and give us a week of northern lights. But the spectacular examples are misleading. They wouldn't happen if anger had not settled in as part of everyday life. New Anger in this sense is all around us all the time, invisible to the eye though we breathe it in like air pollution. On a particularly bad day, we may notice it. People around us seem especially rude and unpleasant; we encounter road rage (or worse, commit it); or we unexpectedly run into an anger exhibitionist. But generally the smog stays just below the threshold of what we notice. We've grown used to it, and having breathed it so long, we've actually made it part of ourselves.

Across the street from the young man and woman, near Fenway Park, a man was selling "Yankees Suck" ball caps.

Nearby, a car CD system was humping the rhythms of the rapper 50 Cent:

> ...control your jealousy
> 'Cause I can't control my temper, I'm fittin' to catch a felony
> Pistol in hand homie, I'm down to get it poppin'
> Once I squeeze the first shot [gun shot], you know I ain't
>   stoppin'
> Till my clip is empty, I'm simply
> Not that nigga you should try your luck with, or fuck with
> Hollow-tip shells struck you with your bones broken, gun
>   smokin', still locin...

Hip-hop is music of self-aggrandizement and power and sex; but it is mostly anger music. Not that it is alone in this category. The teenage and young adult audience has among its alternatives old thrashers such as Metallica's "St. Anger," Ablaze My Sorrow's "Anger Hate and Fury" (AMS's anger seemingly extends to commas), Flake's "Wild Cool Anger," the Anger Brothers pop act, and the Ministers of Anger. Matisyahu, a Jewish rapper from Crown Heights, in a recent song advises, "Slam your fist on the table and make your demand."

An MBTA bus rumbled by, its side emblazoned with an ad for FCUK—which stands for "French Connection United Kingdom," the hip purveyor of clothing, cosmetics, and accessories to those whose tastes in acronyms run to the puerile. FCUK's website offers games as well as merchandise. In "Not Idol," for example, the player can use "FCUK's instruments of torture" to eliminate "Barry," a cartoon character who auditions for the popular TV show *American Idol* even though "his voice sucks big time." The theme seems to be that buyers of FCUK merchandise are the folks cool enough to humiliate those who, though lacking talent, have the audacity to seek attention. Anger at attention seekers in those who themselves seek attention by wearing FCUK-emblazoned clothes may seem perilously close to home, but the French Connection United Kingdom calculates that teenagers draw fine distinctions among forms of self-advertisement.

At the corner was a row of plastic news boxes with the week's supply of free tabloids. Here for sure was a distillation of fashionable attitudes. The *Weekly Dig* commenced with Ted Rall's cartoon depicting Americans torturing Iraqis; plugged an anti-Bush product, "National EmbarrassMints"; and reviewed local music and art. In her column, "Screaming from the Gallery," Kate Ledogar framed her review of a photography show by grousing that her car had been towed because she hadn't paid her tickets. One of the photographs praising Snow White's evil stepmother as "beautiful, assertive, and constantly asking questions" prompted Ledogar to reflect, "There it is! It's all those fairy tales that poisoned me into passivity, made me think that some big, shiny man would come and rescue me from my predicaments. That's why I've been getting all these parking tickets...."[3]

Ledogar's tone was not anger but ironic helplessness. That theme in a way ties together the culture reviews, the sex ads ("I'm temporarily yours"), the comics page (Bush feeding American soldiers into a giant meat grinder), and the personals ("I'm not angry! Just wanna have fun!"). If these folks are not *exactly* angry, anger is the sun around which they orbit, and in its heat they feel their own torpor, self-contempt, disdain for others, and longing for escape.

The newspaper vending machines themselves have been defaced and the original defacements themselves defaced with stickers for alternative rock bands and the scrawled initials of kids desperate to make a mark somewhere. But perhaps it is too much to read "anger" into www.coppermine.com's attempt to snag a little free attention with its sticker on the vending machine. The stealing of a few square inches of public space *feels* like an act of aggression, but is it?

On this particular day, I see no road-raging drivers, no pushing matches, and no lovers' jagged quarrels in Kenmore Square. If anger is present, it is only in the small texture of things, where lives and artifacts mingle, for the moment unnoticed, except by someone bent on noticing. This subtexture of the world that humans create for themselves is one of the meanings we anthropologists give to the word *culture*.[4]

Ambient Anger

Culture in this sense may not intrude into our conscious thought very often. It is rather a context that we take for granted, save when we deliberately place it on display to affirm it, or on those infrequent occasions when it erupts by itself. Angri-culture, however, surrounds contemporary Americans. It is, of course, most visible in our politics, where its icon is probably the face of the former presidential candidate and Vermont governor Howard Dean, brows arched, eyes aflame, veins bulging, and maxillary muscles stretched to their extremes in a rictus of rage. But Dean crossed some invisible line: anger is OK up to the point where it becomes genuinely scary—and just there the angri-culture draws its limits.

The Dean-style rage assumes an audience of people who respond positively to the histrionics of extreme anger; but the example of a public figure abandoning himself so completely, in turn, gives everyday anger a lift. It says, in effect, "Society is run by conniving people who are in it for themselves. You are being screwed. Your anger is justified." Then if we are not actually feeling angry, we can at least pay homage to the emotion with the little flags of anger pasted to our cars or stitched into our skin.

Is this ambient anger really justified? Anger in a certain sense is always hanging around waiting for the opportunity to take charge. Often all that is needed to turn an underlying frustration into an outbreak of real anger is someone to enunciate the grievance. A key difference between New Anger and old anger, however, is the vagueness and elasticity of the grievances. Angri-culture issues an extremely broad warrant for getting angry and a still broader one for striking angry poses even when we are not actually angry. The angri-culture is more a pervasive attitude than a specific grievance. Indeed, the word "attitude" has recently emerged as a synonym for a generally surly disposition—for example, "That girl has attitude."

Consider the contrast between "that girl" and the six-foot Carry Nation, dressed in crepe, chopping her impressions into the saloons of the 1890s with her trademark hatchet. Carry Nation was an angry woman, and her hymn-singing female vanguard conveyed a righteous contempt for men who drank, whether a shot of whiskey or a growler of beer. But the anger of the Prohibitionists was focused and specific. Can we say the same of Rage Against the Machine? We now live in a society in which a great many people *seem* angry for trivial reasons or no reason at all.

In the winter of 2003–2004, Governor Dean became the political face of some of this anger. He took hold of a particular theme, opposition to the war in Iraq, and fused it with what had been until that moment the inchoate contempt that many Democrats felt toward President Bush. As a candidate, however, Dean proved maladroit, stumbling for an untimely consistency, for example, when he responded dismissively to the capture of Saddam Hussein. Dean summoned the sea monster of anger into a presidential campaign, but he had no ability to control the beast. His loss in the primaries came as Democrats worried that a candidate whose main talent was to galvanize the wrathful would not be able to win the votes of calmer, more pragmatic centrists.

The Dean campaign was thus one of those instances in which widespread but typically invisible attitudes suddenly emerge in spectacular form. Governor Dean didn't invent contemporary angri-culture; he just gave it political salience. But if the good doctor from Vermont was only channeling an anger that already existed, where did that anger start? The two most direct sources were opposition to the wars in Afghanistan and Iraq, along with the domestic security policies enacted after 9/11; and the resentments of Gore supporters over the U.S. Supreme Court's intervention in the 2000 presidential election. Dean, however, supported the Afghan war, only later taking issue with the follow-up. In a 2003 interview, he said that the best policy for the United

States in Afghanistan would be to build a middle class "where women fully participate in the government."[5] And as recently as December 2005, he called for an additional twenty thousand American troops to be sent to Afghanistan.[6] These views have sometimes irritated Dean's own supporters.[7] So Dean did not rise as the personification of the Angry Left by identifying himself with its whole agenda at the time.

These two grievances were well articulated and lodged like a bone in the throats of some political partisans by the summer of 2003, but they had yet to become themes that defined a broader political movement. That was Dean's accomplishment in winter 2003–2004, and it was all the more remarkable in light of his ignoring all of the actual grievances (with the exception of Iraq) in favor of simply channeling the anger. Anger over the 2000 presidential election had not really settled into a longing for Al Gore as president. Democrats regretted no longer holding the White House, but it was hard to detect nostalgia for the scandal-ridden Clinton administration. Opposition to the wars in Afghanistan and Iraq likewise had an elusive quality: the anger was far more apparent than its source. No one wished to defend the regimes of the Taliban and Saddam Hussein; and very few held that "the War on Terror" was itself a mistake. The denunciation of the Department of Homeland Security and the actions of Attorney General Ashcroft as present dangers to domestic civil rights similarly seemed far angrier than could be justified by a list of specific abuses.

The Patriot Act, passed in the weeks following 9/11, gradually emerged as the Left's symbol of the supposed erosion of American rights and freedom under the Bush administration. But frequently people became angry about the Patriot Act without being able to give any instance of how it had damaged civil rights. The consequences were occasionally peculiar. In mid-December 2005, for example, a University of Massachusetts at Dartmouth professor told a local reporter that one of his students had been interrogated by federal agents after trying to borrow a copy of a book by Mao Tse-tung. The story spread quickly and was repeated by

Senator Edward Kennedy in an anti-Bush op-ed article in the *Boston Globe*, just before the student confessed that the whole matter was a hoax.[8] Before the hoax was revealed, the story had already spread through the national media and an account had been posted on the American Library Association website. Why the readiness to believe a story that didn't even pass muster with the *Boston Globe*'s editors? Perhaps there is a thirst for evidence to substantiate a strongly held but weakly supported suspicion that the federal government is abusing its powers under the Patriot Act.

The magnitude of much of today's announced anger mismatches the apparent motives. Something is missing. To explain the electoral anger that Governor Dean tapped as the reservoir of bad feeling among opponents to the War on Terror and as lingering resentment over the 2000 Florida recount fails to register the eagerness with which some Americans moved from disappointment and disagreement to a caustic and often aggressive form of anger.

The Left's politics, in other words, seems to fall far short as explanation for the emotional tone that has emerged in the last few years. Just how did we become so infatuated with anger?

To answer this question, we have to start with a wider-ranging exploration of the angri-culture. I have mentioned its subtexture (its all-but-invisible background in our everyday lives); the feedback loop between public exemplars of New Anger and ordinary folks foregoing patience for petulance; the vagueness and elasticity of its grievances; and its disproportionate quality. We need to look also at cultural changes in the assessment of angry people; a flattening of the American emotional range; the therapeutic rationales for anger—and the newer therapeutic "anger management's" ambiguous repudiation of some of those rationales; the "liberating" quality now assigned to anger, along with its exhibitionist and theatrical forms; the notion of anger as "authenticating," and its related roles as a badge of identity and a credential for group membership. As the angri-culture has risen to a national ideal, it has also connected to and partially transformed old fantasies of righteous revenge. And all of these factors play into the delight that the true embracers of New Anger feel with their uninhibited rage. The angri-culture is, in this sense, an overthrow of older ideals of temperance and self-control.

The best way to get a sense of the angri-culture is to contrast some of the older forms of anger and resistance to anger with their counterparts today. Chapter Two provides some of those contrasts—in our imagined views of anger, in our actual behavior, and in our moralistic and therapeutic responses. Chapter Three explores the differences between acting angry and being angry, and reaches back to the American Revolution to illuminate what it means *not* to act angry when one really is. Chapter Four explores the arrival of New Anger at the center of American politics, with particular attention to Bush-hatred. Chapter Five examines anger in popular American music. Anger enters into all of the arts, but music most directly captures and shapes our emotional repertoire. Chapter Six examines the ways in which Americans explain and justify their anger—often by characterizing it as self-empowering. The patterns of self-justification differ among men and women, and feminism has played a very large part in valorizing women's anger. Chapter Seven offers a historical and generational explanation of how and why New Anger emerged at this point in our history. Broadly, I argue that it is the late-arriving product of the expressive individualism championed in the 1950s by a variety of dissenters from traditional American values. It is late arriving because to achieve cultural salience, it had to await a generation brought up by parents opposed to the older ethic of self-restraint. Chapter Eight examines New Anger as part of our public spectacle: in sports and the media, with special attention to the newest medium, the blogosphere.

TWO

POLLYANNA MEETS TAR-BABY

I n 1913, on the eve of World War I, an American novelist named Eleanor Porter published a children's book
about the orphaned daughter of a missionary who goes
to live with her crabby but well-off aunt in Vermont.
The child, dressed in donated clothes and sent on her way
by the Ladies' Aid Society, has endured a lot, but she is surprisingly cheerful. Consigned to a bare garret in her aunt's
house, she exults in the view from its window. Assigned as
punishment to read a pamphlet on the filthiness of flies, she
declares, "I love to read!" Her secret? She confides to the
housemaid, Nancy, that her father taught her a game: "to just
find something about everything to be glad about—no matter what 'twas."

The name of Porter's heroine, Pollyanna, has long since
become a byword for naïve optimism in the face of grim facts.
Pollyanna's aunt and partial namesake, Polly—austere, punc-
tual, and perhaps a bit *too* concerned with houseflies—may
not be entirely to our taste either, but at least she *is* angry.
Pollyanna cannot seem to rise to life's provocations with anything more extreme than a tearful smile. As conceived by
Eleanor Porter, however, Pollyanna is not the simpleton of our
catchphrase, "Don't be a Pollyanna." She is rather a strong-
willed child who succeeds in bringing adults, including Aunt
Polly, around to her side. Steadfast, tough-minded optimism
proves more potent than self-pity or angry complaint.

Our ancestors were not oblivious to the seductions of anger. They understood that some people get accustomed to expressing harsh feelings and enjoy the petty tyranny that this gives them over meeker people, whether members of their family or employees. The angry husband or wife, the angry parent, and the angry boss were familiar figures in life and in fiction. Dickens' Scrooge is a man driven much more by anger than by greed. Milton's Satan is a figure in which anger is built on a foundation of envy and pride. Shakespeare gives us a whole gallery of angry characters.

Hotspur, in *Henry IV, Part I,* enters a scene reading a letter from a lord who declines to join his plot. Muttering, "He shows in this he loves his own barn better than he loves our house," Hotspur listens with half an ear as his wife, Lady Percy, complains about his sleepless preoccupation with battle, which diverts him even from the marriage bed. As she realizes he isn't listening because of his angry fixation, she too gets (mock) angry:

> Out, you mad-headed ape!
> A weasel hath not such a deal of spleen
> As you are tossed with.

And he replies in banter that mixes his euphoria over the coming battle with his affection for her. What we see in Hotspur is a man in whom anger is a tonic. It makes him sparkle with energy and wit. He likes his anger.

Another of Shakespeare's history plays, *King Richard the Second,* opens with the king hearing two angry young men, Bolingbroke and Mowbray, accuse each other of lying and treason. As King Richard puts it, they are "full of ire, / In rage deaf as the sea, hasty as fire." He orders the pair of "wrath-kindled gentlemen" to forgo a duel and to forgive each other. Mowbray, however, says he can't forgive Bolingbroke's insult, which "no balm can cure but his heart-blood," and, hearing this, Bolingbroke won't back down either. The king then agrees to their settling the matter by combat—though he later exiles them instead. Anger seems to give both young men a force that King Richard does not know properly how to deal with.

It might be possible to create a taxonomy of anger using Shakespeare's characters—Titus, Timon, Coriolanus, Lear, Antony over Caesar's body, Othello, Shylock, Caliban—but, despite the variety, anger in Shakespeare's characters always seems a dangerous intoxicant that variously blights good judgment, stirs destructive passions, and gives a false clarity to the world. Shakespeare, of course, drew on the medieval theory of the humors, in which anger was traced to an excess of "choler." An angry person was literally "out of balance."

The rewards of anger for the person who indulges it were the same then as now: a feeling of domination, at least for the passing moment; frustration giving way to a sense of power; and a surge of clarity. The angry person is decisive. He knows what is to be done and who is to blame. Anger makes things happen.

But the habitually angry person was also seen as weak and unhappy as well as troublesome to others. The heroic figures in the eyes of Americans from the eighteenth through much of the twentieth century generally were not angry men. Although they may have been men who had good grounds for grievance, most kept their wrath from getting the better of them. Dignity, manliness, and wisdom called for self-control and coolness of temper. Exceptions, such as Aaron Burr and John Brown, come to mind—but they stood out to their contemporaries *as* exceptions. Burr was a man whose frustrated ambitions led him angrily into disloyalty to the country he had served as vice president. John Brown was maddened with divine fury against slavery, but such frenzy was its own lesson: Brown destroyed his family and himself. As Hawthorne said of him, "Nobody was ever more justly hanged."[1] Better to consult Teddy Roosevelt's mantra of national self-control, "Walk softly and carry a big stick." In Owen Wister's novel *The Virginian,* the hero offers what became classic advice to those who test the limits of familiarity. A fellow addresses him "you son-of-a-___," to which the Virginian answers, "When you call me that, *smile.*" Anger is ready and waiting in that answer, but quiet strength comes first.

America has its own history of anger as yet largely unwritten, but it is woven into our politics, sermons, literature, and behavior. John Wise was a Puritan cleric born in Roxbury, Massachusetts, in 1652. He was imprisoned for a time for agitating against the royal governor, Sir Edmund Andros, whom the king imposed on Massachusetts Bay Colony. Later, Wise wrote a pamphlet defending "The Churches' Quarrel" with the monarchy. Even the idea of arbitrary government, he said in 1710, puts "an Englishman's blood into a fermentation." But when such a government actually comes along and "shakes its whip over their ears, and tells them it is their master, it makes them stark mad." The "Englishmen" that Wise refers to are Americans, and he warns that they have a "memical genius" that will lead them, angrily, to respond to arbitrary government by turning "arbitrary too." Sixty-six years before the Revolution, Wise provided a pretty precise account of what makes Americans angry.

Wise's text ought to be better known than it is, but we do have a national fable known to almost all Americans that encodes our best wisdom about anger. It is Joel Chandler Harris's retelling of an African American folk tale, "Brer Rabbit and Tar-Baby." Brer Fox "fix up a contrapshun w'at he call a Tar-Baby" and puts Tar-Baby on the side of the road. Brer Rabbit comes pacing down the road and is astonished to see Tar-Baby, but shows his good manners:

> "Mawnin'!" sez Brer Rabbit, sezee—"nice wedder dis mawnin'," sezee.
> Tar-Baby ain't sayin' nothin', and Brer Fox, he lay low.

Brer Rabbit grows exasperated in trying to make conversation with Tar-Baby; Brer Fox continues to lie low; and Brer Rabbit, losing his temper, punches Tar-Baby:

> Present'y Brer Rabbit draw back wid his fis', he did, en blip he tuck 'er side we de head. Right dar's whar he broke his merlasses jug. His fis' stuck, en he can't pull loose. De tar hilt 'im. But Tar-Baby, she stay still, en Brer Fox, he lay low.

Brer Rabbit, enmired in his own anger, becomes angrier still, kicks Tar-Baby, and becomes completely trapped.

"Did the Fox eat the Rabbit?" asked the little boy to whom Uncle Remus has told the story. "Dat's all de fur de tale goes," replied the old man.[2]

American popular literature offers many other fables that give instruction about anger, but one more that is certainly still alive in popular memory is the closing scene of Dashiell Hammett's *The Maltese Falcon.*

> Spade pulled his hand out of hers [Brigid O'Shaughnessy's]. He no longer either smiled or grimaced. His wet yellow face was hard set and deeply lined. His eyes burned madly. He said, "Listen. This isn't a damned bit of good. You'll never understand me, but I'll try once more and then we'll give it up. Listen. When a man's partner is killed he's supposed to do something about it. It doesn't make any difference what you thought of him. He was your partner and you're supposed to do something about it."[3]

The movie version with Sam Spade played by Humphrey Bogart is completely faithful to Hammett's text, which continues with Spade's reasons why he intends to hand over O'Shaughnessy to the police.

Spade's monologue isn't angry, but that's the point: he is subduing his passions to his code. The proper response to the murder of his partner isn't anger but "to do something about it." The skein of betrayals that have led to this crisis in his life might prompt him to be furious—and he may love the murderess, though Hammett hasn't been very convincing on that point. But instead of declaring his feelings, he almost desperately spins out his analysis of why he must act as he does.

Brer Rabbit traps himself in anger, Brer Spade steels himself against it and becomes the original of the hard-boiled detective. We still have this archetype who refuses to indulge anger, but he is increasingly giving way to the Hulk, the Punisher, and a myriad of other characters for whom, to the contrary, the anger just can't be controlled.

If we want to understand today's angri-culture, we need to develop this sense of how different it is from views that prevailed in the past. Anger has always been part of both private and public life, but in our time it has gained a wholly new status.

Don't Forgive My Anger

The 2004 presidential election turned anger into a topic of political debate in the United States. The "Angry Left" attacked President Bush with a vitriolic gusto not seen since the far-off days when demonstrators chanted, "Hey, hey, LBJ, how many kids did you kill today?" After the election, the mood on the left only darkened. The senior managing editor of the *Boston Phoenix,* Clif Garboden, summed up his view of Bush's victory under the headline, "Screw You America: Sometimes the Fish in the Barrel Deserve to Die." Mr. Garboden began his screed, "Don't forgive my anger."

Domestic politics, however, isn't the only venue for bruised and bruising feelings. Anger bubbles up in nearly all contexts of American life. When the Indiana Pacers guard Ron Artest leapt into the stands at the basketball game with the Detroit Pistons on November 19, 2004, to pummel a spectator he wrongly believed had thrown a plastic cup of beer at him, he lived up to his reputation for hot-headedness. Artest was known for confrontations on and off the court; on a previous occasion, after his team had lost, he smashed a $100,000 television camera. But the brawl he started that November night was more than just the antics of one player lacking self-control. Rather, it reflected a deeper change in one of America's popular sports.

The National Basketball Association in recent years has shed its image of graceful teamwork and players with nicknames like "Magic" and sunny smiles, in favor of what many call a "thug league." One sportswriter calls it "gangstaball." Games feature hip-hop music and tattooed players who exhibit tough-guy attitudes. An investigative journalist, Jeff Benedict, reports that "40 percent of the NBA players have a police record for serious offenses such as assault, rape and robbery." The mood of spectators at basketball games has likewise shifted to courser expressions of antagonism—such as hurling cups of beer.

Angry sports fans, of course, are not limited to America. Foul-mouthed, bumptious, and angry fans have turned some European soccer games into melees. But the resemblance may be misleading. What's happening in the United States is a generational change that has made open displays of anger stylish. The NBA is only one organization that has attempted to keep up with the times by exploiting the new style.

Anger in America also has flavors besides that of stale, airborne beer. Americans have mastered a kind of exuberant show-off anger. It is as if the sunnier side of our national disposition got in the way of the grimmer forms of crankiness. Hollywood has discovered the humorous potential of the emotion in such films as *Anger Management* (2003) and, more recently, *The Upside of Anger* (2005). The latter presents Terry (played by Joan Allen) as a wife deserted by her husband and left with four daughters. The trailer begins with the line, "Terry is mad at the world," but her anger leads to romance with her ex-ballplayer neighbor Denny (played by Kevin Costner). Another 2005 movie took the romance of domestic anger up several notches. In *Mr. and Mrs. Smith,* husband-and-wife professional assassins played by Brad Pitt and Angelina Jolie rekindle the spark in their marriage by attempting to kill each other with weapons ranging from a bazooka to an exploding elevator. It's played for laughs, but part of the joke is that the characters indeed come alive—and feel sexual attraction—only after becoming murderously enraged. If we can make light of it, how mad at the world and at each other can we really be? Is American anger real or is it a pretense?

The anger that now plays such a large role in our public life, our sports and entertainment, our work, and our domestic lives is in fact a mix of wrath and swagger. While people have always gotten angry and expressed their anger (e.g. John Wise's 1710 tract, Aaron Burr's 1804 duel with

Hamilton, and John Brown's 1859 raid on Harpers Ferry), something about today's expressions of anger *is* new: anger has been transformed from a suspect emotion that most people struggled to keep under control, to a fashionable attitude that many people strive to "get in touch with" and exhibit in public. The imaginary Vermonter, Pollyanna, has been replaced with the incendiary Vermonter, Howard Dean.

This transformation enters into our culture in all sorts of ways. The *Wall Street Journal* recently took notice of one unexpected outlet for our new fascination with all things angry. In "Why Cars Got Angry," Jonathan Welsh explains, "Car makers used to strive for an inviting face, but lately they're pushing an edgier look: Car faces that look meaner, angrier and, at times, even downright evil." Accompanying photos show model years of the BMW 3 Series sports sedan beginning in 1968, getting meaner and meaner over time. Welsh quotes Kirk Perry, a business owner in Lake Owassa, New Jersey, professing his attraction to the "wide, snarling look" of the Audi Q7. The Hyundai HCD9, the 2005 Dodge Charger, and the Chrysler 300 sedan ("gaping grille and headlights that seem to scowl") also make the grade. Of course, anger isn't for everybody. Mini Coopers and Volvos, according to Welsh, are resisting the trend.[4]

Not so long ago—a matter of a few decades—a person giving free vent to anger was seen as weak and rather pathetic. The anger-prone who did not control their wrath were disdained as having a character flaw. Religions—Protestant, Catholic, and Jewish—taught that most anger was a sin; and the secular world pronounced intemperate anger as a sign of immaturity or sometimes an illness. The heroes of America, from George Washington to Jackie Robinson, were self-controlled individuals, who if roused to anger, kept it in its place and outsmarted or outplayed their foes. Should it light, the bee of anger was crushed, not cosseted.

Today, many Americans have adopted an entirely different view of anger. We feel entitled to *express* that emotion, and perhaps more importantly, we feel justified in *feeling* it in the first place in contexts where earlier generations would have felt ashamed. Clif Garboden, in responding to President Bush's electoral victory, gloats in having feelings that better men would be ashamed of. For some of us it goes even further: beyond feeling and verbal expression to outright acts of angry aggression. But the bee in the mouth, rather than the gun in the hand, is the most conspicuous sign of the newness of New Anger. The anger we speak (and write, gesture, sing, growl, and shout) in both private and public now comes in many flavors: multicultural righteous; leftist sneer; right-wing snivel; patriotic rage; ironic cooler-than-thou; and designer flavors like Paul Krugman's contempt, Ann Coulter's lividness, and Rev. Pat Robertson's prophetic-unhinged.

New Anger tends more to the political left than to the political right—the conservative "angry white male" of a few years ago having turned much of his attention back to Home Depot and bass fishing. At center stage today are the virulent Bush-haters, with their buttons ("Bush Lied, People Died"; "Hail to the Thief"; "Bush is a Dumbass"); bumper stickers ("Compassionate Conservatism is an Oxymoron, George Bush is Just a Moron"); and boutique conspiracy theories (e.g. Michael Moore's idea that the war against the Taliban in Afghanistan was motivated by Bush's desire to help a company that builds oil pipelines). This is not to say that New Anger is absent on the right. In fact, right-wing New Anger has its own websites (e.g. *Little Green Footballs*), its own demons (Ted Kennedy, Noam Chomsky, Jane Fonda), and its own bumper stickers ("Stop Global Whining"; "I ♥ Gitmo"; "Guns Don't Kill People, Abortion Clinics Kill People"). But perhaps because I have spent most of my time in the last decade in Massachusetts, Vermont, and New York, I have to work hard to spot public displays of New Anger on the right, while the public displays of New Anger on the left are as common as Che Guevara T–shirts.

Is the political polarization of the United States the root cause of New Anger that is just spilling over into nonpolitical domains of life? Or did New Anger precede the specific distempers of Clinton-hating and Bush-hating? When we take a close look, I think it is unmistakable that New Anger came *before* the political inflammations in which it is most conspicuous, and that New Anger is broader and more *pervasive* than politics.

My view runs squarely against what many political observers are saying. They think this national epidemic of anger is mainly the creation of political elites and their ratings-conscious friends in the national media. But New Anger was preening itself in many contexts before it ran for office or auditioned for prime time.

This is not to minimize the political aspect of New Anger. Our politics are now angrified to an extraordinary degree and in a new and dangerous way. New Anger in politics means that we have discovered a new kind of political satisfaction: deriding an opponent for the sheer pleasure of expressing contempt for other people.

As a nation we have had many previous occasions of public rancor. The most rancorous in the estimate of many historians was the period leading up to and following the presidential election of 1800 between John Adams and Thomas Jefferson. Adams' commercially minded, mainly northern supporters viewed Jefferson as a would-be tyrant, a man of low morals, and a closet atheist. Jefferson's agrarian, mainly southern supporters viewed Adams as a hypocritical betrayer of the Revolution, ready to sell the nation back to the British. The two candidates tied in the Electoral College, and the tie was broken only by a secret deal that got one of Adams' supporters to switch his vote. The bitterness endured for years. Can today's anger top this?

In truth, there is no way of knowing. We can't count units of anger. Then as now, partisan feeling ran high and many people publicly declared things that in calmer times they would regret. What really distinguishes New Anger from the anger circa 1800 is *the embrace of anger on a mass scale as a positive sentiment*—as a way of feeling good about oneself and coping with everyday life.

I don't mean to say there are no legitimate reasons for political excitement in opposing views and candidates we disagree with. But that excitement has been spiked with a new ingredient that has changed its character. Some observers thought the anger in the 2004 presidential election was merely an especially intense version of the usual political pulse. But that was a misreading of the situation. What really happened in 2004 was that New Anger passed the threshold from being a phenomenon of the political fringe to being mainstream. Major political figures adopted New Anger postures as part of their political repertoire, and advocacy groups that rejected old forms of political suasion in favor of New Anger tactics—groups such as MoveOn.org and America Coming Together—ended up as the dominant voice of the Democratic Party. As a result, even politicians who are not by temperament suited to New Anger theatrics, such as Senator Hillary Clinton, have begun to adopt the mannerisms of New Anger, as when Senator Clinton went to a church in Harlem for the Martin Luther King Jr. Day celebration in 2006 and said that the U.S. House of Representatives "has been run like a plantation, and you know what I'm talkin' about."[5]

New Anger will continue to add its distinctive kick to the divisive arguments between left and right, turning political defeats into occasions of vicious rebukes and victories into fleering smugness. This indeed has happened in earlier times in our Republic, but never with such relaxed self-approval, as though anger were its own vindication and savory reward. New Anger is by no means exclusively or even primarily a political concoction. It is, rather, the expression of a new cultural ideal that emphasizes the importance of individual authenticity achieved through the projection of personal power over others. New Anger is a modality—perhaps the most important modality—of an increasingly common personality type. It is the type that the historian Christopher Lasch called "narcissistic" a generation ago, but in the intervening years we have had the chance to get to know these narcissists a little better, and especially to see how their stance toward the world plays out in their lives and relationships.[6]

But precisely because New Anger is everywhere, it is also part of American politics, and in the political context it achieves a kind of mutant grandiosity. New Anger politics is the fusion of the "red state"/"blue state" cultural divide with the narcissism of the 1970s human potential movement. Differences of political opinion, which were in principle negotiable, are transformed into claims of identity, which cannot be negotiated. We are watching the emergence of a ferocious politics of "I am right because I am me." Cross that line or even hint that a compromise may be in order and you unleash a political rage founded on the Newly Angered person's sense of being personally threatened.

New Anger is anger that congratulates itself. It is as though the person with the bee in his mouth mistook the repeated stings for the sweetness of the honeycomb. An administrative assistant in Harvard's social studies department, Norah Burch, lost her job in May 2004 when her supervisor read her blog, www.AnnoyYourFriends.com, which was linked to her e-mail signature via her homepage.[7] Ms. Burch's blog contained some disturbing declarations:

> I'm two nasty e-mails from professors away from bombing the entire Harvard campus.[8]

> I was ready to get a shotgun and declare open season on all senior faculty members and students who dared cross me.

Personnel matters are usually pretty discreet. We know about Ms. Burch's dismissal because she published a self-defense in the *Boston Globe,* and her justification captures perfectly the complacencies of the New Anger–prone:

> I used my online diary as a steam valve for my administrative assistant job.... Dealing with obstinate and nasty professors and students, I found that a quick one—or two— minute rant in my blog would calm my nerves enough so that I could return to productivity.... To me, blogging became a sort of electronic primal scream, one that saved the eardrums of my neighbors and co-workers.

Ms. Burch's tone of wounded innocence—the death threats were, after all, a service to her employer, since they helped her return to productivity—is the crucial thing. She was admittedly angry, but not dangerous. Her employer "couldn't prove [her] performance suffered in any way." No harm, no foul, at least in her sense of the situation. Upon getting reprimanded, she "was in shock and felt a little humiliated."

Ms. Burch was shocked because she lives in a world where expressing anger—even in the hyperbolic terms of bombs and shotguns—is a legitimate form of self-expression. How can self-expression that doesn't involve actual dynamite or bullets be taken amiss?

New Anger, Left and Right

The same question hangs over a recent book, *Checkpoint,* by the novelist Nicholson Baker. *Checkpoint* is a conversation between two old friends, Jay and Ben, about murdering President George W. Bush with a variety of lethal weapons. It is very hard to imagine that a respectable publisher—*Checkpoint* was issued by Alfred A. Knopf—would have put its name on such a lurid fiction in the days of FDR, Eisenhower, or Kennedy. But Knopf now speaks with a voice much like Ms. Burch's. The publisher blurbs the book as the "most audacious novel yet" by the "most original writer of his generation." Audacious, apparently, but well within the range of current literary sensibilities. *"L'audace, l'audace, toujours l'audace,"* the cry of yesterday's avant-garde, has become the tinkling of today's cash register.

On news of the book's impending publication, a speechwriter for the first President Bush, Mark Davis, took urgent notice of the cultural shift that Nicholas Baker and Knopf were partly surfing, partly accelerating:

> *Checkpoint,* whatever its literary conceits, will be an act of linguistic terrorism. "He is beyond the beyond," the *Washington Post* reports the main character saying of Bush. "What he's done with this war. The murder of the innocent. And now the prisons. It makes me so angry. And it's a new kind of anger, too."[9]

Mark Davis was himself angry about the book, but clearly he expressed an old anger, one that catches itself and fears excess. He conjured a time when most partisans had "an internalized reality check," and those who didn't were brushed off rather than published by Knopf. He concludes, "Today's Left has lost its way."

Well, yes. The left is especially lost in New Anger, but, once again, it is not *just* the left. New Anger is more comprehensive, reaching down to the one- and two-minute anger breaks demanded by administrative assistants like Ms. Burch. But the political side of New Anger does divide into two very different emotional styles.

In broad terms, the left is angry because it had incorrectly assumed that it had won all the important debates and deserved to hold political power. But in 2001, it found that the House and the presidency were in the hands of Republicans, and the Senate (with the defection of formerly Republican Senator Jeffords of Vermont to the status of "Independent") evenly divided. Worse still, culturally conservative Republicans held the key positions. The left, comfortable in its long dominance of the media and the universities and convinced that any opposition was founded on some combination of stupidity, ignorance, and corruption, responded to the new situation with incredulity. How could this have happened? And it answered its own question by insisting that it hadn't happened. Bush was not "elected." Rather, he stole the election with the help of the U.S. Supreme Court and gained public backing only by deception. Thus the anger motto of the left became "Bush lies." In the light of unclouded truth, the left would have its legitimate place in command of the government and in the hearts of all worthy Americans.

The emotional center of the left's anger is an unbridled fury at having been dispossessed of a birthright. The left generally cannot conceive that its opponents are intelligent or possess well-reasoned arguments, and losing to an inferior is a bitter thing. The response, focusing on President Bush, is to insist ceaselessly that conservatives *are* inferior, in both intellect ("Bush is a moron") and moral stature ("The murder of the innocent. And now the prisons."). This form of anger combines righteous indignation with utter contempt for the adversary.

Meanwhile on the right, a very different set of irritations have produced a different kind of anger. Conservatives have achieved a measure of political power, but they continue to feel their marginalization by the arbiters of culture. Whether they turn to TV news or Hollywood movies, they find their views ignored or derided. In college classrooms, they are often caricatured as racist, sexist, environment-despoiling, militaristic jerks. Intellectually serious conservative arguments are airbrushed out of the *New York Times* picture of America, and the great herd of newspapers, newsmagazines, and television newsrooms that take their lead from the *Times* follow suit. Rock and hip-hop merit the attention of savvy critics, while country music, despite its immense popularity, is treated as having the cultural significance of monster truck rallies. The conservative churches typically find themselves treated by the leftist establishment as a looming danger to American rights and freedoms. When a cultural event that is rooted in conservative ideals breaks through to a mass audience, as happened with Mel Gibson's *The Passion of the Christ,* the cultural establishment hammers it with full force.

Issues that conservatives take as profoundly serious, such as the defense of the traditional family against court-ordered gay marriage, get muffled and distorted in the mainstream press. In the gay-marriage debate, for example, the mainstream press unrelentingly framed the issue as "civil rights" for gays vs. the Religious Right's biblically based bigotry. Even after the U.S. Senate's two-day debate on the Federal Marriage Amendment put a plainly secular argument on the table (that gay marriage in Scandinavia and the Netherlands has sent heterosexual marriage into a nosedive and hugely increased the percentage of children who grow up in one-parent households), the press stuck fast to its presumption that the debate was really nothing but a matter of enlightened advocates of civil rights facing off a rabble of homophobes.

Conservatives are used to this treatment, and it extends to numerous issues such as abortion, school prayer, gun ownership, school choice, immigration, and affirmative action. The right responds to this broad exclusion of its views from the zone of cultural respectability partly by evoking an imaginary world (Rush Limbaugh, FOX News) where its views are quietly dominant, and partly by getting angry. The right's anger, however, is heavily tinged with gloom—at least among older conservatives. Even as people on the right press their points, their tone often suggests that the larger battle may already be lost. And the dissonance between these two acts puts bees in their mouths. Their ideal of a world of deeper unity between transcendent ideals (freedom, equality) and ordinary life seems to be hastening away into impossibility. Even with both houses of Congress and the presidency in supposedly conservative hands, the *diversity* doctrine got elevated to constitutional status by the U.S. Supreme Court in *Grutter v. Bollinger* in June 2003, and gay marriage gathers the momentum of established fact in the wake of the gay nuptials in Massachusetts following the November 2003 *Goodridge* ruling.

The anger of the right thus springs from a double resentment: the resentment aimed at the liberal elite's day-in-and-day-out condescension toward hometown America, and the more punishing resentment that is directed inward at the inability of conservatives to win cultural respect and gain any cultural traction even as they win elections. Not all of the right's anger is New Anger, but some of it definitely is. The anger of conservative pundits such as Ann Coulter (*Treason*) and Mona Charon (*Useful Idiots*) is meant to punish the punishers, and it has the quality of unstoppable glee that is the signature of New Anger. At one level, the left in the United States is angry and the right is self-effacing; but look again, and the right is rousing itself to anger as well.

Dreadful Temper

One way to draw the contrast between New Anger and older forms of anger is to read what people used to say about their emotions and to consider the characters in popular books. But these aren't our only clues.

In writing *Anger: The Struggle for Emotional Control in America's History* (1986), psychiatrist Carol Zisowitz Stearns and historian Peter Stearns combed through self-help manuals, books of advice to husbands and wives, articles on child care, and magazine fiction to tease out a history of how popular attitudes toward anger developed through American history. The portrait they offer is subtle and complicated, but their essential point is that Americans of generations past saw anger as a powerful and disruptive force that individuals had to learn to control. That lesson was perennial in stories for American children. The Stearnses cite, for example, Louisa May Alcott's *Little Women*. Jo's mother counsels her about her "dreadful temper," saying, "You think your temper is the worst in the world, but mine used to be just like it. I've been trying to cure it for forty years, and have only succeeded in controlling it. I am angry nearly every day of my life, but I have learned not to show it; and I still hope to learn not to feel it, though it may take me another forty years to do so."[10]

In fact, the Stearnses divide American history into several epochs characterized by shifting "emotionologies"— their term for the conventions and standards by which people evaluate anger and the institutions that "reflect and encourage these standards." For the period 1750–1860, they find an intensifying effort to banish anger from marital relationships, to prevent children from developing habits of angry expression, and to punish the child who gives in to anger. They note along the way that the word "tantrum" (initially applied to adults, though the origin is unknown) was coined in the eighteenth century as a way to characterize a kind of overflowing anger. According to the Stearnses, the period 1860–1940 saw a moderation of the earlier attitude, toward the view that anger was a natural part of the personality and that, rather than strive to eradicate it, we ought to channel anger into constructive activities. This idea applied more to boys than to girls, and often involved encouraging a spirit of competition in affairs outside the home.[11]

The Stearnses invoke one more epoch, "1940 and following," divided between a "permissive subperiod" ending in
the late 1950s and a "somewhat strict subperiod" up to the
mid-1980s, when they were writing their book. During the
permissive subperiod, they say, Americans abandoned the
goal of teaching children to channel their anger and focused
instead on showing that anger was an unpleasant experience,
best to be avoided. Parents were counseled to show sympathy
with angry children, along the lines of "I know how you
feel." By the late 1950s, Americans began to feel a need to
intervene more actively to control and deflect anger, both
among children and between spouses. But at this point, the
analysis seems to blur. The Stearnses are aware that Americans of their time express anger a lot more freely than earlier
generations, but they edge to the conclusion that our society is still too censorious. "One of the most insidious features
of the anger-control campaign, certainly," they write, "has
been its potentially paralyzing insistence that anger is an
internal problem rather than a normal response to external
stimulus."[12]

The Stearnses' book is more helpful in describing *what*
happened than in explaining *why* it happened—although in
the opening pages they avow that "the historian must also
shed light on why expressions of anger have changed and
how these changes are connected."[13] They give considerable
weight to experts who directly shape emotional attitudes—
ministers, psychologists, and other advice givers—but they
also view such experts as often racing to catch up with
changes that have already occurred in family structure or
popular mores. Moreover, the Stearnses say they "don't aspire
to a precision" that would allow them to link specific forms
of anger to specific periods of American history such as "Jacksonian anger and Reconstruction anger." They merely see
some general connection between emotional configurations
and, for example, "the excitement of the Civil War,"
unspecified aspects of Progressivism, and "the steady unfolding of American industrialization."[14]

Their reluctance to pursue "precision" or to hypothesize

why Americans have reformulated anger leaves a question that perhaps anthropologists are better suited than historians to answer. Why have Americans divested themselves of so many of their earlier taboos on how and when to express anger? Because we have, in a slow-moving cultural revolution, redefined the self, its boundaries, and the cultural ideals to which it can aspire. This revolution is necessarily slow moving because it takes *at least* two generations for such a transformation to occur. First, one generation must pioneer a break with the older traditions. But the pioneers, having been nurtured and raised in those traditions, can never entirely divest themselves of the habits of inner governance that those traditions fostered. When the pioneers have their own children and raise them according to their new ideals, however, those ideals themselves define the child's emotional horizons.

The pioneer generation can and often does provide spectacular examples of its new ideals: events in which those ideals reach an efflorescence, a Woodstock of perfected expression. But cultural efflorescence doesn't last long enough to plant itself in the personalities of children or to rewrite the rules of social interaction. Those are bigger projects that involve redefining roles in the family, schools, music, work, and other cultural domains. Valuable as I think the Stearnses' contribution is, I don't think they manage the task of tracing the connections across generations and through cultural domains in quite this way.

Perhaps one reason why they missed this larger story is that they emerge, in the end, as apologists for loosening taboos against anger. Since they are partial advocates of the cultural change, they are not well situated to be its critics. They favor a more free-wheeling emotional style as good for individuals and good for society. Individuals have "paid a heavy price in the loss of emotional richness and clarity" because of America's longstanding demand for "facile emotional control." And society too suffers as the effort to wean people from anger undermines "the emotional basis for grievance."[15] They write off the "somewhat strict" approach as hypocritical, covertly hierarchical, and managerial.

I admire much of what the Stearnses accomplished in *Anger: The Struggle for Emotional Control in America's History*, but their concluding comments are as wrongheaded as could be. We live in an era flooded with self-indulgent and often trivial claims of grievance, but the Stearnses see only a parched field in need of irrigation with still more grievance. At a time when millions of Americans have been flattening their emotional range into an angry monotone, they call for—what else?—more anger. In any case, writing in 2006, I find that the wish expressed by the Stearnses sixteen years ago, that Americans would open their emotional lives to the "richness and clarity" of anger, has been amply rewarded. To paraphrase Ronald Reagan (against whom much anger was directed), are we better off now than we were sixteen years ago?

Gentlers vs. Purgationists

All this excess anger in America hasn't gone unnoticed. A therapeutic industry has burgeoned, with promises to help people get the better of their own anger and to deal more effectively with the anger of their spouses, children, and coworkers.

Of course, the existence of a therapeutic industry implies a substantial number of people who are unhappy with the anger in their lives, and we might take the *anger management* movement, at one level, to be a repudiation of the angri-culture. But the situation is actually more complicated. Anger management smoothes some of the rough edges of the angri-culture. Most importantly, it provides help for those whose anger threatens to overwhelm their personal lives. Therapeutic approaches to anger, however, generally do not challenge either the background radiation of New Anger—the bumper stickers, the music, the manners, the clothing, et cetera—its political prominence, or its somewhat disguised role in the workplace. Rather than offering a repudiation of the angri-culture, anger management turns out to be part of that culture: a combination of New Anger's designated driver for nights on the town and dry cleaner for the morning after.

The touchstone for this popular therapeutic movement is Carol Tavris's *Anger: The Misunderstood Emotion* (1982), which renewed the call of all those earlier authors to bring anger under control. Tavris's book has remained in print for more than twenty years, and justly so. It is an intellectually rich and wide-ranging exploration of anger. Tavris positioned her advice as a challenge to the view that had gained ground in the 1970s that open expression of angry feelings was generally healthy and often constructive. She had in mind get-it-off-your-chest authorities such as Dr. Theodore Rubin ("blocks of unexpressed anger actually inhibit the free flow of loving feelings") and Paul Popenoe ("Many intelligent men and women are under the mistaken impression that expressing anger is dangerous and destructive to a marital relationship").[16]

Tavris's commonsensical advice about reining in anger inspired a great many similar self-help books in the last two decades—and more recently, websites. Among the most popular of the manuals are Harriet Lerner's *The Dance of Anger: A Woman's Guide to Changing the Patterns of Intimate Relationships* (1985) and Reneau Z. Peurifoy's *Anger: Taming the Beast* (1999). But it is a crowded field. If Lerner or Peurifoy don't appeal, try Ron Potter-Efron's *Stop the Anger Now* (2001) or Albert Ellis's *How to Control Your Anger before It Controls You* (1998). The genre extends to warnings about the dire health consequences of overindulged anger, such as Redford Williams' *Anger Kills* (1993), and more specialized ventures such as Suzette Haden Elgin's *You Can't Say That to Me: Stopping the Pain of Verbal Abuse* (1995).[17]

Those who counsel against giving free rein to anger, however, do not have the field to themselves. Dr. Theodore Rubin never relented in his quest to increase our loving feelings by helping us connect with our anger. Rubin's *The Angry Book*, first published in 1969, has run through many printings. And various thinkers have offered strangely refined defenses of rage. The clinical psychologist Stephen Diamond, for example, argues for the creative side of choler in *Anger, Madness, and the Daimonic;* and, in *Popular Music, Gender, and Postmodernism: Anger Is Energy,* Neil Nehring attempts to defend the anger in angry versions of rock 'n' roll from the strictures of postmodernists who find it all too ironic, or insufficiently ironic, or something. Still other writers propose to rechannel anger away from its destructive path into wholesome assertiveness. Neil Clark Warren, for example, in *Make Anger Your Ally* (1990), declares, "I believe anger is a God-given capacity—a neutral force that offers magnificent possibilities."[18]

In the debate between those who hope to gentle us down and those who wish we would unleash our too-hushed hurts, I'd say the Gentlers dominate, though the Unleashers and Purgationists have not fled the field. The relative success of those who would teach us how best to keep a lid on our anger, however, is itself evidence of a widespread sense among Americans that anger is in plentiful supply.

After Tavris, the most important popular writer on anger is Daniel Goleman, whose 1995 book, *Emotional Intelligence: Why It Can Matter More Than IQ,* remained atop the bestseller list for nearly a year. The title aside, Goleman is a sophisticated writer who lucidly presents an account of recent scientific findings on the physiology of rage, as well as quietly compelling advice on how and why to quell the impulse to get angry. Physiologically, "anger builds on anger." The initial bodily triggers, says Goleman, prime the body to be extra-sensitive to the next provocation to anger. The individual who gives in to that next provocation, in turn, physically primes his body for an even greater emotional storm. Walk away, he suggests—literally. Walking is one of the best ways to get your mind out of the body's insistence on upping the ante of anger.[19]

Goleman is the Gentler *par excellence,* so much so that another writer on emotions, Tom Lutz, takes the success of *Emotional Intelligence* as evidence that "we are in the midst of a transition away from the cathartic beliefs of the 1970s."[20] I suspect that is true as far as self-help books go, but not true as a measure of popular attitudes. A book that proposes to explain why "emotional intelligence" matters more than IQ sells because large numbers of people are, in fact, enchanted with the ideal of highly emotive styles of decision making. Something similar happened with the success of Rick Warren's Christian self-help book, *The Purpose-Driven Life* (2002). Its appeal is to those who feel disconnected from a deeper purpose in life, not to self-directed go-getters.

How much weight can we give the proliferation of self-help books and therapeutic services? The best gauge may be the scarcity of self-help books offering counsel about other troubling emotions. Those who feel burdened with an excess of envy, greed, pride, shame, disgust, or apathy, for example, find slimmer pickings in the local Barnes & Noble. Fear and worry, however, do considerably better. W. H. Auden characterized the Cold War era as "the age of anxiety," and his phrase has been lofted into the titles of more than a dozen self-help books. *Consuming Passions: Food in the Age of Anxiety* leads to *Mindblowing Sex in the Real World: Hot Tips for Doing It in the Age of Anxiety.* And if that works out, the reader can turn to *Worried All the Time: Rediscovering the Joy of Parenthood in an Age of Anxiety.*[21]

Part of the anxiety appears to be worry about time itself: the difficulty of scheduling a life that has numerous competing demands between work and family. Can a satisfying emotional life be lived on a corporate schedule? Is "quality time" really what children need? For a lot of people, the answer is a disconcerting "No!" Faced with irresolvable conflicts, they find one more reason to live in a state of near-constant irritation with their spouses and children.

The many books assuaging our many separate worries, however, are really piecemeal approaches to happiness. They deal with troubles that seem within reach of a good, long conversation, but they don't vault to the larger question of how to attain happiness itself, or its darker counterpart, how to overcome the pervasive sadness and depression that settle over many lives. We do, however, have self-help books that soar to these higher goals, instructing you how to banish your blues and live a fulfilled life. And these happy/sad books, it turns out, frequently bring us full circle to advice about anger. A theory about depression marketed through much of the therapeutic world is that depression is the result of anger turned inward. According to this view, someone who suffers depression can overcome it by figuring out the real target of anger (mom, dad, spouse, etc.) and then expressing the misdirected emotion to the right cosmic Zip Code. Thus within the most common therapeutic worldview, our two prevailing ailments—anger and depression—are really two faces of the same thing.

Tavris, incidentally, disagrees with this psychoanalytic cliché, saying that it confuses two separate emotions. "Why not argue anger is depression turned outward?" In fact, people can be simultaneously angry *and* depressed, and the two feelings involve different responses to psychological realities.[22]

The popularity of anger management therapists, support groups, self-help books and websites testify that Americans today tend to see excess anger as more of a mental-health problem than a moral issue. If your temper has cost you your job or threatens your marriage in contemporary America, you will almost certainly be advised by family and friends to seek counseling. In this case, the shift away from an older approach of moral censure toward the professional channeler is part of a larger transformation that was noticed and named as long ago as 1966, when Philip Rieff memorably dubbed it *The Triumph of the Therapeutic.*[23]

Angri-culture leans toward these therapeutic cultural premises for some purposes and away from them for others. The ambivalence is nicely displayed in the comic movie *Anger Management* (2003), about a chain of seeming accidents that lead the innocent and angerless Dave Buznik, played by Adam Sandler, to receive intensive therapy from a bizarrely uninhibited and confrontational doctor, Buddy Rydell, played by Jack Nicholson. The comic premise of the movie is that the therapist aims not to cure Dave of his "rage" (he has none) but to help him achieve self-respect, which he can do only by getting appropriately angry at the kid who bullied him in fifth grade, his exploitative boss, his girlfriend's obnoxious ex-boyfriend, and ultimately Dr. Rydell himself.

While the movie makes light fun of anger management therapy, the plot ultimately vindicates the angri-cultural assumptions that nice guys are simply self-loathing repressors of their authentic angry selves; that no one can really love another person without embracing anger too; and that anger is the true liberating force in our lives. Dave has to be tricked into discovering these "facts," but once he grasps them, he becomes a full man—tells off his boss, punches out the ex-boyfriend, and wins the girl.

The put-upon and anger-less Dave who inevitably redeems himself by getting angry also shows us the double-sided quality of "therapy" within the angri-culture. On one hand, we see a version of therapist-driven therapy, which is good-humoredly burlesqued. Nicholson's Dr. Rydell is manic and strange. His therapeutic techniques include teaching his patients to chant a supposed Eskimo phrase ("goosfrabba") to calm them down and interrupting tense moments to have grown men sing Stephen Sondheim's "I Feel Pretty." On the other hand, "therapy" is also the welling up of authentic self-assertion in Dave—with the help of Dr. Rydell's wise provocation.

The comedy in *Anger Management* probably wouldn't work without an audience that already accepts both angri-cultural premises: that formal counseling is a little bit silly, but learning to release one's anger is liberating and good. The Gentlers may be prevailing in the bookstores and actual therapist offices, but, judging by *Anger Management,* the Unleashers are winning at the box office. The 2004 thriller *Paparazzi* can stand for a whole genre of films. It presents a celebrity assigned to anger management for roughing up an intrusive photographer; he finds a more satisfying way to deal with his anger by killing off his tormentors.

American ambivalence about glib, therapeutic approaches received another nice twist in 2005, when the freelance journalist Steve Salerno published *Sham: How the*

Self-Help Movement Made America Helpless. "Sham" is Salerno's acronym for Self-Help and Actualization Movement. The book is a caustic survey of the fatuities of the self-help industry, which rakes in many millions selling clichés and meaningless nostrums to the gullible. But Salerno's own book, laced with angry indignation at the self-help racket, is yet another exercise in pointing out the obvious; it is a self-help book for those addicted to self-help books.

Legacies

The rise of the angri-culture was helped along by the therapeutic worldview. Even though particular psychologists such as Carol Tavris have counseled strongly against the Purgationist approach, modern psychology as a whole seems to have provided the angri-culture with a tissue of rationalizations and excuses for dispensing with the old inhibitions against anger. The figure of Pollyanna comes back to us in Adam Sandler's Dave Buznik, but this time, instead of Pollyanna teaching her aunt Polly how to overcome anger, the Pollyanna-ish Dave learns how to tap into his own, long-suppressed angry inner child.

I don't want to oversimplify angri-culture's origins or flatten it by emphasizing only its personal-liberation side. Anger therapies, real or fictional, tend to lift anger out of its historical and social contexts and make it a matter of an individual's efforts to cope with life's checkerboard challenges. But therapeutic assumptions explain only one aspect of our culture's current infatuation with anger. Some other aspects are plainly political, and one of these grew directly out of Cold War divisions in America.

For instance, during the McCarthy era, many Americans were angry at Communist subversives—angry enough that the government executed Julius and Ethel Rosenberg and blacklisted various academics and, notoriously, a handful of Hollywood screenwriters. And numerous American Communists, ex-Communists, and fellow travelers were angry at both the American government and the citizens who shunned them. The anger on both sides left wounds that lasted the lifetimes of the participants, and then some. In 1952, the movie director Elia Kazan testified to the U.S. House Committee on Un-American Activities, naming eleven screenwriters and actors as current or former Communists. Kazan never wavered in his conviction that he acted rightly. His longtime friend Arthur Miller, however, sharply disagreed, and he put his anger on stage in 1953 with *The Crucible,* implicitly likening the House inquiry into Communist subversion to the 1692 Salem witch trials.

Kazan held his ground. The witches in Salem were a popular delusion; the Communists in Hollywood and elsewhere in American life were real. Kazan put his righteous anger into his 1954 movie, *On the Waterfront,* implicitly likening his HUAC testimony to longshoreman Terry Molloy's decision to take a stand against a thuggish and corrupt union.

Their friendship was finished, but Kazan and Miller overcame their mutual hostility to the extent that Kazan agreed in 1964 to direct Miller's play *After the Fall.* Nothing, however, could redeem Kazan in the eyes of many on the left, who viewed his willingness to "name names" to the House committee as utterly unforgivable.

The story of these old animosities is well known, and I don't take the original animosities as New Anger. They were plain old anger to start with, although with a seed of sourness on the left that would eventually ripen into full-blown New Anger.

In 1999, Kazan at eighty-nine received a lifetime achievement Oscar from the Academy of Motion Pictures, and the memory of that old anger came flooding back. Not only did it flood back: it was now celebrated, enacted, and put on display, as though it were a national treasure. Some 250 protesters gathered outside the Dorothy Candler Pavilion on Oscar night to denounce the award. An eighty-year-old screenwriter, Bernard Gordon, who had been blacklisted in the 1950s, led the protest, joined by other octogenarians such as Bob Lees, another blacklisted writer, who said that

"Kazan ruined people's lives." The protesters chanted, "No Oscars for rats." Inside the Dorothy Candler Pavilion, some guests stood up and turned their backs when Kazan received the award. Their staged anger became a news story that won equal billing with the award itself.[24]

Kazan's Oscar also stirred vitriol in some segments of the press. The *Boston Globe* columnist Thomas Oliphant, for example, wrote that "Kazan is also a pathetically prototypical rat-fink of the anticommunist hysteria." David Aaronovitch, writing in the *Independent* (London), took the occasion to characterize Kazan's testimony forty-seven years earlier as "a cowardly choice, a choice to be on the side of the bully, and not the bullied."[25]

One of the threads in Aaronovitch's comments is worth following a little further. He recalled that a month after Kazan's HUAC testimony, the playwright Lillian Hellman, who was one of the people Kazan named as a former Communist, also testified to the committee. Hellman, however, refused to name names, scornfully telling her interrogators, "I cannot and will not cut my conscience to fit this year's fashions."

This sentence is frequently quoted by leftists both in contrast to Kazan's supposed cowardice and to exemplify a kind of heroism. Aaronovitch does not say but I will add that Hellman, a stalwart Stalinist, was not otherwise known to possess much of a conscience, at least not one that flinched at mass murder or political tyranny. But why do Hellman's fierce words to HUAC continue to reverberate decades later? Aaronovitch thinks it is because the relativist left, having few firm principles to stand on, has discovered that anger itself can substitute for principle in some situations. How else to explain the admiration accorded to figures such as "that totally uncompromising American feminist, Andrea Dworkin?" These instances, he says, show "how some now value anger and authenticity over respectability."

The word "respectability" isn't exactly right. It is a slightly dismissive substitute for the more daunting word *truthfulness*. For what Hellman exemplifies for the left is a facts-be-damned victory of attitude over substance. Hellman found a way to sound angrily high-minded about covering up Communist subversion.

I don't want to pause at this point for the late and now passé Andrea Dworkin, who built a career on angry pronouncements of risible theories about sex and marriage, except to register Aaronovitch's insight. Dworkin is perhaps most famous for her declaration that "Marriage as an institution developed from rape as a practice. Rape, originally defined as abduction, became marriage by capture." Anthropologically speaking, there is no evidence whatsoever that marriage derives from capture, abduction, or rape, but then the purpose of making such counterfactual declarations is not to deepen understanding. They simply demonstrate the writer's outrageousness as a kind of emotional credential.

The feud between Miller and Kazan is part of the story of anger in America now because it is one of the events in the historical memory of the left that continues to shape a specific kind of anger. The angri-culture is not a single endlessly repeated jeer, but a cacophony of rude noises, blaring insults, and staccato vituperation. The nearly half a century that the left spent hating Kazan, praising Hellman, and sentimentalizing Hollywood Communists perfected one distinct note in that cacophony: the angri-culture gained its sense of anger as something one could subscribe to and wear as a badge of membership. The Cold War provided several other events that played in much the same way: Alger Hiss's conviction for perjury; the execution of the Rosenbergs for spying; the derailed careers of people like Owen Lattimore. But Kazan's longevity carried his case over the decades and made it a particularly powerful opportunity for turning long-standing political enmity into theatrical New Anger.

THREE

SELF-GOVERNMENT

On August 16, 2004, a German truck driver transporting a fifteen-ton load of jam jars through Berlin attempted to swat a wasp that had flown into his cab. He missed the wasp but hit the guardrail, spilling his cargo of jam over the highway. The road was closed for two hours, the cleanup hindered by thousands of wasps that arrived to feast on the sweet mess.[1]

The wasp may have merely been acting as wasps do, but perhaps it deserves more credit. It may have been a master strategist, a Machiavelli or Sun Tzu of the hymenoptera, who understood that provoking one man to flail in anger could unlock a kingdom of sweetness.

In contrast to the wasp's wisdom, we might consider Turo Herala, a theater director in Helsinki who offers lessons to Finns on how to get angry. "Anger in Finland is a bigger taboo than sex," he says.[2] Finns are unfailingly polite to each other, and Herala would like to change that. But so far he has attracted few converts. Perhaps Americans, in a spirit of international friendship, ought to offer the Finns some technical assistance. The difference between the near-panic of real anger and labored efforts to mimic anger may not be as wide as it seems.

Anger's Omnibus

When expressing anger becomes a badge of loyalty to an

ideology or to a political faction, people have a motive to adopt angry styles even if they do not inwardly feel angry. But only a very talented actor can routinely simulate anger without, in time, feeling the emotion itself. Perhaps not even a very talented actor can do it. In Bernardo Bertolucci's film *Last Tango in Paris* (1972), Marlon Brando gave what many critics regarded as his finest performance, as Paul, a man raging "against himself and the women he famously seduced and abandoned." Brando said in his autobiography that when the film was finished, "I decided that I wasn't ever again going to destroy myself emotionally to make a movie."[3]

When politics gets angry, individual people do as well, but whether they stroke and pet this anger the way they do the insufferable grievances of personal life depends. Some people master an angry public style and leave it on the street corner or at the front door of their lives; others invite it inside. Cable television and the Internet, both stuffed with angry exchanges, have no doubt helped political anger find a place in the living room and the den.

The angri-culture thus experiences a kind of suburban sprawl. It moves beyond the particular issues in their original contexts to clutter the countryside with its pervasive resentments. It is "out there" as well as "in here." Real anger mixes with the imitations of anger, but the imitations in turn provoke their own rage until it is difficult to tell who is really angry and who is just dressing the part.

The mixture of actual feeling and mere acting, of course, is nothing new. Social anthropologists (like me) long shied away from emphasizing the emotional side of culture precisely because of this conundrum. When a culture mandates a particular emotional expression—joy at a homecoming, pride at a graduation—do people necessarily feel the emotion? Or do they often just go through the motions? In some cultures, people can hire professional mourners to weep at funerals. The paid-for tears still express "grief," but in the manner that a prerecorded laugh track on a TV sit-com expresses surprise and delight. The outward form conveys a culturally standardized attitude, but the inner human reality of the hired mourner may be very different.

Not all anthropologists have regarded this disjunction between conventional form and inner feeling as a big issue. In 1934, the anthropologist Ruth Benedict wrote one of the discipline's all-time bestsellers, *Patterns of Culture,* in which she argued that cultures typically shape the individual's emotions to fit a larger prevailing ideal. Benedict cited the Zuni, for example, as a people who favor a tightly self-controlled style, and she claimed that all but a handful of "deviant" Zunis mildly fall in line with what is expected of them. Likewise, Benedict described the Melanesian inhabitants of the island of Dobu as schemers who inwardly live in deep fear of the people around them but outwardly express an attitude of polite friendliness. Dobuan culture raises every child to be a conniving hypocrite, and few Dobuans disappoint.

Benedict's approach, which aimed to capture what is central to a culture and to downplay its ambiguities, is very much out of favor in today's anthropology.[4] Not all Zuni are so tightly wrapped or all Dobuans the model of Machiavellian cunning. But Benedict did offer an interesting way to think about group psychology. In effect, she minimized the distinction that psychologists usually draw between emotional dispositions and actual episodes of emotion, usually phrased as the difference between emotional "traits" and emotional "states."[5] And indeed, New Anger involves both traits and states, or dispositions and episodes—as well as a third element that Benedict emphasized and most psychologists do not: the surrounding ambiance that teaches, prompts, and continually reinforces the dominant emotional styles.

To understand contemporary angri-culture, we need to give due weight both to the radically skeptical view that anger is often performed according to a cultural script without the performer necessarily feeling it *and* to the Benedict-like view that people generally follow such scripts because they *do* feel the appropriate emotions. On one hand, outward displays of anger are not always what they seem. On the other hand, the angri-culture does impose a kind of conformity. The calmly reflective soul rarely shows up on *Hardball* or *Hannity and Colmes*. We expect titanic clashes on *The O'Reilly Factor*. The angri-culture feeds on conflict and rewards those who can best play the role of gladiators—those who, like the professional weepers at funerals, play the role just far enough. The gladiatorial spirit is to play the game roughly but never with total abandon.

The gladiatorial quality of New Anger, however, doesn't mean that New Anger is always a game or a perpetual conflict. It can and does lead to final outcomes: people acting on New Anger make key life decisions. New Anger offers a doctrine of self-empowerment and all those empowered selves in America are indeed *doing* something, even if it is mostly contributing to the divorce rate, the number of children raised by single parents, and the fluidity of the job market.

America *has* an angri-culture but this doesn't mean that all Americans are perpetually angry or on the verge of anger. Nor does it mean that the angri-culture is the only cultural mode available to us. Rather, it is a kind of emotional air pollution that forms dense smog in some contexts and mere haze in others. The angri-culture doesn't prevent Americans from being friendly to strangers (some of the time) or opening their hearts to victims of tsunamis and hurricanes. But it also never quite goes away. Almost any event, including the December 2004 tsunami in the Indian Ocean and Hurricane Katrina's devastation of Louisiana in August 2005, can be swept up in the grandstanding recriminations of the angri-culture.

Is this really any different from earlier epochs? Are we actually angrier than people in the 1950s—or 1930s, or 1860s, or 1770s? It is hard to imagine an objective measure of the sheer quantity of anger, or even a subjective measure that could be adjusted for changes in historical circumstances. Were disappointed Confederate veterans angrier than the World War I veterans who camped in Washington D.C. to demand additional benefits? A popular song in the South in 1870, "Good Old Rebel" by Innes Randolph, offers lines that strut with anger, such as, "I killed a chance of Yankees and I wish I'd killed some mo'!"; but lyrical defiance and venom are to be found in every decade. Can we find benchmarks that distinguish contemporary anger from angers past? Or has America always been, at some level, an angri-culture?

The explosion of anger in American politics in the last few years has prompted several scholars, besides Carol Zisowitz Stearns and Peter Stearns, to take up the historical question and to answer—I think superficially—that national life in the aftermath of the presidential elections of 1800 and 1860 was exceptionally acrimonious. Indeed it was. But that paints the situation with too broad a brush. What we really want to know is how the acrimony during Jefferson's administration and the Civil War reflected the emotional texture of American culture at those times. Counter to the view that America has always been an angri-culture is that once strong but now radically diminished emphasis on holding anger in check.

Through wars, strikes, riots, and political unrest, anger in the past was either an occasional thing—an eruption of a specific group with a powerful grievance, such as the Pullman Strike of 1894 or the riots at the Chicago Democratic convention in 1968—or a malady limited to specific people, such as the feud between the Appalachian Hatfield and McCoy families, 1878–1897. Even though they were sometimes turned into approving legends of vigilantes seeking frontier justice, none of these events made anger into a national ideal. They were on the whole seen as regrettable and sometimes tragic violations of the standards of civilized life. It is telling that the angriest factions in American society, from Know-Nothings and the Ku Klux Klan to Weatherman and the militia movement, almost always organized themselves as secret societies. In the past, those who decided that they would act on anger hid their faces.

One genre depicts "Indian haters" who, having lost family members to an Indian massacre, devote themselves to a solitary career of vengeance. Herman Melville in *The Confidence Man* captured the genre well when he put the story of the (real-life) Colonel John Moredock in the mouth of an inept hustler. Moredock, an Illinois pioneer in the early nineteenth century, tracked a band of Indians who had killed his mother and siblings. Eventually, having killed all twenty members of the band, Moredock supposedly made a practice of hunting down and killing any Indians he could find.

Moredock-like figures continue to inhabit some dark place in the American soul. Ethan Edwards in John Ford's classic Western *The Searchers* (1956) reminds some of Moredock, but he is present in any number of revenge movies that have nothing to do with Native Americans. The angry anti-hero of *Paparazzi* (2004) who dispatches annoying photographers is a modern Moredock, as are the numerous triggermen of "first-person shooter" video games. The figure has been with us at least since Thomas Kyd wrote *The Spanish Tragedy* (c. 1594), the first Renaissance revenge play.

All this is to say that New Anger has one of its roots in an old form of virulent anger in which some Americans imagined an enemy so vile that nothing short of serial or collective murder was warranted. But Moredock was never an American hero. He and his copies have existed in the American imagination primarily as a type to be repudiated, although the repudiation has recently taken a new direction.[6] A view currently popular within the field of (anti-)American studies is that America has long been a hateful place filled with incitements to genocidal violence. Richard Slotkin's 1973 book, *Regeneration through Violence: The Mythology of the American Frontier, 1600–1860*, provided one of the original sources of this revisionist thesis, and Slotkin built on it in later works, including most recently *Gunfighter Nation: The Myth of the Frontier in Twentieth-Century America* (1998). The latter concludes with images of the My Lai massacre in Vietnam as the practical result of America's supposed obsession with "redemptive" violence.

Slotkin himself, however, can stand as the purveyor of a certain version of New Anger, one that looks at the history of the United States mainly in order to debunk the nation's older, positive images of itself. In the world of American studies these days, we are asked by some historians to see our past as driven in no small part by delusional madmen who killed in order to achieve an ecstasy of revenge. The theme has traveled well beyond academic journals. A recent novel by Sherman Alexie, *Indian Killer* (1998), gives us a new Moredock-like character, an Indian in contemporary Seattle who is a serial killer and hunts down, murders, and mutilates whites, exulting in his acts of vengeance against the race that perpetrated so many massacres against Native Americans. The tone in which Alexie evokes the unnamed killer borders on adulation:

> The killer's mouth is dry, tastes of blood and sweat. The killer carries a pack filled with a change of clothes, a few books, dozens of owl feathers, a scrapbook, and two bloody scalps in a plastic bag. Beneath the killer's jacket, the beautiful knife, with three turquoise gems inlaid in the handle, sits comfortably in its homemade sheath.

And the book ends with a phantasmagoric vision of the serial killer, who has gotten away with his crimes, mystically calling other Indians to join his vendetta:

> The killer sings and dances for hours, days. Other Indians arrive and quickly learn the song. A dozen Indians, then hundreds, and more, all learning the same song, the exact dance.[7]

This fantasy violence of punishing America for its sins is central to the multicultural version of New Anger. Violent fantasies generally rate pretty low on the scale of literary achievement these days, except when the violence arises from the anger of someone who purports to speak for an oppressed group. So Sherman Alexie, properly framed as a Spokane/Coeur d'Alene Indian and "Native American novelist" (*Publishers Weekly, Booklist, Kirkus Reviews*) is excused for his bloodthirsty tale:

> It displays a brilliant eye for telling detail...(*Publishers Weekly*)
>
> ...the grinding of Alexie's axe is sometimes a bit loud. Still

> this is a fine novel by an up-and-coming writer.... (*Library Journal*)

> It's also difficult not to make the novel seem more angry than reflective. But Sherman Alexie is too good a writer, too devoted to the complexities of a story, to settle for a diatribe. (*New York Times Book Review*)

> Anger is rarely an endearing trait—it tends to flatten even the most well-rounded characters—and this novel is populated almost completely by angry people.... But the anger and the fear smell so real, so shockingly familiar, that we resist the temptation to turn away. (*Booklist*)

> ...a haunting, challenging articulation of the plight and the pride of contemporary Native Americans. (*Kirkus Reviews*)

I have mined these snippets from the editorial reviews on Amazon.com only to illustrate one small department of the angri-culture at work. The reviewers recoil from Alexie's grim, angry story, but they seem to take it as their duty to make allowances. "He's an Indian. He's angry. It's OK." I imagine the reactions would have been a bit different if *Indian Killer* had instead been a story by a non-Indian sympathetically recounting the troubled life of Colonel John Moredock.

Angri-culture does not lift up and celebrate just any old anger. Rather it focuses on certain kinds of grievances. The suffering of blacklisted Hollywood screenwriters is a just cause for anger against "rats" like Kazan. But the suffering of, say, Budd Schulberg isn't part of the angri-culture repertoire at all. Schulberg was a screenwriter in the 1930s (*Little Orphan Annie*, 1938; *White Carnival*, 1939) who had belonged to the Communist Party for several years and had gone on to become a successful novelist (*What Makes Sammy Run?* 1941; *The Harder They Fall*, 1947). In 1940, when he decided to try his hand at writing a novel, the Communist Party attempted to tell him what to say. Two CP members, Richard Collins and John Howard Lawson, for example, pressured him to submit an outline of the prospective book for Party inspection and approval. Schulberg broke with the Party and left Hollywood as the only way to preserve his artistic freedom. His brush with the Communist Party's thuggish methods of controlling his work left Schulberg angry enough that he telegraphed the House Committee on Un-American Activities in April 1961 volunteering to cooperate with its investigation of Communist influence in Hollywood.

Schulberg's story is about outrage over censorship as much as any of the stories about Hollywood blacklisting, but somehow angri-culture doesn't find in Schulberg's particular case exactly the right stimulus for righteous indignation.

The suffering of oppressed minorities is another good source for the angri-culture anger. It isn't always an easy card to play, but it is usually in the deck. In October 1995, when Johnnie Cochran convinced the jury in the O. J. Simpson murder trial that his spectacularly unoppressed client was the victim of racist cops, New Anger produced a verdict of not guilty. Angri-culture has its uses. Meanwhile the anger of Nicole Simpson's parents has been portrayed as excessively "vindictive."[8]

Although the grievances celebrated by angri-culture are very numerous, sometimes New Anger appears in the form of delight in anger itself. Another literary example: a new genre emerged in 1981 with the publication of *Tygers of Wrath: Poems of Hate, Anger, and Invective,* an anthology edited by X. J. Kennedy. A poet himself, Kennedy explains in his introduction, "So many anthologies have been devoted to the poetry of love that it seemed high time for the poetry of hate to have one."[9]

Success breeds imitators and now there is also *I Have No Gun But I Can Spit: An Anthology of Satirical and Abusive Verse* (1991). In combing through literature in search of expressions of anger, publishers must sense a market hungry for articulate nastiness. We also, however, have a kids' division starting with *I'm Mad at You: Verses* (1978) and the more recent *Poems about Anger by American Children* (2002), which seem to be aimed mainly at chasing the demons away.[10]

One publisher—Farrar, Straus and Giroux—declined to grant permission to classify any of its poets as "haters" in Kennedy's anthology. But that was twenty-five years ago and doesn't necessarily mean that FSG is out of touch with today's angri-culture. The publisher's current offerings include a new edition of Robert Fitzgerald's translation of *The Iliad:*

> Anger be now your song, immortal one,
> Akhilleus' anger, doomed and ruinous,
> that caused the Akhaians loss on bitter loss
> and crowded brave souls into the undergloom,
> leaving so many dead men-carrion
> for dogs and birds; and the will of Zeus was done.
> *(Lines 1–6)*

And there is the novel *21 Grams* by Guillermo Arriaga, in which "the widowed Christina descends onto a dangerous cycle of grief, rage, and drug abuse." But perhaps this points to an aesthetic distinction between plain old anger and New Anger. Some literary and popular expressions of anger are smirky and show enjoyment in displaying anger for its own sake. To be a literary anthology of "poems of hate, anger, and invective" is like being in a WWF Smackdown: everything becomes a matter of flamboyant posturing. But other literary and popular expressions of anger are serious and aim to reveal our profound discontents. Homer's depiction of Achilles' anger has traveled down the millennia because we can recognize the destructive petulance of a man capable of grandeur. Achilles' anger brings "bitter loss" to his own countrymen; New Anger vainly imagines that anger has no cost at all.[11]

To understand the American angri-culture, we will need to keep in mind this distinction between mere showmanship and expressions of deeply felt human realities. Still, the border between simply *acting* angry and actually *being* angry is unmarked and people stray over it in both directions. This is because of the theatricality of much of modern life. We have learned to live in an unending orgy of self-dramatization and self-creation.

Our historical moment is distinguished by the *way* we think about anger as much as it is by the magnitude of our ire. We have somehow arrived at a society in which anger has gained a high degree of approval and public respect. Anger is fashionable; within limits, anger is good. Anger has become legitimate and no longer apologetic about itself. This is what it means to have an angri-culture.

Founding Anger

Where can we find a plausible standard for the *right* form of anger in a society like ours? Our Republic, founded in revolution, owes something to the anger of men aroused by injustice. Quantifying the amount of anger is, once again, a historical dead end. Although we can see clearly that the French Revolution resulted in fiercer rhetoric and bloodier consequences, we have no way of saying that the Jacobins were intrinsically angrier than the Sons of Liberty—only that the French Revolution licensed a frenzy of angry expression and cruelty that the American Revolution generally avoided.

The success of the American Revolution in forestalling a descent into unbridled anger is especially interesting in view of the pent-up frustration of the generation of Americans who joined in the revolt against Britain, the angry temperament of some of the leaders, and the quarrelsomeness that flowered in the early Republic. All three factors point to the emotional powder keg that somehow did not ignite over the course of six years of armed conflict. There are two conventional explanations for this. First, the colonies and their internal factions (with the exception of Tories) united against a common external enemy. Benjamin Franklin's quip at the signing of the Declaration of Independence, "We must indeed all hang together, or, most assuredly, we shall all hang separately," captures that necessary putting aside of local quarrels for the time being. Second, the Founders as creatures of the Enlightenment explicitly conceptualized their revolt as founded in law and reason, not in what they called the passions. To a large extent, they played against the anger of their countrymen and took considerable effort to keep their own passions under control.

As far back as John Wise's 1710 admonition that the idea of arbitrary government puts "an Englishman's blood into a fermentation," Americans had shown a readiness to respond to injustice with anger. And the lead-up to the Revolution included plenty of American words and acts redolent with anger. The Boston Tea Party was organized fermentation: anger staged as a public spectacle.

One of the angriest of American leaders was James Otis, the author of the well-worn sentence, "Taxation without representation is tyranny." Otis had been the Crown's advocate general in the Vice Admiralty Court in Massachusetts, but he resigned in 1761 when he was ordered to defend the Writs of Assistance, which in effect allowed colonial officials to search private houses for smuggled goods without evidence of wrongdoing and without search warrants. Otis not only resigned, but volunteered his services as counsel to some Boston merchants; from this vantage, he gave a five-hour speech on February 24, 1761, in which he expressed—and evoked in his listeners—fury against the government that had imposed the Writs of Assistance. He said that the writs promoted "revenge, ill-humour, or wantonness" among some, causing others to use the law in self-defense, and so on in reprisal; so "one arbitrary exertion will provoke another, until society be involved in tumult and in blood."

Otis is not well known today, but among those in that audience in 1761 was the young John Adams, who later wrote that "the child of independence was born" in Otis's diatribe against the Writs of Assistance. Otis was provocative on more than one occasion, and through the 1760s he was one of the key leaders in opposition to British impositions. In 1769, however, a customs house official enraged by one of Otis's newspaper articles beat him severely over the head with his cane. Badly injured, Otis never fully recovered his intellectual powers, but drifted in and out of sanity. During lucid intervals, he still served the cause. He served, for example, at Bunker Hill. But Otis the revolutionary lightning bolt was dimmed. A dinner with Governor Hancock in 1783 stirred up old memories and so disturbed him that he was put under the watchful care of an old friend in Andover, Massachusetts. Standing in the doorway of the friend's house while telling a story to the friend's family, he was appropriately discharged by a bolt from a passing thunderstorm.

The American Revolution was not lacking for other temperamental hotheads, such as Patrick Henry and Thomas Paine. And it may be that the Revolution would not have succeeded without their capacity to distill the cause down to a fiery essence. But their provocations seem less central to the event than the cerebral coolness of Jefferson, for example, who could calmly subordinate revolutionary anger to abstract principle. Jefferson's draft of the Declaration of Independence is a manifesto of revolution, but it deliberately backs away from anger as a reason to rebel. Instead, it advances the claims of "duty":

> Prudence, indeed, will dictate that Governments long established should not be changed for light and transient Causes; and accordingly all Experience hath shewn, that mankind are more disposed to suffer, while Evils are sufferable, than to right themselves by abolishing the Forms to which they are accustomed. But when a long Train of Abuses and Usurpations, pursuing invariably the same Object, evinces a Design to reduce them under absolute Despotism, it is their Right, it is their Duty to throw off such Government, and to provide new Guards for their future Security.

The call to "Duty," of course, does not mean that the American Revolution was anger-free. Otis, the Boston Tea Party, and others had already seen to that. But the word "Duty," in a way, repudiates anger, even as the Declaration goes on in a litany of twenty-seven clauses naming various abuses by "the present king of Great Britain."

That list accuses the Crown of serious infractions and neglect, and concludes with reminders that Americans have "petitioned for redress" and, when those failed, warned their British brethren of trouble to come. In a sense, the body of the Declaration is *objectively* angry, in that its details incite a kind of righteous wrath. But the details are also securely under Jefferson's control. This seething list of grievances and might-have-beens is recited under the rubric of performing a public "Duty" by showing "a decent respect for the opinions of mankind."

Is the Declaration of Independence an angry document? It is surprisingly hard to say. It contains a cargo of angry complaints in a ship of legal and dispassionate reasoning. Perhaps that's the key to understanding not just Jefferson's view of the Revolution but the guiding ethos of the whole generation of Founders.

This is not to say that the Founders were, as individuals, either angry by nature or cheerful. Individuals varied.

The last of the Declaration's clauses that condemn King George III begins, "He has excited domestic insurrection among us," and goes on to mention frontier wars with Indians. Domestic insurrection was a real possibility. Their Tory opponents often characterized the revolutionaries as wild, intemperate, and willing to license the passions of the mob. The Maryland planter James Chalmers, for example, penned a seventy-page pamphlet titled *Plain Truth* under the pseudonym Candidus, to refute Paine's *Common Sense*. He warned that the revolutionaries were "demagogues" who "to seduce the people into their criminal designs ever hold up democracy to them," but intend really to bring despotism. Chalmers was not eloquent but he *was* angry, ending his screed, "INDEPENDENCE AND SLAVERY ARE SYNONYMOUS TERMS."

The revolutionaries, though indeed in love with liberty, also feared what was wild and unrestrained in American life. In the rambunctious history of the quarter-century following the Declaration, the vituperative rivalry between partisans of Adams and Jefferson as well as Burr's killing of Hamilton in a duel testify to a society in which anger coursed through both public and private life.

One reason for this was that the American Revolution itself aimed at political liberty, not at replacing the basic values of respect, dignity, kindness, and honor that suffused ideals for both political authority and private conduct in eighteenth-century America. The Revolution was intended to create a new regime, not a new culture, much less a new emotional stance toward life. All those emotions that the Founders held at arm's length as "passions" were in fact vitally part of their culture and bound to affect the political order. The closest they came to finding a constructive place for the passions was in *Federalist No. 10,* where Madison defines a faction as a number of citizens "united and actuated by some common impulse of passion." That passion is not necessarily anger, though it might be: he mentions, for example, "parties inflamed with mutual animosities." Madison famously goes on to argue that in the large republic contemplated in the Constitution, the sheer multiplicity of factions will help to prevent any one faction—even an angry one—from dominating. Anger is, so to speak, diffused by its own futility.

Madison's theory was wise statesmanship, but it still leaves a curiously flattened view of human nature—a view that acknowledges the passions but firmly pushes them into the realm of dangers to be managed, *not* defects to be corrected, *not* qualities to be cultivated, and *not* exuberances to be, on occasion, celebrated. Madison aims to address the "fractious spirit" that has "tainted our public administrations." But since "the causes of faction" are "sown in the nature of man," we are best advised, as far as politics go, to set aside the causes and focus instead on how to handle the consequences. This framing of the issue politely but firmly closes the door on a deeper inquiry into those human qualities that *make* us fractious.

The inability or unwillingness of Madison, Jefferson, Adams, and their peers to speak more directly about the passionate nature of the Revolution and the buried animosities that reemerged after the nation won its independence left a peculiar gap in our sense of national identity—a gap that the twenty-eight-year-old Abraham Lincoln famously noted in his Lyceum Address in 1838.

A mob in St. Louis had taken hold of an African American freedman suspected of murder and had burned him alive. Lincoln said that this outrage was one of many across the country that demonstrated "the growing disposition to substitute the wild and furious passions, in lieu of the sober judgment of Courts," and he saw disaster ahead for the nation if Americans did not learn to cherish the law. The problem, in Lincoln's view, stemmed from the passing of the generation that had fought for the Revolution.

That revolutionary generation had staked everything on proving "the capability of a people to govern themselves." Although they preached reason, they were moved by pride, ambition, and fear of shame if they should fail. "If they succeeded, they were to be immortalized; their names were to be transferred to counties and cities, and rivers and mountains.... If they failed, they were to be called knaves and fools, and fanatics for a fleeting hour; then to sink and be forgotten." Lincoln adds that the "passions of the people" in the American Revolution "as distinguished from the judgment" were united with the great cause, and channeled away from domestic acrimony:

> By this influence, the jealousy, envy, and avarice, incident to our nature, and so common to a state of peace, prosperity, and conscious strength, were, for the time, in great measure smothered and rendered inactive; while the deep-rooted principles of hate, and the powerful motive of revenge, instead of being turned against each other, were directed exclusively against the British nation.

But as the events of the Revolution receded and the patriots died off ("a forest of giant oaks" swept over by "the all-resistless hurricane" of mortality), the powerful emotions that had held these divisive passions at bay dissipated. "But this state of feeling," says Lincoln, "must fade, is fading, has faded, with the circumstances that produced it."

The young lawyer from Springfield, Illinois, had deep admiration for the achievement of the Founders, but he was worlds away from them on the issue of "passion." For the Founders, with their Enlightenment faith in reason, *feelings* were to be self-governed by the responsible individual and held in check for everyone else by good government. But for Lincoln, the "passion" of the patriots was what made them "the pillars of the temple of liberty." He concludes—rather unconvincingly—that the only recourse for his own generation, who could not experience that original passion, would be general intelligence, sound morality, and "reverence for the constitution and laws." Perhaps this wasn't an entirely vain hope in 1838, with the Civil War more than two decades away, but it seems unlikely that intelligence, morality, and reverence would ever be enough, by themselves, to galvanize a people into active commitment to the rule of law.

A counsel of temperance in an angry time was surely not out of place. The lynch mobs that prompted Lincoln's speech were, after all, assuming a kind of perverted moral authority, and his task was to convince his listeners that that authority was false and illegitimate. The broader problem, of course, has not gone away. Today we have vigilantes of other sorts—radical environmentalists who burn houses and cars, computer hackers who "punish" corporations, animal rights activists who invade research labs—turning their anger into lawless attacks on those they accuse of injustice. What exactly *do* you say to people so convinced of the righteousness of their cause and the lameness of the law that they strike directly at their opponents?

In his Lyceum speech, Lincoln suggested that the Founders were able to brush aside the complicated issues of the emotional cohesion of the country because the birthpangs of the new republic practically guaranteed an intense common commitment. But the result was a nation in which the bonds of citizenship lacked a certain kind of emotional definition. The cardinal principles articulated in the founding documents and in the nation at large were (and are) liberty and equality. But what was the founding's emotional stance?

I am not sure this question has an exact answer, but the society that emerged from a long and bloody war was far from a calm, reason-doting constitutional seminar. It had complicated emotional qualities even if its leaders lacked an overt vocabulary for this aspect of collective life. And the most important of those qualities were, in a way, on display in George Washington, the Founding Father who seems more than any other to have shaped the character of the American people.

Washington was a man burdened throughout his life with a quick temper. In 1748, when he was sixteen, he was hired by Thomas, Lord Fairfax, a relative of his, to survey some property. Fairfax sent Washington's mother a letter, observing, "I wish I could say that he governs his temper. He is subject to attacks of anger on provocation, sometimes without just cause." Fairfax predicted that Washington would get control of his anger but "go to school all his life."[12]

And indeed, all his life Washington did struggle with his tissue-thin sensitivity to slights. The dignified and reserved George Washington that looks out from his portrait on the dollar bill is a man who fought his fiercest battles in mastering himself. He was a huge man (for his day) at six foot two, powerfully built, physically tough, and renowned for his horsemanship. Such a man in a burst of anger surely intimidates, but just as surely is shunned. But Washington didn't become the eighteenth-century equivalent of a Hell's Angel on the Appalachian frontier. Instead, he bound his temper with the steel hoops of a code of respect for other people.

This by no means meant that he smothered his temper entirely. Jefferson noted Washington's extreme sensitivity to criticism, and others saw in him a restrained fierceness and a habit of fighting and mastering his passions. In his recent biography of Washington, Richard Brookhiser remarks, "His temperament had its raw edges, however, and when they were incautiously touched, he could become dangerous to those around him." During the war, Alexander Hamilton, serving as his aide, found Washington testy and direct, and resigned when Washington angrily accused the younger man of "disrespect" for being moments late for a meeting. The incident, of course, did not tear Washington and Hamilton apart permanently, but Hamilton knew better than most the barely bridled temper in the commanding general.[13]

David Hackett Fischer in *Washington's Crossing* describes several episodes of Washington struggling—successfully—to control his rage. On Christmas Eve 1776, as Washington was about to have his troops cross the Delaware for a surprise attack on the Hessian soldiers in Trenton, New Jersey, he received word that a freelancing subordinate, Adam Stephen, had sent his own raiding party across the Delaware on a tit-for-tat mission of revenge. Stephen's raiders had roused the whole Hessian garrison in Trenton, which chased them away. Washington then

> summoned Stephen from the column and asked if it was so. Stephen confirmed the truth of it. The general grew very angry. "You, Sir!" he raged. "You, Sir, may have ruined all my plans by having put them on their guard." Others remembered that they had never seen Washington in such a fury. The more he thought about what Stephen had done, the more infuriated he became.

Then something remarkable occurred:

> But in a moment, Washington mastered his anger. He calmed himself by turning away from Adam Stephen and talking to the bewildered men in Captain Wallis's company [who had carried out Stephen's raid]. He spoke kindly to them and personally invited these proud Virginia soldiers to join his column.[14]

George Washington comes down to us, however, not as the Enlightenment guru of anger management but as Father of the Country. The phrase, worn out by repetition, is not easily understood today, but somewhere in it is the sense of a fierce and destructive power held in check by a man determined to do what's right. This determination cost Washington something that today we often value more: his "authenticity." Washington frequently buried his feelings and retreated behind manners and formality. He adopted a stiff dignity, when all who knew him commented on his physical grace and fluidity. He disappeared behind his mask—almost.

For an odd aspect of such masks as public figures wear is that we almost always see behind them. The heartfelt respect that his contemporaries felt for Washington was not just for the figure who defined the plain republican ideal of President of the United States, but for the man who mastered himself. This would have meant little had self-mastery come easily or had he never faced serious temptation. His contemporaries, however, realized that Washington triumphed by conquering the proud, ambitious, and fierce man that lay within.

Spitoons

Americans over the last two centuries have had many occasions to be angry, and have usually passed the test by not enslaving themselves to anger. They learned in time to put it aside and get on with life. They learned to bear with some afflictions; to rise to anger for a just cause and to swallow it sometimes; and occasionally to forgive.

I don't wish to make saints out of earlier generations. A great many individuals also lived lives of bitterness, drank themselves to oblivion, or poisoned their lives with unconquerable hatreds. Unable to resolve their differences over slavery and states' rights, one generation precipitated the agony of the Civil War. Unable to open their hearts to African Americans as free and equal fellow citizens, several generations of white Americans angrily impeded the spirit of political and social equality. Anger has been enlisted in many generations both as a motive for transgression and as a fierce determination to end those transgressions.

But that said, Americans have not been by temperament an angry people, and still are not. Foreign observers from the eighteenth century on discerned numerous collective qualities, not all of them pleasant. Tocqueville was mightily impressed with our individualism; Dickens with our then public habit of spitting tobacco juice. A wild rambunctiousness struck many refined visitors. But none characterized Americans as a sullen, angry people. Are we now?

George Anderson, the president of Anderson & Anderson, a California-based anger management firm, recently told a reporter, "Things really changed after 9–11, and we saw an overwhelming number of referrals. Companies and organizations started to recognize there was a need for this kind of service and that it could be truly beneficial."[15] The terrorist attack of September 2001 may well have aroused new interest in anger management, as it certainly aroused a lot of new anger. As those "companies and organizations" were busy sending grumpy employees to ten weeks of anger counseling, Toby Keith was selling a lot of copies of his song "Courtesy of the Red, White, and Blue (The Angry American)":

> Ohhh Justice will be served
> And the battle will rage.
> This big dog will fight
> When you rattle his cage.
> And you'll be sorry that you messed with
> The U.S. of A.
> 'Cause we'll put a boot in your ass;
> It's the American way.

But Anderson also explained, "About 40 percent of my business comes from court-ordered referrals." Road rage, barroom fights, and domestic violence are the usual doors to anger management. A special door is held open for celebrities who thereby escape jail time: actress Shannen Doherty (who threw a beer can through a car window) was sentenced to anger management, as were rapper Tone Loc (a woman's car met his baseball bat—repeatedly), and boxer Mike Tyson (need you ask?). Whether these referrals do much good is another matter. Roberta Kyman, commissioner of Los Angeles Superior Court, told the *Los Angles Times* in October 2001 that in four years she had sentenced two hundred defendants to anger management, advising them to "choose a class from the approved list and report back after finishing." Unfortunately, it wasn't until late August 2001 that Commissioner Kyman realized "there was no such list."[16]

I understand Commissioner Kyman's perplexity. We hear so much about "anger management" and we experience so often the promptings of the angri-culture that it is easy to suppose that the therapeutic industry is on top of this phenomenon. But oddly, the professional psychiatrists and most of the scholarly psychologists keep the subject of anger at arm's length. The American Psychiatric Association, speaking for 35,000 doctors, does not regard anger itself as a treatable disorder, and the American Psychological Association takes no official position. Anger management classes are simply taught by anyone who decides to teach them. As far as mental-health professionals are concerned, certain kinds of "anger" may be a symptom of some psychological disorder, but most often anger is just a normal human emotion.

This is a pretty sensible judgment, and it means that to understand New Anger, we ought not to go in search of some hitherto unrecognized psychiatric disorder. Americans have not gone collectively crazy; we have simply adopted the attitudes, the styles, and the premises of the angri-culture. We do need to account for an important change in our society, but it is a cultural change, not a pathology. Dickens today would find us spitting more epithets than tobacco juice, and we possibly have undergone a metamorphosis from the admonition "Don't tread on me" to "You wanna piece of me?" belligerence. But this change is easy to overstate. Despite the angri-culture's pervasiveness in public space, a placid temperament does somehow survive in much of American life, beneath the appearance of a bickering, all-anger-all-the-time politics and everyday *attitude*.

The kid who dresses angry, listens to anger music, and sports fashionably angry opinions may be a cheerful, good-natured fellow beneath his tattoos. But then what sense can we make of his tastes and his decisions to present himself in the guise of hooded anger? Despite his superficial insignia of alienation, he has thoroughly acclimated to his country's angri-culture. What prompts that disguise?

FOUR

WACKADOO POLITICS
America's Uncivil Liberties

"Heroic Bee Stops Man from Singing Crappy Song." This headline, tacked on to an AP wire story by an anonymous wit, referred to the sad fate of John L. Nunes, nineteen, who crashed his car into a tree in Days Creek, Oregon, on September 18, 2003, when a bee flew into his mouth. Mr. Nunes had been singing along with Justin Timberlake's song "Rock Your Body."[1]

Mr. Nunes avoided a sting, but bit his tongue in the crash and had to get it stitched.

A bee in the mouth apparently isn't *always* bad.

Some, indeed, perform a public service. The bees in our mouths when we talk politics, however, always sting. The angry tone of contemporary politics shuts down many conversations before they can begin. People simply don't want to risk exposing themselves to the bottled brine that is passed around as though it were sparkling wit. Enjoying the company of acquaintances who espouse political opinions that differ from one's own is a civilized art fast fading from the vicinity of the backyard barbeque and the park bench—and nearly extinct in the op-ed pages. The deftness required in ribbing the other guy and responding in good humor when he ribs you back has all too often been replaced by callow mockery, sneering self-righteousness, and annihilating fury.

Mockery, self-righteousness, and fury are not exactly new, of course. At the beginning of the nineteenth century, an opinionated country lawyer named Thomas Green Fessenden (1771–1837) had these sorts of bees in his mouth. Fessenden started out writing vernacular verse that lightheartedly picked up the vocabulary and accents of rural folks in his native New Hampshire and Vermont, but then turned to intellectual and political satire. In 1803, he published a poem lampooning the medical profession, *Terrible Tractoration!* and then hit his stride with *Democracy Unveiled or, Tyranny Stripped of the Garb of Patriotism,* which he published in 1805 under the pseudonym Christopher Caustic.

Democracy Unveiled may be among America's strangest literary works. It consists, like Vladimir Nabokov's novel *Pale Fire,* of a poem accompanied by a self-commentary in the form of footnotes. The form imposes just a little control over Fessenden's almost voluptuous hatred for Thomas Jefferson and his party. The poet:

> Commences war with certain brats,
> Who stile themselves good Democrats.

He elaborates:

> And I'll unmask the Democrat
> Your sometimes this thing, sometimes that,
> Whose life is one dishonest shuffle,
> Lest he perchance the *mob* should ruffle.

Footnotes explain that the Democrats (i.e. Jefferson's Democratic-Republican Party) shift identities for political expediency and that "the mob" is made up of those who are destitute both "of property and of principle."

This is strong stuff, calculated to offend lots of people. Some of it is political diatribe, but Fessenden's satire also aims at the intellectual roots of Jeffersonian democracy. He begins an attack on Rousseau:

> There was a gaunt Genevan priest,
> Mad as our Methodists at least,
> Much learning had, but no pretence
> To wisdom, or to common sense.

And he works his way through dozens of French, German, and English social thinkers, with venom and with glee.

In his later years, Fessenden mellowed into the genial editor of *The New England Farmer's Almanack* (1828–1836) and the author of successful how-to books such as *The New American Gardener* (1828). Nathaniel Hawthorne met Fessenden in January 1836, and when the sometime poet died in November of that year, Hawthorne wrote a memorial essay that praised Fessenden's spirit—his "guileless simplicity"—but adroitly managed not to quote a single line of his "jog-trot stanzas." Hawthorne was a Jacksonian Democrat.

Fessenden is an American original, one of our home-grown eccentrics who presents an unsettling mixture of gullibility and intellectual acuteness. He was scammed by bogus inventors and he enthusiastically promoted medical quackery. (*Terrible Tractoration!* savages physicians who doubted a popular cure-all device that Fessenden believed in.) His verse has charm only for those who take pleasure in rough originality. And his political opinions probably put him somewhere to the right of today's *Free Republic* readers.

But if he was sometimes the cranky "Christopher Caustic," Fessenden was also a rustic poet with a deft touch for traditional themes. "A Pastoral Dialogue. Scene—Vermont" begins:

> Yonder tiny insect ranging,
> Flits about on filmy wing,
> Fickle Sophy, ever changing,
> Is exactly such a thing.

His college poem, "The Country Lovers or Mr. Jonathan Jolthead's Courtship with Miss Sally Snapper" (1795), was a newspaper staple for half a century. As Hawthorne observed, Fessenden caught "the very spirit of society as it existed around him," and every line of the poem has "a peculiar, yet perfectly natural and homely humor."

Fessenden was far from alone in the early days of the Republic in adopting a hyperbolic contempt for his political opponents. He wasn't even alone in composing satiric verses roughly modeled on Samuel Butler's comic send-up of Cromwell's supporters, *Hudibras*. A group of Yale graduates, the Hartford Wits—John Trumbull, Timothy Dwight, and

Joel Barlow—similarly attacked Jefferson in Butlerian rhyme. But Fessenden stands out as the rustic original, and because he wrote so much in other veins, we can put his political screeds into a broader psychological context. Fessenden, the farmer of *The New England Farmer's Almanack,* the gullible enthusiast for medical quackery, and the chronicler of Jonathan Jolthead's courtship, was that odd combination of quick-witted skepticism and wide-eyed credulity that was to become an essential part of American character. His anger at the Jeffersonians clearly did not consume him.

In describing today's vitriolic political rhetoric, Alan Wolfe recently invoked the eighteenth-century pamphleteers who warmed up the American public for the Revolution and their nineteenth-century successors who struggled to define the character of the Republic:

> We had partisanship even before we had parties. Our framers warned against the dangers of faction because we so rarely stood together. If you prefer your invective unseasoned by decorum, check out what the anti-Federalists had to say about the Constitution or how Whigs treated "King Andrew" Jackson.[2]

And it is true. Mud-flinging and apocalyptic pronouncements are two key ingredients in the American political tradition. They are the sauce in which we have cooked many capitol geese.

But if we take Fessenden as representative of the old pamphleteers, Wolfe is only half right. Then as now, political diatribes could be wildly over-the-top; and then as now, righteous anger was on display and the polemicists could seem distempered. But in one key respect, the pamphleteers of yesterday and the pundits of today seem to inhabit different worlds. The pamphleteers lacked the elaborate self-centeredness of today's media-savvy screech owls. They offered arguments—often wobbly, overstated, and tedious arguments—but arguments nonetheless. And as far as I can tell, nowhere did Fessenden or any of his fellow pamphleteers resort to today's most familiar conceit, in which the writer says, in effect, "I am right because I am personally very, very angry."

Fessenden, with his self-mocking pseudonym Christopher Caustic, does not make himself the center of his attack
on the Jeffersonians. It is worth seeing an example of his typical mode to make the contrast with today's polemicists
completely clear. Here are four lines from *Democracy Unveiled,*
along with Fessenden's footnotes:

> Those who assume, at Faction's call,
> A *right* t'infringe on rights of all,[a]
> Who swear all honesty a hum,[b]
> Who rise because they are the scum,[c]

> a   *A right t'infringe on rights of all*
> See a Charge delivered to the Grand Jury in Pennsylvania,
> by the Honorable Alexander Addison, in which the dis-
> tinction between liberty and licentiousness, the dangers
> to be apprehended from the tyranny of the MANY, ever
> more dreadful than that of the FEW, are pointed out in a
> perspicuous and masterly manner.
>
> b   *Who swear all honesty a hum*
> Declarations to this effect, I have repeatedly heard made
> by those who stiled themselves Democrats, friends to the
> people, real patriots, &c. &c. That there is no such thing
> as honesty in politics; that in the scramble for power, bad
> means were justifiable to obtain the good end in view, to
> wit, the aggrandizement of the party making use of such
> means; and that they have ever acted in conformity to
> these tenets, an impartial history of the party will amply
> testify.
>
> c   *Who rise because they are the scum*
> "When the political pot boils, the scum rises."

Fessenden continues in this vein for more than two hundred
pages in what amounts to a filibuster in doggerel.

At first glance this *does* resemble Paul Krugman declaring in the *New York Times,* "No question: John Ashcroft is
the worst attorney general in history." Or Al Gore saying of
President George W. Bush, "He has created more anger and
righteous indignation against us as Americans than any
leader of our country in the 228 years of our existence as a
nation." But the degree of sheer vitriol isn't the right measure. The old pamphleteers were loud and vehement; they
were, often as not, unscrupulous; and they frequently saw

their opponents not just as wrongheaded but as scoundrels too. That much hasn't changed, but New Anger has added to the mix a lavish I-hate-therefore-I-am joyful smugness.

Here, for instance, are the opening lines of Jonathan Chait's pivotal article, "Mad about You," which appeared in September 2003 in the *New Republic:*

> I hate President George W. Bush. There, I said it. I think his policies rank him among the worst presidents in U.S. history. And, while I am tempted to leave it at that, the truth is that I hate him for less substantive reasons, too. I hate the inequitable way he has come to his economic and political achievements and his utter lack of humility....

Chait is a serious political commentator, not a barroom drunk, and the *New Republic* is a serious political magazine, not a MoveOn.org contest for Angry Left jeremiads. The publication of Chait's "I hate President George W. Bush" manifesto in the *New Republic* may have been one of the decisive moments in unleashing New Anger into the Democratic presidential primaries. Outright Bush-hatred was already well established on the fringes of the American left, but mainstream political commentators held back out of a slight and lingering sense of decorum. Chait's essay announced that it was now permissible, or perhaps even "responsible," for the left to embrace its hatred of Bush publicly. And the left, with a gleeful whoop, all at once abandoned what remained of its emotional restraint.

In the weeks and months that followed, fellow writers on the left cited Chait's article again and again as though it officially granted permission to turn loose. What mattered was that Chait was not known as a hothead, but as a serious political writer. His "I hate President George W. Bush" thus came as an enunciation that people who were eager to maintain a view of themselves as "serious" and "thoughtful" could, without risk to self-image or reputation, indulge in public vituperation of President Bush. Chait's article is a landmark in the history of *anger chic.*

The left's anger was self-evident at one level, but also slightly out of focus for political observers, just as the right's anger had been during the various scandals of the Clinton administration. In both cases, political theory revealed some bafflement at a popular enthusiasm that seemed ill calculated to achieve any practical end. Had President Clinton been driven from office, the Republicans would have faced an incumbent President Al Gore in the 2000 election. Clinton-hatred failed to produce the backlash that many Democrats hoped for, but it did leave conservatives feeling demoralized. In the 1996 presidential election, Republican candidate Bob Dole famously complained, "Where's the outrage?" In fact, he handily captured the voters who were outraged by Clinton's dishonesty, but outrage proved too narrow an appeal to win the election, and people who voted their outrage were especially prone to a sense of despondency in defeat. They felt as if the nation had lost its moral center and was making fateful decisions on the basis of expediency rather than judgments of right and wrong.

Old Woes

Like swimmers pushing off a wall as they turn to do another lap, angry Democrats routinely touch on the era of Clinton-bashing. Recalling the nasty treatment of Clinton provides an extra thrust for the next lap of flailing against Bush. Writes one angry leftist:

> Clinton revilers were animated by matters mostly unrelated to his presidential performance. He was a saxophone-playing hedonist, a pot smoker, a womanizer, a child of the '60s; he was also, in Toni Morrison's words, our "first black president."[3]

Writes another:

> Hatred is a very contagious thing. Republicans are hurt that a few entertainers, using some blue language, have expressed their displeasure with the Bush administration's radical right-wing policies.
>
> Hmmm, hate-talk, insulting innuendo, and even murder accusations were thrown at President Clinton for eight years. Citizens of the party that brought my grandfather and millions

of others out of poverty with the New Deal were called treason-
ous, sick, abnormal, unpatriotic, America-haters.

This vilification made me feel disgust and hatred toward
conservatives.[4]

And yet another:

After eight years of incessant Clinton-bashing (accusing him
of everything from rape to murder), turnabout is fair play.
Depicting our current chief executive as stupid and incompe-
tent is probably a bit harsh, but any objective observer had
to be appalled by Bush's recent pathetic performances on
Meet the Press and his last press conference. The inept mismanagement of the Iraq war and the constant shirking of
accountability in this administration convey a woeful lack of
leadership....[5]

The *memory* of the conservative anger against Clinton provides to these individuals a sense of moral justification for
feeling angry against Bush. "Turnabout is fair play," however,
is a pretty shaky principle. To escape the implication that
Bush-bashing is merely revenge for Clinton-bashing, the
writers have to dwell on the memory a little longer. They
need to spot a difference that makes their anger *better* than
the anger against Clinton.

The anger that arose on the left during the Florida election in November and December 2000 and that continued
into the first months of the Bush presidency was obviously
not a point-by-point recapitulation of the earlier Clinton-
hatred transferred to Bush. The substantive complaints were
dissimilar and—more significantly for my purposes—the
emotional style differed too. In both cases, people who
should have known better indulged in foolish excesses of
anger and imagined lurid conspiracies among their opponents. At the fringes of the conservative attacks on Clinton,
people spoke about his having Vince Foster murdered; connected the president to cocaine traffickers at the Mena
Airport in Arkansas; and speculated that he had had Secretary
Ron Brown assassinated. At the fringes of the left's attacks
on Bush, we get the crackpot theories of people like Michael
Moore speculating that Bush was in league with the Saudis

and that the war in Afghanistan was motivated by an obsolete bid by an American company to build an oil pipeline.

At some level, excess just looks like excess, no matter who is indulging in it. But an account of the angry right and the angry left that treats their antics as merely the contemporary version of the age-old spoiled-sportsmanship of American politics is too blunt. I don't deny Alan Wolfe's observation that rhetorical excesses of anger are a longstanding part of the American political tradition, but I do think something new has entered the picture. The rioting outside the 1968 Democratic National Convention in Chicago by some ten thousand protesters was an early manifestation of a new kind of anger: anger that fused into one Molotov cocktail the political antipathies of the antiwar movement, the theatrics of the counterculture, and the preening self-satisfaction of those for whom expressing anger was a new way of defining self.

This exhibit of New Anger in 1968, however, offended and puzzled millions who saw it on TV. Polls showed that Americans backed Mayor Richard Daley's use of police against the rioters by nearly two to one. And the trial that followed of some of the riot's instigators, the "Chicago Seven," put this stylized anger into even sharper focus. The political version of New Anger then faded out for a while. Actually, it went into a long period of quiet growth as its youthful avatars began their careers and emerged at last in the candidacy of our first president to come of age in the 1960s, Bill Clinton. He introduced an overt form of emotional transactionalism ("I feel your pain") into American politics, one that was instantly recognizable as a 1960s style. The growing Republican anger (in effect, "You cause our pain") during his two terms oddly mirrored Clinton's own emphasis on the authenticity of his emotions.

By suggesting that the 1968 Democratic National Convention ought to be understood as the touchstone for contemporary anger in American politics, I don't mean either to slight Alan Wolfe's point or to overlook forerunners. Any attempt to trace a history of emotional styles faces a challenge in drawing distinctions. Consider for example the contrast between the anger of some of the protesters at the 1968 Democratic convention, and the anger of a protester at an earlier Democratic convention in Chicago.

William Jennings Bryan, at the 1896 Democratic National Convention, declared on behalf of struggling midwestern farmers, "You shall not press down upon the brow of labor this crown of thorns, you shall not crucify mankind upon a cross of gold." *The Yippie Manifesto,* published eight months before the 1968 Democratic National Convention in an effort to attract protesters to the event, commands, "Rise up and abandon the creeping meatball!" The two statements are worlds apart in political context and content, but let's focus on their distinctive emotive appeals. Both express political anger, but it differs radically in character.

Bryan's language, full of righteous indignation and bleeding with Christian imagery, aims to establish a boundary. It is line-in-the-sand rhetoric. Note that nothing in it (or anywhere else in Bryan's speech) reveals the inner life and yearnings of William Jennings Bryan. He is on display as an orator, not as autobiographical subject. *The Yippie Manifesto,* on the other hand, is jokey and at pains to display its irreverence. The term "creeping meatball," incidentally, while not as famous as Bryan's "cross of gold," is repeated to this day by those who look back fondly to the Chicago '68 convention and cite *The Yippie Manifesto.* It has inspired a folk lyric, a recurrent free-verse motif, and the name of a blog. The radio humorist Jean Shepherd (1921–1999), who had a rich vocabulary of derision, is credited with inventing the expression, which moved on to become a kind of all-purpose sneer at American mass culture.

"Rise up and abandon the creeping meatball!" initially doesn't sound angry at all, but of course it is addressed to companions, not to adversaries. The *Manifesto* continues, "Come all you rebels, youth spirits, rock minstrels, truth seekers, peacock freaks, poets, barricade jumpers, dancers, lovers, and artists." But by the *Manifesto*'s last paragraph, the happy countercultural parade gives way to a harder, more vehement tone, on the verge of incoherence:

> The life of the American spirit is being torn asunder by the forces of violence, decay, and the napalm-cancer fiend. We demand the politics of ecstasy! We are the delicate spores of the new fierceness that will change America. We will create our own reality, we are Free America! And we will not accept the false theater of the Death Convention.
>
> We will be in Chicago. Begin preparations now! Chicago is yours! Do it!

Is "napalm-cancer fiend" intrinsically more vehement than comparing advocates of the gold standard to crucifiers of Christ? Probably not, but something is different. Bryan's anger focused on real people who advocated a particular policy he disagreed with; *The Yippie Manifesto* attacks a literally demonized vagueness and instantly turns to its psychedelic demand for "the politics of ecstasy." Bryan worried about midwestern farmers; *The Yippie Manifesto* farms out the "delicate spores of the new fierceness," which is as perfect an instance of the precious, narcissistic, preening New Anger that we are likely to find on the way to creating "our own reality."

Alan Wolfe's reminder that anger has often been part and parcel of American politics thus seems to blur the moment when political anger went from summoning fierceness for a particular cause to imagining fierceness as a permanent form of self-therapy. I can imagine that some anti–New Deal Republicans in the 1930s and 1940s nurtured a loathing for Franklin Roosevelt that came close to defining their own character, much as some on the left in the 1950s conceived a revulsion for Richard Nixon that defined *their* character. These may be genuine precursors to 1960s New Anger, but I see little evidence that hatred of FDR or Nixon in those decades made the additional leap from political antipathy to self-conscious endorsement of ecstatic anger as a mode of political action. From the 1930s through the 1950s, people who were ecstatically angry about political issues would more likely have been hospitalized than treated as political celebrities. Times change.

Here, for example, is H. L. Mencken, writing in his diary on April 15, 1945, on the news that President Roosevelt has died:

> He was always a mite ahead of them [Wendell Wilkie and Thomas Dewey, the Republican candidates for President in 1940 and 1944], finding new victims to loot and new followers to reward, flouting common sense and boldly denying its existence, demonstrating by his anti-logic that two and two made five, promising larger and larger slices of the moon. His career will greatly engage historians, if any good ones ever appear in America, but it will even more interest psychologists. He was the first American to penetrate to the real depths of vulgar stupidity. He never made the mistake of overestimating the intelligence of the American mob. He was its unparalleled professor.[6]

It would be hard to find a more scathing assessment of Roosevelt. Moreover, Mencken is still widely read largely because of his mastery of invective. Mencken's glee and the self-satisfaction in *performing*, even in his diary, are ingredients in what will eventually become New Anger, but this passage represents something else—not anger but the aloof contempt of cynicism. Nothing in the diary entry suggests that he is struggling to control rage. To the contrary, Mencken poses as an Olympian amused at the human comedy, from which he is too far removed to express a personal stake. He mocks Roosevelt without any reference to himself or his feelings. New Anger, by contrast, basks in the speaker's sense of self and how that self feels about the issue at hand.

In the 1990s, a good many Republicans and conservatives seemed to have absorbed the new cultural premise that expressing fury was an appropriate way for adults to engage in politics. By 2000, the nation had turned a cultural corner without even realizing it. Extreme expression of anger was no longer taken as the behavior of the weak-minded and overzealous, but as the authentic deep feeling of people being true to their heartfelt commitments. Extreme anger in politics was now not an exception, but an established *mode,* and one that was legitimate for partisans at all levels, from the neighborhood coffee group to the national candidate.

The corner that we turned in 2000 might be summarized as the difference between the conservatives who expressed *outrage* at Clinton and the leftists who expressed *rage* at Bush. Outrage is anger and resentment framed as indignation over a violation of some principle; rage is uncontrolled anger that, in its frenzy, owes little to violated principles. Republicans attacked Clinton by stating, "He lied under oath." Democrats attacked Bush with the less punctilious, "He lied." Conservatives often looked at Clinton with a mixture of disgust and loathing, as a man whose personal qualities made him unworthy of office. Liberals often look on Bush with a mixture of disdain and mockery, as a man too stupid to be taken seriously.

In examining emotional realities, it is always hard to draw watertight distinctions, and the distinction between Republican outrage over Clinton and Democratic rage over Bush is merely an approximation. Both camps participated in New Anger. They engaged in a mode in which anger was often its own excuse and the angry felt no shame for descending into this emotion. On the contrary, New Anger is proud of itself, and both Clinton-haters and Bush-haters were unapologetic in the license they claimed to declare enmity to their foes.

What kind of description might actually illuminate New Anger's political side? I think we might best get the measure of it by watching the call-and-response of anger politics, as partisans on one side launch rhetorical outbursts and partisans on the other side try to figure out what is happening. The recognition of New Anger in politics was, despite the earlier assaults on President Clinton, surprisingly slow and halting, and even as it came into focus for some observers, others—like Alan Wolfe—continued to deny that anything new or unusual was taking place.

Call-and-Response

As a first step, let's recall a little more precisely the kind of anger that conservatives expressed about Clinton while he was in office. In January 1997, President Clinton was beginning his second term and was greeted by William Safire's column in the *New York Times* wondering how we should answer our children's questions about Clinton's "ethical lapses and moral squalor." He suggested that the kids be told, among other things, that "It is wrong to use tax-exempt money to support political activity."[7] Sandy Grady, writing in a syndicated column, glanced at the Paula Jones allegations, the bribery allegations, and other troubles, and pronounced that "Clinton's second term will be a slog through exploding mines."[8] In March, David Tell, in an editorial for the conservative *Weekly Standard,* commented on the White House defense of providing overnight stays in the Lincoln Bedroom for donors to Clinton's campaign: "And therein lies the most depressing and least soluble aspect of this latest— but certainly not last—scandal surrounding Bill Clinton. Faced with an embarrassing revelation, he and his colleagues have a single, instinctive, and overriding impulse. They lie about it."[9] A few months later, Mary McGrory opined in the *Washington Post* that "This president who prides himself on his pity for others also has the capacity to feel endless pity for himself when things go wrong. Clinton is a child of his age; he believes more in the thrust-out lower lip than the stiff upper one."[10]

These sorts of comments by mainstream journalists treated Clinton disrespectfully, but they do not sound angry. Moreover, the emotions they do convey seem to trail rather than lead the substantive criticisms. These are not statements about what Safire, Grady, and McGrory *feel* about Clinton.

But the tone was changing. A month after McGrory wrote about Clinton's self-pity, she wrote about Clinton's willingness to certify that Paula Jones is "a truthful and moral person." McGrory wondered how Clinton "learned about her probity during a single encounter he denies ever happened, and one she says was given over by his unzipping of a lewd suggestion."[11] The note of disdain seems clear. Grady likewise appeared to be on a path to a much less amused assessment of Clinton. By October 1997, in a column about videotapes of Clinton's White House fundraising parties, Grady wrote, "these tapes show Clinton and his presidency at their grubbiest. Sweating, desperate not to be outspent in the 1996 campaign, he's peddling his charm and clout to bagmen one step away from a police lineup."[12]

A month later, Robert Bork pondered "Should He Be Impeached?" in the magazine that had become the central vehicle of right-wing detestation of Clinton, the *American Spectator*. The article was a fantasy co-authored by the magazine's editor, R. Emmett Tyrrell; and Bork, of course, was the jurist who had been nominated by President Reagan to a seat on the U.S. Supreme Court but failed to win Senate confirmation after a Democratic campaign that vilified him. In Bork's view, "Bill Clinton came to office promising the most ethical administration in our history and has instead given us the sleaziest."[13] Bork made clear that he viewed Clinton as someone who had abused the powers of his office, but this sentence is the closest he got to expressing an emotion.

Harsher words were still to come. The *Weekly Standard* began to look forward to Clinton's removal from office. In May 1998, editor William Kristol prophesied:

> Neither French nor Hollywood mores have taken over the country, and we are not about to have the morality of the casting couch take over the Oval Office. Americans' "wobbly moralism," in the words of Andrew Ferguson, will at last find its legs and reassert itself. Exploitative and adulterous sex; lying; obstruction of justice—Americans will reject them all, and the president who embodies them. That is Clinton's fate.[14]

Journalist Joe Fitzgerald, writing in the *Boston Herald* in September 1988 in the wake of the Starr Report, mocked Clinton's shallow expressions of contrition: "The more he stirs this mess he's made of his life, the more it stinks." Clinton, he added, "is an empty vessel" and his prayer-breakfast request for forgiveness a "scriptural version of three-card monte."[15] Columnist George Will took the occasion to wonder about the willingness of Clinton's staff and cabinet to stick with him: "Clinton's cowardice in sending forth others to absorb pain for him matches his obtuseness." But Will was against impeachment, observing that "impeaching him seems vaguely like using a howitzer against a gnat."[16] David Tell at the *Weekly Standard,* however, was ratcheting up a less forgiving rhetoric:

> Here at THE WEEKLY STANDARD, we no longer much care what party Bill Clinton belongs to. And we have never much cared that his crimes are "about sex." They could be about a lemon meringue pie, and the nation's problem would remain just as severe. The President of the United States is a deliberate and unrepentant perjurer—a man who has thus demonstrated bottomless contempt for the rule of law.[17]

The *New York Times* columnist A. M. Rosenthal observed in December 1998 that "the Clinton story is not the essence of America.... It is one nasty episode...." Rosenthal concluded, "We are ankle-deep in Mr. Clinton's own character-gook."[18] At almost the same moment, David Tell was fiercer, again in the *Weekly Standard,* saying that Clinton:

> has behaved like a decadent king. Bill Clinton, by his actions in 1998, has demonstrated a bottomless contempt for our written law and common language alike. If he is not impeached by the House and convicted by the Senate, Congress will have voiced a shocking formal judgment that it is acceptable to have such rot at the center of the nation's collective enterprise.[19]

This entire litany of criticisms clearly focused on Clinton's character—or actions that exemplified his character. Few critics at that point were dwelling on the consequential political missteps of Clinton's first term, such as his delegation to Hillary of the task of overhauling the American health-care system. It is perhaps worth keeping this in mind as another point of contrast with Bush-hatred. Anger is, by its nature, present-tense, but anger at Clinton was *especially* present-tense. While it kept in mind a long narrative of his previous misdeeds (real and imaginary), it savored the latest scandal and fed on the sense that Clinton continued to lie in order to cover his previous lies. Anger at Bush, by contrast, puts more emphasis on the narrative of past misdeeds. Clinton was attacked for *lying;* Bush for having *lied.*

In March 1999, columnist Jeff Jacoby ruminated about Juanita Broaddrick's accusation that Clinton had raped her in 1978. Like a lot of people, Jacoby found the accusation credible, and commented, "Nobody is shocked. For more than six years, Americans have been pelted with nonstop evidence of Clinton's depravity." In Jacoby's view, Clinton "never admits to the truth. He denies, he lies, he obfuscates, he perjures himself, he wags his finger at the T.V. cameras, he tells his aides and Cabinet secretaries that he is being set up...."[20] "Depravity" was the extreme word in this attack, and an increasingly common one for those who found Clinton unbearable. By November 1999, when the race for the next presidential election was beginning to take shape, Andrew Sullivan wrote in a retrospective tone that "the Clinton-Gore administration has been a domestic success [but] its tawdriness, tackiness and sheer depravity have left a very bad taste."[21]

This sampling of sour views about Clinton during three years of his presidency by no means captures the most vehement expressions of Clinton-aversion. Those probably are to be found in the archives of Internet discussion groups. The statements of mainstream opinion-makers, however, show that the game back then was considerably tamer than today. Indeed, by today's standards the censoriousness of these writers seems almost genteel and the anger tinged with disappointment. After Clinton's reelection in 1996, few of his critics saw a constructive way out of the scandals, which seemed to have a life of their own. Even the saturnine Judge Bork viewed Clinton as unlikely to face a campaign of the kind of intensity that drove Nixon from office. Clinton's "disingenuous protestations" would not save him, wrote Bork, but the diffidence of the press and the people would mean that the "unremitting scandals" would just continue. As conservatives resigned themselves to this prospect, their anger about Clinton became more caustic.

William Safire's January 1997 accusation of "moral

squalor" and Andrew Sullivan's November 1999 summation of "tawdriness, tackiness and sheer depravity" bracket the era of Clinton's biggest scandals and his impeachment. Much of the rhetoric is angry and some of it, in New Anger fashion, reflects showmanship, as writers compete for the image or phrase that most perfectly expresses their contempt for a disgraceful man. And yet none of these attacks has the distilled venom of Jonathan Chait's "I hate President George W. Bush," or the bilious resentment of those on the left who declare that it is "payback time." Clinton-hatred was genuine, but the era had no real equivalent to "Buck Fush" buttons and the five-foot inflatable George W. Bush punching bag, available from bopbush.com for $24 and sold at trendy shops all over Boston.

Anger, Hate, and Fear

The explosion of anger on the left was certainly noticed on the right, and some writers on the left have also remarked on anger's broader currency. The analyses, however, vary a bit in identifying the emotion. Some say *anger;* some say *hate;* a few introduce the idea of *fear;* and *disappointment* and *loathing* show up too. Hatred and anger clearly are not the same thing. We can be angry without hating and, though it is less common, we can hate without anger. Generally, anger denotes a specific and short-lived emotional episode, while hatred denotes a settled disposition. "I hate oranges" does not mean that I am perpetually angry at the fruit and likely to tear off in a rage should I encounter an orange in the supermarket. I might be angry, however, if someone, knowing my dislike of this ostentatious fruit, invited me to dinner and served me a big bright bowl of them.

Still, anger and fear are physiologically related as well as close partners in everyday experience. We often get angry at someone we fear, and most people, at some level, fear their own anger.

Some political theorists such as Thomas Hobbes have made much of the relation between anger and fear, and New

Anger, like all anger, is indeed entangled with fears. The bug-
bears of those who express New Anger are fears of
powerlessness and *irrelevance*. New Anger is narcissistic rage;
it wants to be noticed and it takes reaffirming pleasure in its
own presence. The calamity lurking around the corner is that
no one will care.

New Anger has a special affinity to identity politics at a
time when claims of group rights and group grievances are
losing much of their capacity to compel attention. Fearing
that identity groups will slip still further in political leverage,
their champions respond with a crescendo of New Anger.
Here, for instance, Tim Wise in *LiP Magazine* excoriates Larry
Elder, Shelby Steele, Ken Hamblin, Thomas Sowell, Clarence
Thomas, John McWhorter, and others—all of them black
conservatives—for propagating "myths" that social problems
experienced by African Americans have any sources other
than white racism:

> After all, their hustle has paid enormous dividends. Black
> conservatives, by dint of their hard work on behalf of institu-
> tionalized white domination, have managed to obtain access
> to the halls of white power, and even occasionally positions
> of power themselves. On the one hand, this kind of step'n
> fetchit routine can be lucrative and professionally rewarding
> for those willing to play the game, or [to] convince them-
> selves of the beneficence of their white cocktail party friends,
> it can mean foundation grants, endowed chairs at right-wing
> think tanks, radio shows, syndicated columns and regular
> appearances on Fox.[22]

No evidence contaminates Wise's screed against the character
of the individuals he attacks, and it takes only a moment's
reflection to realize that vastly greater numbers of liberal
African Americans achieve power, get foundation grants, are
appointed to endowed chairs, have radio shows, and write
syndicated columns than do black conservatives. (As to the
percentage of FOX TV appearances, I have no idea, but it is
an odd standard, since black conservatives are a rare sight
on most of the other networks.) Wise, however, is not arguing a case; he is merely acting out a version of New Anger.

In cases like this, New Anger looks so much like hatred or determined loathing that there is little point in trying to draw a strict distinction between how much is really anger and how much is hate. New Anger is anger to the extent that it inflates itself with the rhetoric of rage; it is hate to the extent that it regularly aims its fury at the same detested targets. Because New Anger is planted in a sense of power-lessness, it swells to ever greater heights. But the targets of the wrath often respond in conspicuously tamer language. New Anger claws the air; but its targets often just shake their heads. New Anger is usually found in asymmetrical situations: Rage Against the Machine doesn't expect the Machine to reply in kind.

When President Bush declined for the fourth year in a row to accept an invitation to speak to the NAACP's annual meeting, he was lambasted by the organization's president, Kweisi Mfume, and its chairman, Julian Bond, both of whom had long histories of New Anger attacks on Bush and his sup-porters. Shortly before the NAACP convention, for example, Bond said that Bush Republicans "draw their most rabid sup-porters from the Taliban wing of American politics." Actually, he was recycling a gibe he had first used in February 2001 and repeated with small variations many times since, caricaturing the Bush administration by saying:

> They selected nominees from the Taliban wing of American
> politics, appeased the wretched appetites of the extreme
> right wing and chose Cabinet officials whose devotion to the
> Confederacy is nearly canine in its uncritical affection.

Bond repeated this at Macalester College in March 2001; again at the July 2001 NAACP convention; and again in December 2001, when the United States was at war with the real Taliban in Afghanistan. Apparently he liked the sound of it, and the Bush administration's alleged links with the "Tal-iban wing of American politics" became a staple of Bond's anti-Bush speeches.[23]

After President Bush declined the NAACP invitation in 2004, Mfume said, "We're not fools. If you're going to court us, court us in the daytime, but not like we're a prostitute

where you run around at night or behind closed doors...."
And Bond accused Bush of "outright theft of black votes" in
the 2000 election.[24]

New Anger has perhaps taken us to the point where it
is hard to register just how far Bond and Mfume have moved
in these remarks beyond the older standards of political
decency. Rhetoric of this sort is essentially self-annihilating.
It may please a highly partisan audience, but it also gets
reported in the papers, where it delegitimates the speakers
and the organization they purport to speak for. Under the
circumstances, Secretary of Education Rod Paige's response
was mild:

> I have a message for the NAACP's Julian Bond and Kweisi
> Mfume, who have accused black conservatives of being "pup-
> pets" of white people, unable to think for ourselves. You do
> not own, and you are not the arbiters of, African-American
> authenticity.

Paige also declared that Bond and Mfume had done a "great
disservice" to the NAACP "with their hateful and untruthful
rhetoric about Republicans and President Bush."[25] This is the
language of rebuke, but it is measured in its indignation.
Rather than answering New Anger with New Anger, Paige
stuck with traditional retort.

John McWhorter responded to the NAACP's histrionics
in even more temperate tones:

> Lifting blacks up is no longer a matter of getting whites off
> our necks. We are faced, rather, with the mundane tasks of
> teaching those "left behind" after the civil rights victory how
> to succeed in a complex society—one in which there will
> never be a second civil rights revolution.... Mfume and the
> NAACP's anger-based politics imply that black success can
> only be accidental unless the playing field is completely
> level. Instead of insisting on that, they should be working on
> specific cures to specific ills....[26]

Does a soft answer turn away wrath? Not if it is New Anger
wrath, which seems only to swell. Indeed, since New Anger
wants to elicit anger in return, when it is unrequited it typically tries again.

Conservatives have been relatively slow in realizing that they are up against a new kind of cultural phenomenon. Among the earliest near-recognitions of New Anger by a conservative that I have found is an article by Brian C. Anderson in the spring 2001 issue of *City Journal,* published by the Manhattan Institute.[27] Anderson argued in "Illiberal Liberalism" that the 1990s had brought an increasing volume of name calling, mostly by the left. He mentions the rising use of epithets such as "racist," "homophobe," "sexist," "mean-spirited," and "insensitive," and immediately catches what sets these insults apart from normal political raucousness:

> It has become a habit of left-liberal political argument to use such invective to dismiss conservative beliefs as if they don't deserve an argument and to redefine mainstream conservative arguments as extremism and bigotry. Close-minded and uncivil, this tendency betrays what's liberal in liberalism.

Anderson reviews the older liberal precepts undermined by this new kind of "political argument." (In truth, Anderson errs in calling it an "argument," since it is really just a hardened attitude. The apparatus of actual argument is missing.) The invective, he says, destroys the civility on which democratic government depends, and it dismisses the "belief in the superiority of reasoned argument over force." He offers, as the first of a series of examples, Vice President Gore addressing the NAACP about foes of affirmative action. Gore declared, "They use their 'color blind' the way duck hunters use a duck blind— they hide behind it and hope the ducks won't notice." From this Gore slid into wondering how opponents of affirmative action reacted to the killing of a black man in Virginia who "was doused with gasoline, burned alive, and decapitated."[28]

According to Anderson, such attempts to stigmatize the critics of a position rather than answer the substance of their criticism became standard fare on the left in the 1990s. Anderson's whole article deserves attention as an early warning of New Anger, but perhaps his most important points come near the end. He touches on political theorist Peter Berkowitz's observation that followers of the liberal philosopher John Rawls had adopted a conception of justice that "by fiat proclaims unreasonable and places beyond the pale of public discussion the considered views of many Catholics, Protestants and Jews." And Anderson adds:

> All you can learn from such a conception is how thoughtlessly dismissive is the contemporary liberal attitude, even at its most intellectual, toward principled conservatism. A recent seminar discussion among liberal philosophy professors on how to deal with moral conflicts over abortion, homosexuality, and pornography shows just how thoughtless. One professor, a disciple of John Stuart Mill, argued that in a free society, traditional values at least need debate. The others, Rawlsians to a man, responded: No way. "Why should we listen to loons?" one prominent liberal philosopher opined. "We should just crush them."

Rawls and his followers are noteworthy for providing a veneer of intellectual justification for the new bigotry, but Anderson rightly looks for a source further back:

> The liberals' habits of censoring and discrediting conservative views is a holdover from the 1960s' New Left, whose style and ideology had a profound influence in the late sixties and early seventies on the Democratic Party and on many who now call themselves liberals. The New Left divided the political world into "the good inside and the monstrous outside," in the words of political scientist Richard Ellis.

Once the world is recast as a struggle between "the good guys working for a radiant future" and the bad guys who defend an "unjust and oppressive society," the way is clear not only for name calling but for dispensing with any of the niceties of political argument.

By Anderson's reckoning, the left's success in derailing the appointment of Robert Bork to the Supreme Court in 1987 was the victory that validated the new style. Bork was prevented from winning confirmation not by anyone successfully taking issue with his qualifications, but by an unremitting campaign of vilification. Anderson doesn't quite put it this way, but *anger* worked. A sufficiently loud and vehement chorus of declarations that Bork was "out of the mainstream" made real debate unnecessary.

In his "Illiberal Liberalism" article, Anderson spotted the tsunami racing toward shore, but he failed to identify exactly what it was made of. Rather, he characterized what it was not: *not* classical liberal tolerance, *not* principled commitment to rational debate, and *not* a worldview in which people must act on good faith knowing that humanity is error-prone and largely ignorant about what the future will bring. Beyond this, Anderson only saw that "illiberal liberalism" meant name calling and unscrupulous personal attacks. What he didn't see clearly was the emotional dynamic of this political wave, and beyond that, how the new political absolutism of the left was the product of a cultural transformation.

The Angry Left in Focus

In retrospect, it is easy to see that the New Anger was crystallizing in somewhat different patterns on the right and the left, and that the left was pushing it to a new extreme. But as the call-and-response of anger developed in the first Bush administration, observers were rather slow to comprehend the change. Let's observe the awakening as it occurred.

In the same issue with Jonathan Chait's "I hate President George W. Bush" article, the *New Republic* published a short article by the conservative pundit Ramesh Ponnuru tracing the left's anger back to the contested vote counting in Florida in the 2000 election, but also emphasized the 2002 gubernatorial race in that state. In 2002, the national Democratic Party tried to avenge the 2000 loss in Florida and came up woefully short. Governor Jeb Bush won reelection by thirteen points.[29]

What happened *after* the 2002 Florida gubernatorial election brings to mind a classic sociological study, *When Prophecy Fails* (1956), which examined how the followers of a messianic cult in an American town responded when their leader's predictions repeatedly fell flat. Many of the followers made excuses and redoubled their belief that the prophet would ultimately be vindicated. The failure to unseat Governor Bush likewise seems to have hardened the belief of many Democrats that intense anger would ultimately prove to be an effective political strategy.[30] Ponnuru doesn't cite *When Prophecy Fails,* but he describes a similar spiral of angry feelings:

> Florida is where Bush hatred started, where the Democrats' disdain for an underachieving frat boy began to morph into something more malevolent. Democrats saw Bush's tactics during the recount as an unprincipled, damn-the-conse-quences bid for power. Republicans saw Al Gore's tactics the same way and were as outraged by the Florida Supreme Court's actions as the Democrats were by the U.S. Supreme Court's. But the Republicans won and moved on. Many Democrats didn't.

Ponnuru observes that "Bush hatred has taken on a life of its own" and become "a sentiment that unites the Democra-tic Party." Conservatives, he notes, were mostly baffled by the phenomenon, since Bush campaigned and governed as a "moderate conservative." Liberals, he writes, are mostly frus-trated that Bush co-opted many of their campaign issues (such as the "Patients' Bill of Rights" and prescription drugs), leaving them to dredge up implausible grievances as the only way to clothe a visceral dislike. But Ponnuru adds one more perceptive comment: "At the end of the day," Bush-hatred "seems largely cultural." Bush simply stands for those aspects of America that "blue-state America" hates about "red-state America." Ponnuru ends with a friendly warning to Demo-crats: a political strategy based on antipathy would be unlikely to win the 2004 presidential election.

Ponnuru's analysis improved on Anderson's because in the intervening two and a half years, the emotional basis of the left's illiberalism became more and more evident. In another sense, however, Ponnuru failed to see Bush-hatred in as full a historical light as Anderson did in his earlier arti-cle. For Ponnuru, Bush-hatred is *sui generis*—a particular antipathy aroused against one man who happens to embody the qualities of the country most strongly rejected by the left, and who also personifies the "injustice" of having prevailed in a disputed election. Ponnuru glided by the problem that something like Bush-hatred preceded Bush by five or six years. In that time, the Democratic Party had already turned to what Governor Bill Clinton had labeled early in his 1992 presidential campaign as "the politics of personal destruction." It is useful to recall just what prompted the phrase.

One of Clinton's rivals for the nomination was the former Massachusetts senator Paul Tsongas. By March 1992, accusations of marital infidelity, draft dodging, and dubious business dealings had already surfaced, and Tsongas had run a thirty-second television ad that questioned Clinton's honesty. Reporters followed up with questions for Clinton, who adroitly cast himself as a victim. During a tour of a cheesecake factory in Illinois, he declared that the American people "are tired of the politics of personal destruction." The phrase very quickly became part of the political lexicon of Bill and Hillary Clinton and their supporters as a means of deflecting questions about character, while insinuating that the other side had stooped to an unworthy level. The cheesecake dodge exemplifies a way of fomenting anger under the guise of deflecting it.[31]

In September 2003, Ponnuru was not alone in taking notice of the peculiar intensity of the left's disdain for Bush. The late Robert Bartley, writing in the *Wall Street Journal* that month, diagnosed the Democrats' anger as resentment over a lost "birthright." Bartley suggested that "base Democrats think of themselves as the best people: the most intelligent and informed, the most public spirited, the most morally pure." With loss of power in Washington came loss of something more profound—self-identity:

> It's possible, we've witnessed, to assert moral superiority while defending the Clinton perjury, sexual escapades, vanishing billing records and last-minute pardons. But politicians, pundits and intellectuals with this record shouldn't expect much moral deference from the rest of us. Indeed, inner doubts about their own moral position is one obvious path to anger.

Bartley concluded that Democratic anger is the reflex of "an establishment in the process of being replaced."[32]

Bartley's explanation of rage over a lost "birthright" stops short of invoking psychopathology, but that explanation wasn't far off. Soon afterward, the syndicated columnist Charles Krauthammer suggested that Democrats might be collectively suffering from a syndrome called "secondary mania," which he punditized as "Bush Derangement Syndrome: the acute onset of paranoia in otherwise normal people in reaction to the policies, the presidency—nay—the very existence of George W. Bush." Krauthammer cited Governor Howard Dean's comment on National Public Radio in which he wondered whether Bush "was warned ahead of time [about the 9/11 attack] by the Saudis." He mentioned Barbra Streisand writing to Dick Gephardt in September 2002 to the effect that Bush was planning the war in Iraq to satisfy "the usual corporate malefactors" including the timber industry. And he noticed Bill Moyers "ranting about a 'right-wing wrecking crew' engaged in 'a deliberate, intentional destruction of the United States way of governing.'"[33]

The same December week that Krauthammer's column appeared, *Time* magazine offered a lengthy article, "The Love Him, Hate Him President." Declaring that Bush is "the Great Polarizer" who has "cleaved the nation into two tenaciously opposed camps," the authors saw that Bush has "wrapped his presidency in who he is and what he believes," and that this seems heroic to some and "stubbornly simpleminded" to others. The latter get most of the attention in the article. We meet, for example, Jay Schwartz, who has a bumper sticker on his minivan in Chicago that says Bush is a "Punk Ass Chump." Schwartz told the *Time* reporters that his anger toward Bush is "a very gut-level response to feeling totally disenfranchised and upset with Bush, his Administration and his cocksure attitude."[34]

So where does this anger come from? The article mentions several important considerations. The political parties have gerrymandered safe districts for themselves in almost every state; the "proliferation of the media" means that people no longer need to listen to views they disagree with; Bush is "the most openly religious President in modern times";

and yes, we have seen "The Rise of the Anger Industry," as the journalists titled a sidebar. The "anger industry" turns out to be the flood of politically angry books from both the right and the left. The article concludes with another sidebar recalling that the "American cacophony" is not new; we've been angry before, as witness Father Charles Coughlin's angry radio broadcasts in the 1930s.

The points are all individually well taken, but they seem to gather to a self-canceling conclusion. *Time* ends up saying that anger about Bush is distinct enough to warrant labeling him "the Great Polarizer," but *Time* also says that the anger is just a reflexive response to trivial issues such as congressional gerrymandering and media proliferation; and anyway, we have *always* been angry. Which of these contradictory points does the magazine endorse? Seemingly all at once, but that leads to the bland conclusion that the uninhibited, self-congratulatory, and satisfied anger we have right now is indistinguishable from the hard-won and occasionally lost self-control of decades past. The *Time* article seems to have been written *within* the worldview of New Anger itself, without a glimmer of realization that anything significant had changed on this historical stage.

A few months after Ponnuru's and Bartley's attempts to figure out the Democrats' hatred of President Bush and a few weeks after Krauthammer's satiric jab and *Time*'s blurry roundup, a Stanford linguist and NPR commentator named Geoffrey Nunberg published an essay in the *New York Times* in which he sized up the phenomenon in a dramatically different way.[35] In Nunberg's estimate, the "anger wars" are a Republican fabrication, kicked off in July 2003 by Ed Gillespie's speech to the Republican National Committee. In that speech, Gillespie attacked the Democrats as serving up raw anger in place of argument, and he stuck with the theme subsequently. Nunberg also noticed Marc Racicot, chairman of Bush's reelection committee, inveighing against the "venomous assault from rage-filled Democrats." But in Nunberg's view, the anger of the Democrats is a normal response to "how President Bush came by his job" and "what he's done with it since." Moreover, Democratic anger is of a piece with Republican anger:

> The left is expressing itself with the same pugnacity as the right, Democrats say. If the tone comes out sounding angry in Democrats and merely aggressive in Republicans, that's because of the discrepancies in power between the two, not because of any temperamental difference between the sides.

Nunberg also correctly pointed out that many of the epithets Democrats use against Bush are the same as those Republicans used against Clinton: liar, phony, hypocrite. He concluded that the Republicans are really hoping to stigmatize legitimate Democratic rhetoric by invoking "civil rights" words like "hate speech" that are inapplicable in this new context. "Hate speech," for instance, properly applies to "disparaged social groups on the basis of race, sex, religion and the like" and not to "personal antipathy to the president."

The trick of stealing an opponent's catchphrase and redefining it to suit one's own purposes was surely on the minds of Republicans who appropriated "hate speech" as a characterization of the left's particular form of anger. But both sides play that game; the more interesting issue is whether the left's anger against Bush in 2003 and 2004 can properly be characterized as simply the Democrats' version of an established political mode, available to and exploited by both parties. Nunberg is nearer the truth than conservative partisans would like to admit, but he also overstates his case.

Conservatives had certainly wandered into New Anger territory during the scandal that culminated in the Clinton impeachment. But contrary to Nunberg, this does not make the kind of anger we are now witnessing an age-old politics-as-usual mode of expression; nor does it mean that Clinton-hating and Bush-hating are identical in emotional character. I'll return to the contrast in due course. The task at hand is to capture the historical moment when at least some Americans began to realize that our politics had been invaded by New Anger. The key to this is the widespread recognition that the Democrats' anger was more and more concerned with its own performance than with any specific grievances.

As a conservative critique of the Democrats' debauch into rage-politics began to take shape, the rage itself simply intensified. During the Democratic primary in the fall of 2003 and through January 2004, Howard Dean, growing ever more histrionic in his anger, remained the dominant figure. And the Internet-based leftist organization MoveOn.org ardently exacerbated the situation. In January, for example, MoveOn announced the winner of a contest for a thirty-second anti-Bush advertisement, for which they had set aside $15 million. The winner, "Child's Play," depicts young children working on assembly lines and as janitors "to pay off President Bush's $1 trillion deficit." MoveOn also posted many of the 1,500 entries on its website, including two that compare Bush to Hitler. Jack Pitney, a political scientist at the Claremont Colleges, told a reporter, "The MoveOn material in general and the ads in particular are designed to make angry people even angrier, but they don't necessarily broaden the anti-Bush coalition."[36]

That description seems to fit the emotional trajectory of New Anger as a spectacle to be witnessed by an appreciative audience, not an attempt to win over the uncommitted. For anger to persuade, it has to be held back and forced to fuel more subtle suasions. Anger unleashed can hope only to intimidate a foe or impress a friend. It is not a strategy for winning over the undecided.

And before long, many observers were remarking the peculiar futility of the left's rage.

Anger Is "In"

Shortly after John Kerry sealed the Democratic presidential nomination in the primaries, *USA Today* ran an article under the headline "Voter Anger Alone Can't Capture the White House." *USA Today,* which is seldom mistaken for a source of cutting-edge insights, warned, "Elections are won by attracting the political moderates and independents who can be turned off by over-the-top partisan rage." The article took as plain fact that the Democratic primaries had been shaped by "fury toward Bush," which it compared vaguely to the earlier fury toward Clinton.[37]

This article, which ran on March 3, came roughly six months after Jonathan Chait's "I hate President George W. Bush" manifesto in the *New Republic* and Robert Bartley's "Angry Democrats—Lost Birthright" column in the *Wall Street Journal.* In those six months, the assessment of the Democrats as seething with anger had moved from the elite opinion makers to the *USA Today*'s version of received wisdom. By March, no one was echoing Nunberg's December declarations in the *New York Times* that the "anger wars" were a "Republican fabrication." *USA Today* did, however, support the idea retailed by Nunberg and *Time* magazine that the Democrats' anger was not so different from Republican anger over Clinton.

After the beginning of March, the recognition in the American press of the anger fueling the Democratic campaign became widespread, but a handful of articles stand out for their authors' attempts to make sense of this new political style. For example, a few weeks after the *USA Today* article, Stephen Miller, an independent scholar and fellow at the American Enterprise Institute, published a commentary in the *Wall Street Journal* under the title "Anger Mismanagement." Rather than just lambaste Democrats for excessive anger, Miller steps back and considers the cultural shift. He begins by noticing the histrionic quality of the anger: "John Kerry is angry—and he wants voters to know it." In other words, the anger in question is not a matter of private seething, nor is it focused primarily on an opponent. Rather, it is anger intended for display. It says, in effect, "Look at me. I'm angry."[38]

Miller also observes that "Righteous anger is for many Americans a good thing: a sign of one's commitment and integrity, and not just in politics." He cites, as an example, Gerald Green's 1956 novel, *The Last Angry Man,* in which the protagonist is "an elderly Brooklyn doctor, [who] is angry because he cares deeply about the community." But Miller nonetheless senses a shift:

> In the past year, I've noticed that many friends of mine—

Republican and Democratic alike—get truly angry when discussing politics. A Democratic friend calls George W. Bush a usurper and liar. A Republican friend calls Mr. Kerry a liar (about Vietnam) and a waffler. Which side is angrier? I don't know, but anger definitely is "in."

Miller notes that Howard Dean's anger "was a symbol of his *authenticity* as an 'outsider' candidate," and he quotes the *New York Times* columnist Paul Krugman sneering at those who reproved the flood of angry pronouncements:

"All this fuss about civility," wrote Mr. Krugman, angrily, "...is an attempt to bully critics into unilaterally disarming— into being demure and respectful of the president."

Miller's article thus far strikes me as exactly on target. He has captured three of the key qualities of New Anger: that it is performed for an audience; that it extends across party lines and into domains beyond politics; and that it is grounded at a deep level on claims of personal authenticity.

Miller also takes up the vexing question of whether this kind of anger in American politics is actually new. He cites nineteenth-century English visitors (Mrs. Trollope and Charles Dickens) on the "electioneering madness" of Americans and our "injurious Party Spirit," and he quotes candidate Rutherford B. Hayes predicting in the 1876 presidential race that a victory by the Democrat, Samuel Tilden, would be an "irretrievable calamity." Yet, says Miller,

in the 19th century there was not what might be called an ideology of anger, as there seems to be now. In the past 40 years, countercultural theorists, psychologists, rappers and talk-show hosts have acted as if expressing one's anger is good for the psyche and good for the nation. In his (sadly) influential essay "The White Negro" (1957), Norman Mailer said: "To be an existentialist, one must be able to feel oneself—one must know one's desires, one's rages, one's anguish, one must be aware of the character of one's frustration and know what would satisfy it." Existentialist here is a fancy term for a person who gets in touch with his feelings. And feelings are everywhere now, with plenty of fuel to keep the angry fires burning.

Miller deserves the credit for publishing the first full recognition that the Democrats' rage in the 2004 presidential race has to be understood as one manifestation of a broader cultural development—the development of what I have labeled "New Anger."

The recognition of an unusual intensity of anger continued to spread during the late spring and summer of 2004. The *Los Angeles Times* editorialized, under the headline "Rage Is All the Rage," that Howard Dean "didn't invent public anger when he lost Iowa and his temper. But his late-night fist-waving punched the campaign fast-forward button." The editorial balanced a jaundiced view of American politics ("American candidates prefer divisive stances to steel their core supporters") with the suggestion that the anger was spreading beyond its usual political precincts. An anger management assembly in Woodlawn, Maryland, for example, provoked "a fist-throwing, sneaker-swinging melee" among 750 students, resulting in two arrests and eleven suspensions.[39]

In late May, another campaign event solidified public recognition that the nation had wandered into a kind of emotional Bermuda Triangle in which the normal gauges and controls were malfunctioning. On May 26, Al Gore gave a 6,500-word speech to MoveOn.org full of thundering denunciations of Bush and the Republicans. His performance was so angrily excessive that the reliably left-leaning *New York Times* pundit Maureen Dowd said that Gore now represents "the wackadoo wing of the Democratic Party." The *Wall Street Journal's* official blogger, James Taranto, observed that "the immoderation of Gore's words, combined with the fury of his tone, puts him in a class by himself, or very nearly so, even among angry Dems."[40] What exactly did Gore say to provoke such reactions? Among the most quoted lines was a declaration that President Bush "has brought deep dishonor to our country and built a durable reputation as the most dishonest president since Richard Nixon." This is also where Gore spoke the line I quoted earlier, that Bush "has created more anger and righteous indignation against us as Americans than any leader of our country in the 228 years of our existence as a nation." And he compared Bush somewhat bizarrely to the Marquis de Sade for creating "an American gulag" full of torturers.[41]

Polarization

In June 2004, as public recognition of an exceptional degree of anger was settling in, John Tierney in the *New York Times* offered a fresh rebuttal. Drawing on the work of several scholars, including Alan Wolfe, Tierney focused on studies purporting to show "that the polarized nation is largely a myth created by people inside the Beltway talking to each other or, more precisely, shouting at each other." In this account, the anger is real but mostly confined to political elites. The general public consists of a majority of "centrists" in both parties who agree on most issues. Party leaders, however, have a strong interest in provoking and exaggerating differences. The "culture wars" are therefore an illusion, maintained by the elite politicos but not rooted in the experience of ordinary people.[42]

Tierney's main source for this picture was a Stanford University political scientist, Morris P. Fioina, who with two colleagues, Samuel J. Abrams and Jeremy C. Pope, had written a book, *Culture War? The Myth of a Polarized America*, attempting to demonstrate that large majorities support stricter gun control, the death penalty, and legal abortion, and oppose racial preferences in hiring. Tierney also found support for his picture of an un-polarized nation in the work of a sociologist at Princeton, Paul DiMaggio, who has found that the range of opinions among Americans divided by race, age, sex, education, religion, and region has been steadily diminishing over the last several decades. And Tierney cites the views of Alan Wolfe that I referred to at the beginning of this chapter—that "our disagreements now are not that deep," especially in comparison with earlier periods. The exception, says Wolfe, is gay marriage, which really is polarizing.

Tierney then turns to the question, "Why, if the public is tolerant, would the political elites be so angry?" He offers five reasons: "the decline of party bosses" who could promote centrist candidates; the rise of special-interest groups focused on ideologies; permanent lobbies that can use their defeats as a way of spurring donations from their supporters; media professionals who use anger to entertain their audiences; and gerrymandering, which protects incumbents in general elections but forces them "to appeal to the partisan voters who dominate primaries." Professor Fioina returns at the end of the article to offer a sixth reason: "voters are merely responding to a president who is more partisan than virtually all of his modern predecessors."

A certain amount of self-contradiction slips into Tierney's picture of American political culture. If large majorities have, in effect, reached consensus on the supposedly contentious issues, where do these ideological "interest groups" get their popular support? Who are the donors that are so moved by the defeat of their ideas that they redouble their contributions? Who are the readers, listeners, and watchers who provide such lucrative livings to the media hotheads? Who are the "partisan voters" that turn out for the primaries? These people collectively may be, in sheer numbers, smaller segments of the population than those who veer toward the consensus "moderate" positions identified by researchers such as Professors Fioina, DiMaggio, and Wolfe, but they are obviously not all members of the "political elite."

If we go look for the culture war as a matter of constant and heated disagreement among ordinary people, we will indeed fail to find it. That's for several reasons. First, most American people are passive consumers of culture rather than active combatants. They go along with their neighbors and they participate in the culture war only to the extent they cannot avoid it. The existence of noncombatants, however, doesn't mean there's no war. Gettysburg had noncombatants too.

Second, opinion surveys are a weak way to get at some of the deep disagreements in American life. One person may support "gun control" in the sense of keeping guns out of the hands of criminals, while another who supports "gun control" is thinking about the dangers of domestic violence. Two people may agree that abortion should be legal, one believing in an unconditional "woman's right to choose," the other favoring strict laws on parental consent. Surveys can tease out such differences only if the survey is designed to look for them, and often what appears to the pollsters as "broad agreement" masks important splits in premises and logic.

And the "war"—if we have to call it that—is really about these premises and logic. America is divided not by the percentage of people who range on one side or another of a pollster's question, but by two incompatible views of the world. One view emphasizes injustices in American history and the continuing systemic oppression of women and minorities; the other celebrates American freedom and accomplishment. Those who focus on a history of injustice tend to look with pleasure on the crumbling of traditional American culture from the 1960s on. Those who celebrate American freedom tend to look on the last forty years as a period of sharp decline. One side champions the expansion of state-sponsored "rights"; the other champions individual responsibility. One side tends to view the family as an obstacle to personal liberation; the other views the family as the key social institution. Within these two broad frameworks, of course, people disagree about a lot of specific issues. Occasionally people on opposite sides of the division find common ground. But the division itself is nothing trivial: it guides emotional attachments, tastes, lifestyles, and personal decisions as well as political attitudes. The culture war in this sense is perfectly obvious to almost everyone in America, since it is experienced the moment one turns on the television or steps out into the street.

The views of Fioina, DiMaggio, and Wolfe have not gone unchallenged. In a recent article, "How Divided Are We?" Professor James Q. Wilson of Pepperdine University challenges Fioina's views in particular. Wilson argues that the United States is in fact polarized and far from its historical norms in the handling of political disagreements. He cites a Gallup poll in spring 2005 that showed Bush's approval rating among Republicans at 94 percent and among Democrats at 18 percent, "the largest such gap in the history of the Gallup poll." He also examines the growing tendency of Americans to line up along party lines on issues ranging from abortion to the war in Iraq. In Wilson's view, the polarization extends far beyond the narrow opinion-enunciating elite, out to the common voters in both parties.[43]

Wilson explains the growth in divisiveness as the result of three shifts: the political parties evolving from each being a "coalition of dissimilar forces" to each being dominated by ideological concerns; the news media evolving from a relatively few mass-market ventures aimed at the political center to a more plentiful supply of media that "find their markets at the ideological extremes"; and the shift from major interest groups such as the chambers of commerce and the AFL-CIO, focused primarily on material gains, to interest groups "focused on social and cultural matters," such as civil rights and the role of women. These new interest groups are intrinsically less able to compromise since they are rooted in claims about rights and morality.

All three shifts are, I think, real and worth keeping in mind as regards the social changes that underlie polarization. But I also think they stop short of a deep explanation of what has happened, and Wilson's three proposed *causes* for polarization may themselves be *effects* of cultural shifts that also created New Anger and the broader reign of expressive individualism that we are living through. Notwithstanding Wilson's criticisms of Fioina's views, it is easy to see why the hypothesis that the elites are angry and the people aren't has a certain appeal. It reassures us that the genuinely nasty side of the culture war—the calumnies and the vengeful anger—are someone else's fault. The elites, driven by dishonest and selfish motives, are foisting this division upon us. Deep down we are peaceable, friendly folk who would agree on the important things if talk radio and Internet bloggers would let us.

Most people understand that to get along with each other on a daily basis they need to find opaque ways to phrase certain issues that would otherwise embroil coworkers and neighbors in constant acrimony. We don't tear at each other day in and day out on matters such as immigration, the environment, school choice, health-care reform, Social Security, globalization, climate change, homeland security, and the projection of U.S. military power abroad because we know the arguments won't end. Usually we hold back and offer bland bromides instead of jalapeno harangues. But let someone raise one of these issues in a bar, at a party, or in an Internet discussion, and the truce is over. These issues truly do divide the nation into complex and sometimes fiercely opposed communities of opinion that generally fit right inside the culture-war divisions.

Finally, "polarization" and anger are not the same thing. The elites are indeed polarized from each other as well as angry. But if "polarity" means a generalized and total opposition, we can have anger without polarity and polarity without anger. Opposition itself is not necessarily a source of anger. The North Pole is not usually thought of as angry with its Antarctic counterpart, and people (even today) disagree about a lot of things without getting angry. The opposition between fans of hip-hop and fans of country music might well be described as a polarization, but neither cohort seems specifically angry at the other. Indeed, anger sometimes blooms more furiously when people agree about a great deal but unexpectedly find themselves in opposition on some relatively minor point. East Coast and West Coast rappers shoot at each other. The Dixie Chicks and Toby Keith were, for a while, in mutual enmity. Or, for a political example, conservatives who favor tightly closed borders and policies that aim at repatriating significant numbers of illegal aliens are very angry at conservatives who favor amnesty for illegal aliens and relatively relaxed policies toward additional immigration. The anti-immigration conservatives disagree with opponents on the left as well, some of whom favor policies that would considerably extend public benefits to illegal immigrants. But these conservatives are far angrier at fellow conservatives than they are at their leftist opponents.

I certainly don't want to dismiss the connection between polarization and anger. The New Anger does have roots in the cultural polarization of the last half-century. But it has since gone on to a life of its own, and some of the performances of extreme rage on the political scene are more about the hyperinflation in our emotional currency than about the polarization of our politics.

This refutation of the Fioina, DiMaggio, and Wolfe theses stands complete, but it may help to add that at least in the case of Alan Wolfe, his thesis seems to sit awkwardly with his own pronouncements. He long counseled patience and deliberation in public debate but seems lately to have decided, "What the hell. Wrath works." The old Wolfe opined in 1994:

> American politics does seem to have reached a new stage of partisan ugliness, as political parties and interest groups noisily exaggerate their own case and denigrate the case of their opponents. There is considerable polling evidence that Americans are disgusted by the whole spectacle. And the reminder that this kind of public bickering is as old as the republic, and may have healthy consequences for the body politic, falls on deaf ears. Americans hate politics because they detest the conversational style in which it takes place.[44]

Wolfe never opposed ordinary conflict in politics. He regularly chastised those who try to bypass the rough-and-tumble of democratic decision making in favor of artificial consensus. Bickering has its place, according to Wolfe, but how large a place? His model seems to be that the hotheads and extremists will duke it out with each other while a small group of wiser and more temperate thinkers will hold the polity together.

But these days Wolfe also seems to take little time-outs from his job as Mature Advocate of Better Politics to pour battery acid into the aftershave of Bush Republicans. Here he is in 2002, for example, with an early formulation of what would become a leitmotif of the Angry Left:

> During the 2000 election, Bush's advisers discovered something that no one before had ever quite known: there are simply no limits to how much you can lie in American politics and get away with it. And it is the transposition of that approach to politics into policy that constitutes the disgrace of the Bush method.[45]

In the same article, Wolfe asserts:

> The presidents with the lowest reputations over the past hundred or so years were all Republicans, and they were all guided by the conviction that their job was to side with the powerful in any potential conflict with the poor....

> George W. Bush will be lucky if his presidency ever rises to the level of Taft's or Harding's....

> The business of the Bush administration is not just business, but sleazy business. America's worst firms picked America's most complaisant politicians (and vice versa) because they knew that they could work with each other.

And a great deal more in a similar spirit. So much for eschewing "partisan ugliness." The puzzled, aloof sensibility here makes room for the vehement castigator. Nor is this growling version of Wolfe's persona "winking at his own foibles." He is, rather, dead certain of what he says and plainly angry.

Wolfe is but one example of a cultural critic who, having built a career attempting to stand above America's political and social divisions, has lately seized the pitchfork or the broken whiskey bottle to dive into the frenzy.[46] If the apostles of civility cannot abide by their own message, it seems unlikely that the message is going to persuade lots of other angry people to calm down.

Storm Warnings and Fair Weather

John Tierney's *New York Times* article received considerable attention but, of course, did not end the argument over whether the Democrats or the left in general were acting exceptionally angry or, alternatively, simply expressing justified indignation. As the Democratic National Convention approached in the last week of July, conservatives stepped up their commentary on the phenomenon. Michael Novak observed that the "rabid hatred for George Bush that drives Democrats has spread like an infection, farther and farther." And:

> In the past, liberals made a point of hating hatred. They imagined that the forces of hate were entirely on the other side: "Right-wing hate merchants." Now they have begun publicly to glory in hate, first writing articles explaining why hatred of Bush is okay, then being pleasured by the ferocity of their own hatred, then competing with others to see who can voice the most intense disdain, and who can curl from his lips the most deliciously forbidden insults. The Left has engaged in an orgy of hatred. And enjoyed it, really enjoyed it.

Novak explained this in pure culture-war terms: The reason the left hates Bush is that he stands for those aspects of America that the left despises, including "innocence" and "boyishness." The left also sees Bush as the embodiment of qualities it associates with the right: "mean, narrow, selfish, evil," and stupid.[47]

William Bennett, writing the same day as Novak, offered an "open letter to the Democratic Party" urging it to eschew the "hate-filled rhetoric" at the national convention. Bennett reviewed the anger campaign from the beginning of the Bush presidency ("bumper stickers such as 'Hail to the Thief' were in proliferation") through the various inflammatory statements by Democrats during the primary season. He cited, for example, Al Gore's comparison of Bush to Hitler ("The Administration works closely with a network of rapid response digital Brown Shirts...").[48]

The columnist Jeff Jacoby chimed in: "The left's bitter fury toward Bush is more than just atmospherics. It is the big political story of the past two years. The visceral revulsion Bush provokes in so many Democrats fuels the passion that has had such a seismic effect on the presidential campaign."[49]

At receptions and parties around Boston, the anger stars of the Democrats kept up their diatribes, and the leftists continued to feel good about their anger. One angry fellow explained:

> Clinton's enemies practically shut down the federal govern-
> ment in 1995; they spent millions on partisan investigations
> and tried to chase him out of the White House with a semen-
> stained dress. Disgust with Bush, by contrast, has mobilized
> grass-roots activism on issues ranging from environmental
> policy to foreign policy. It can get nasty, but it has never
> been frivolous.[50]

The tactical decision to exclude such anger from emphatic display at the convention acknowledged in a way that Democrats were in danger of having no real message other than Chait's "I hate President George W. Bush." New Anger, for all its determination to perform for a public audience and its pride in not being "frivolous," turns out to have very little to say.

The week after the convention, Gary Alan Fine, a sociology professor at Northwestern University, published an article in the *Washington Post* ("Ire to the Chief") ruminating on Bush-hatred. Fine said he realized the depth of hostility when a "distinguished social scientist" (he doesn't name her) "without preface or embarrassment" declared that she "hated" Bush. Fine remonstrated: surely she meant that she disagreed with Bush's policies, found him unappealing, was "vexed by the outcome of the 2000 election," for example. No, she "hated" Bush. "She felt nauseated and angry when she watched him. She was not just intellectually offended but morally so."[51]

Fine ventures an intriguing but I think incomplete explanation. Drawing on his earlier work about "Nixon haters," he suggests that "presidential hatred" develops from the public's "images of the president as a young adult," which in turn capture "critical cultural divisions that were never fully healed." Nixon was hated for his role in McCarthyism; Clinton was hated for his radical, hippie past; and Bush is hated as a rich, feckless boy who succeeded in life despite his manifest failures.

We do indeed think of our presidents not just in light of their actions in office but as embodiments of their whole biographies, and their life stories take on the kinds of cultural significance that Fine describes. But this was true no less of George Washington, Thomas Jefferson, and, for that matter, Grover Cleveland. The distinguished social scientist who, unembarrassed, declared her visceral loathing of George W. Bush in all likelihood does think of him as a drunken frat boy and inept businessman who got by on family connections. President Bush's "biography" is a potent element in Bush-hatred, where it is used to make him a ripe symbol for the autocracy of the rich as well as a proof that conservatives are stupid people who get ahead on connections rather than real academic and intellectual achievement. Fine is certainly right that disdain for Bush makes prominent use of all these elements.

But while Fine's observations pry open some of the cultural discontents that live inside Bush-hatred, they do not explain the license that a distinguished social scientist felt to allow her distastes and disapprovals to fester into "hatred" or the legitimacy she felt in expressing that hatred as though it were a perfectly acceptable form of opinion. Her ease about "hating"—and her evident pleasure and satisfaction in both harboring it and telling others—is something new. The old practice of seizing the biographies of presidents either to praise or denigrate them has been marshaled into the culture wars and armed with the weaponry of existential fury.

That early versions of this weaponry were used against Nixon and Clinton is undeniable. One of the birthplaces of New Anger was the left's response to the McCarthy hearings in the 1950s, and the campaign to drive Nixon from office had some hints of the self-righteous, triumphal anger to come. But to understand American anger today, we need to recognize that these histrionic elements are now dominant. For the first time in our political history, declaring absolute hatred for one's opponent has become a sign not of sad excess but of good character.

After Anger

In the summer of 2004, the former Clinton strategist and

newspaper columnist E. J. Dionne published *Stand Up Fight Back: Republican Toughs, Democratic Wimps, and the Politics of Revenge,* a book that, despite its pugnacious title, is really an effort to move Democrats out of the futility of mere anger-politics and toward some sort of constructive agenda:

> But if anger, properly directed, can be politically useful and even necessary, it cannot, all by itself, create a political movement or inspire a country. As Todd Gitlin put it—he was talking about the dangers of anti-Americanism—"You can fall in love with your outrage."[52]

Dionne is not exactly against anger; he merely wishes it to be "properly directed," which is to say harnessed to his ten-point "The Right Stuff" agenda. (No. 2: "Against Right-Wing Judges Making Law"; No. 9: "Tolerant Traditionalism: Strengthening Families, Accepting Diversity.")

Dionne may be best known for a book published in the pre-Clinton days of 1991, *Why Americans Hate Politics,* which presented a theme that we have already encountered at several stages: that the great majority of Americans enjoy near-consensus on the major political issues, and that the so-called divisions are "false choices" foisted on the public by self-interested political elites. In a fashion very similar to Alan Wolfe, Dionne called for an end to polarization. He acknowledges his former position in his new book, but now believes "there are good reasons for liberal and Democratic alienation and anger." About half of *Stand Up Fight Back* consists of his account of how conservatives kept up an unrelenting attack on Clinton to ensure that not only his character but also his policies would be permanently discredited; how Bush (in the 2000 race) "ran as a moderate," but once in office governed as a conservative, and in so doing invited the anger that burgeoned around him; how the nation's political mood following 9/11 offered an opportunity for a genuine foreign policy consensus that Bush squandered in favor of his own partisan agenda; and how Bush sowed particular rancor by his nationwide campaigning in the 2002 midterm election, where, for example, he endorsed the congressional campaign of the Republican challenger Saxby Chambliss against Max Cleland, a Vietnam War veteran and triple amputee. Representative Cleland had voted against Bush's homeland security measures, but Democrats were outraged that the Republicans turned this vote against him. Cleland, who lost the election, then became a potent symbol for Bush-haters and a prominent figure in the Democratic National Committee.

Dionne's recounting of this sequence of events is fascinating precisely because he does not, like Nunberg, Wolfe, and several other observers, attempt to play down the exceptional anger on the left. Rather, he attempts to justify it as a reasonable response to a set of unbearable provocations. To recall the distinction I suggested earlier, Dionne is trying to turn Democratic *rage* back into *outrage* by giving it narrative coherence. He would like to replace histrionic New Anger with something approaching plain old anger grounded in explicit principles and moderated by self-control.

Which, Republicans under Clinton or Democrats under Bush, suffered more grievously at the insolence of the other or responded more petulantly? I doubt that any objective standard could be found to evaluate such rock fights. In both cases, older ideals of circumspection and restraint collapsed. As Wolfe rightly points out, decorum in American politics was a weak reed to begin with: we have long had the habit of speaking harshly about each other's failings and have often descended into personal attacks. But the eruptions of anger against Clinton and Bush took us beyond vituperation to a kind of anger that luxuriated in its own vehemence. New Anger is almost always more about the fellow with the bee in his mouth than about the person he rails against. Anger always has content as well as style, but New Anger elevates style to a new prominence. Being angry with New Anger is as much about declaring one's identity as it is about taking umbrage at someone else's infraction.

Although I have necessarily spent much time here detailing the New Anger endemic to the left, I hope it is clear that New Anger is not exclusively a Democratic disease. It is bipartisan in its epidemiology, but naturally more salient in whatever party is currently out of power. New Anger does, however, have deeper roots on the left. We can trace it back at least to the 1968 Democratic National Convention in Chicago. On the right, it seems to have emerged into mainstream prominence only during the Clinton years. The angry right of previous decades—the John Birch Society and kindred anti-Communist and anti-civil-rights organizations— was politically marginal and focused much more on advancing an ideology than on New Anger. New Anger shifts the emphasis to public projection of one's feelings, in a manner that may wrap in some political ideals but that nonetheless makes the matter personal. In this sense, Clinton was a revelation for American conservatives. He held up a mirror that showed conservatives that they too had been deeply changed by the transformation of American culture in which everything had somehow become personal.

Clinton stood for millions of conservatives as an embodiment of a loathsome personality, a man who careened recklessly across the landscape indulging his appetites and, with no twinge of compunction, lying about it. Anger against Clinton was rarely and only superficially directed at his policies, although these too could be swept into an indictment of his lack of principles. Conservatives saw Clinton as a man seducing the country into a cheaper version of itself—and, what was more galling still, succeeding. They saw the leaders of elite institutions shrugging off or temporizing with Clinton's personal corruption and feared this meant that older traditions of moral probity had lost their grip on America.

Bush stands for millions of Democrats as an embodiment of the callow and ignorant side of American life, a man moved by the pursuit of money and cronyism, and contemptuous of social justice, international law, and other enlightened ideals. In the place of serious secular thought, he offers evangelical Christian piety; and in the place of a sophisticated grasp of culture, he offers catchphrases and slogans. Democrats see Bush as tricking the country into becoming a meaner version of itself—and using the war on terror to make that change permanent. They fear that he is displacing the people who by virtue of education and commitment to liberal ideals ought to be guiding America's institutions.

These really are polarized views. It is hard to imagine that any single American subscribes to both of them simultaneously or that there are large numbers of Americans who do not lean more to one or the other. Each offers a moral picture of the United States as corrupted at the very top. And each invites us to participate as an agent of moral cleansing by joining in a wrathful purging of political opposition. Neither view invites us to consider the advantages of compromise, negotiation, patience, or temperance.

The anger in our politics thus has a great deal to do with rival visions of what the nation should be and who Americans actually are. Part of Bush-hatred is the depiction of Bush himself as exceptionally stupid—the "village idiot" on many bumper stickers and buttons—and his supporters as "morons." In early May 2004, a story raced around the Internet and was even published in the *Economist,* saying that a study had proven that states with higher average IQs had voted for Gore and states with lower average IQs had voted for Bush. The left is usually not too keen on using IQs as a measure of anything, but in a matter of days, the red-states-have-low-IQs story was posted on several hundred liberal websites. It might have spread still further except that journalist Steve Sailer exposed the claim as a hoax.[53]

If, in your anger, you reduce your opponent to the status of someone unworthy or unable to engage in legitimate exchange, real politics comes to an end. That is the danger we face if we allow New Anger to continue to flourish in our political life. We have now discovered what it is like to be so angry—or self-righteous or condescending—that we hear only our own ravishing anger song. Anger may sharpen the senses in some contexts, but New Anger leads to a kind of cultural obliviousness that cannot be good for a democratic society.

When I began working on this book in the year before the 2004 presidential election, I encountered a fair amount of skepticism from people who, while concurring that the politics of the moment were inflected with anger, believed this was mostly a phenomenon of the election itself and would fade after the race was over. As I write today in 2006, that skepticism has vanished. Bush's election to a second term did not persuade those who adopted the new emotional style to try a calmer approach. A few weeks after the election, the senior managing editor of the *Boston Phoenix* posted an article to an online journal titled "Screw You, America," which began, "Don't forgive my anger," and descended from there. The only new note was that the Angry Left was now angry at Kerry as well as Bush.[54]

In spring 2005, Byron York published an election post-mortem that attributed the Democrats' loss, in part, to the partisans who deluded themselves into believing that the country shared their contempt for Bush. A reviewer of York's book in the *Wall Street Journal*'s online *OpinionJournal* commented that the angry continue to nurture their anger at "the prospect of long-term Republican governance, at John Kerry's inept campaigning. Even, it seems, at being called angry."[55]

Cathy Young, a contributing editor of the libertarian magazine *Reason,* ended the year with a plague-on-both-your-houses review of Michelle Malkin's *Unhinged: Exposing Liberals Gone Wild.* Malkin, a conservative columnist, gathered together instances of the left's angry rhetoric, but, Young says, "what about the unhinged conservatives?" She cites Rush Limbaugh and Ann Coulter, but her more interesting remark is that "everyone seems to agree that there is far too much nastiness in American political discourse today."[56]

No, I don't think everyone agrees. On the contrary, a substantial number of people have found New Anger a satisfying form of political engagement. Governor Dean's attack on Republicans as "brain dead" people who "have never made an honest living in their lives" was received with pleasure by some—perhaps among them the customers of the novelty shop in Berkeley that reported strong Christmas sales of a full line of items, "from cards to action figures to doggy chew toys," mocking Bush. The store sells Bush "Dum Gum," "National EmbarrassMints" with Bush's image on the package, and a Bush air freshener, captioned, "dumbass head on a string."[57] These are small matters—and it is, after all, only a store in Berkeley. Yet they speak to the settling in of a disposition in which puerile insults are mistaken for a kind of angry wit.

During the confirmation hearings for the Supreme Court nominee Judge Samuel Alito in January 2006, several Democratic senators, including Edward Kennedy, Charles Schumer, and Joe Biden, put on yet another display of New Anger, which elicited a rebuke from Dahlia Lithwick, senior editor of the online journal *Slate*. Lithwick warned that Democrats err in supposing that judges who, like Alito, espouse the conservative judicial philosophy of "federalism" are "teeming with hate and rage." Thinking so, she said,

> leads you Senate Democrats to believe that if you can just ask the right question of a federalist, he will erupt into a hissing, spitting parody of Bill O'Reilly and then try to strangle you with his bow tie on C-SPAN. As you observe the federalists here today, you will learn that they love their families and do *not* devote their careers to systematically holding back women, persecuting minorities, and stealing wheelchairs from the disabled.[58]

Angrily depicting federalists as dedicated to "raging misogyny or racism," said Lithwick, was likely to backfire.

The self-defeating behavior of the Democrats on the Senate Judiciary Committee, however, is only one small instance of how New Anger stymies those who might, with less anger and more careful attention to actual circumstances, persuade other people of the merits of their views. New Anger has eroded our collective capacity to advance worthy political aspirations. This is true for conservatives as well as liberals, though liberals right now are paying the bigger price because they have more ardently embraced New Anger. But whoever embraces it is bound to find that, at least in the political realm, he has traded the possibility of real influence for the momentary satisfactions of self-expression.

The dustup in February 2006 over the Republican National Committee chairman, Ken Mehlman, saying on TV that Hillary Clinton "seems to have a lot of anger" and that angry people don't get elected president opened another window on New Anger in American politics. Democrats by and large came to Hillary's defense and attempted to throw the onus of anger back on the Republicans. The lessons in the episode are subtle. Both sides see the advantages of deploying New Anger, but both sides are also eager to portray themselves as calm and deliberative and righteously indignant at the other side's misbehavior. New Anger attempts to perform a vanishing act while standing midstage.

This was nowhere better illustrated than when Jonathan ("I-hate-President-George-W.-Bush") Chait went on Hugh Hewitt's radio interview show on February 14, 2006. He declared that Hillary is "just the opposite of angry. I think she's robotic, passionless, dull." Chait then went on to say the concept of anger in politics doesn't really make sense. "The whole notion of anger is just weird and misplaced." Al Gore, he allowed, has "visceral passion in his voice when he is denouncing Bush. It seems, you know, like he's really feeling something, unlike Hillary Clinton, who could just as well be ordering from a restaurant menu when she's talking."

Hewitt repeatedly pressed Chait to explain what he meant by "anger," since he simultaneously was disavowing the concept and applying it. Chait asserted, "There are millions of angry conservatives out there," and seconds later added, "This whole anger thing is just a weird way of thinking about people who have views about politics."

Chait was adamant that whatever his feelings, they didn't get in the way of his being "cool and rational in analyzing what Bush does." He felt "aggrieved" at the way the country was being run, but he carefully distinguished that emotion from the "rage" that he saw among Republicans. Hewitt read back to him Chait's own words from the beginning of the "I hate President George W. Bush" article, and succeeded in getting only an admission that the language "might" sound like anger.

So the man who might be said to have played the most important part in conferring mainstream respectability on performing anti-Bush New Anger now performs like a circus contortionist in an effort to deny that anger in American politics even exists (except for the rage on the right); or if it exists, that he ever felt so weird a sensation; or if he did, that it ever influenced his judgment. Say this for New Anger: those who indulge it pay a price.

Americans are faced with plenty of issues in which a certain amount of good old-fashioned anger might be appropriate. Among other things, we are faced with a high tide of corruption in Congress, a poorly run bureaucracy that seems unable to respond well to natural calamities, a federal government that is unwilling or unable to guard the national borders, and an educational system that falls short at every level. But this book is not about advancing my own view of substantive national priorities. Rather, I am concerned that we have, with no real forethought, drifted into a style of political engagement that is very unlikely to prove constructive.

When Thomas Greene Fessenden angrily denounced President Jefferson in his poem *Democracy Unveiled*, the United States had fewer than seven million citizens. Today, we have over three hundred million, and we are divided from one another into more interest groups, factions, and subcultures than Madison could ever have imagined. If we allow New Anger to become the common mode of self-expression in politics, can we hold this enterprise together? Or do we sink into a vast and noisy quarrel in which everyone is so eager to express his personal grievance that we are no longer able to hear ourselves?

Recall the heroic bee at the beginning of this chapter, the bee that stopped young Mr. Nunes from singing along with Justin Timberlake. So many crappy songs, so few heroic bees.

FIVE

ANGER MUSIC

I n 1932, when the Great Depression was settling in for the long haul, a bankrupt electrical supplies salesman named E. Y. Harburg (1896–1981) wrote the lyrics for *Americana*, a musical show that praised the ordinary man beaten down by the capitalists. In one scene, a man standing in a breadline sings:

> Once I built a railroad,
> Made it run,
> Made it race against time.
> Once I built a railroad,
> Now it's done.
> Brother, can you spare a dime?

Though banned by some radio stations, "Brother, Can You Spare a Dime?" became a hit, recorded by Bing Crosby among others. Both the song and the phrase became inseparable from the national response to the Depression.

"Brother, Can You Spare a Dime?" expresses plenty of political anger.

> When there was earth to plow
> Or guns to bear,
> I was always there
> Right on the job.
> They used to tell me
> I was building a dream,
> With peace and glory ahead.
> Why should I be standing in line
> Just waiting for bread?

Harburg was an avowed socialist, destined to be blacklisted in 1950 from Hollywood, where he had been working on films since 1936. His song about the guy on the breadline did not pull any punches. Yet the tone is somehow slightly wistful and the singer's reproach to American society is a call on fellow feeling: "Say, don't you remember / I'm your pal."

Harburg was, not coincidentally, the author of that other great Depression-era standard of yearning for a better world, "Over the Rainbow."[1]

Reproaching society for its callous treatment of the poor never goes entirely out of fashion. The terms of the reproach as phrased by the Wu-Tang Clan in their 1993 rap classic "C.R.E.A.M." are, however, a little different. "C.R.E.A.M." means money and stands for "cash rules everything around me." At one point, Wu-Tang member Raekwon the Chef (Corey Woods) raps:

> Had second-hands, Moms bounced on old man
> So then we moved to Shaolin land
> A young youth, yo rockin' the gold tooth, 'Lo goose
> Only way I begin to G off was drug loot
> And let's start it like this son, rollin' with this one
> And that one, pullin' out gats for fun

The immediate contrast, of course, is language. Harburg aimed for an idiom everyone could understand, and more than seventy years later, he requires no translation. Hip-hop, however, is in vernacular code that is meant to be understood only by insiders.

The Wu-Tang Clan even has a phrase—"Only Built 4 Cuban Linx"—that means "only made for those who understand."[2] Some of the lyrics of "C.R.E.A.M." are nonetheless accessible. Raekwon was poor: he had only second-hand clothing. Moms walked out on (bounced on) his father. "Shaolin" is the Wu-Tang Clan's slang ("Wu-Tang slang" to aficionados) for Staten Island, the group's home base, the name reflecting their fondness for martial arts films. *G* and *gats,* of course, are anachronistic gangster slang that Harburg himself would have recognized, referring to a grand ($1,000) and a gun. So we have a portrait of an impoverished, father-

less boy who turns to drug dealing and gunplay "for fun."
Raekwon continues:

> No question I would flow off
> and try to get the dough off
> Sticking up white boys in ball courts
> My life got no better
> same damn 'Lo sweater
> Times is rough and tough like leather
> Figured out I went the wrong route
> So I got with a sick-ass clique and went all out
> Catchin' ki's from cross seas, Rollin' in MPVs,
> every week we made forty G's
> Yo nigga, respect mine, or anger the Tec-9
> Ch-ch, BLAOW, Wu from the gate now.[3]

Here the singer describes how his efforts to expand his career
into mugging white boys failed to produced a satisfactory
income stream. Aiming to improve his circumstances, he
takes a higher-risk role in drug dealing (importing kilo-
grams—"catchin' ki's"—of cocaine). "Rollin' in MPVs" is a
puzzle. "MPV" was in use in 1993 for "multi-purpose vehicle"—i.e. a minivan. So perhaps we are supposed to imagine
Raekwon driving ("rollin'") around Staten Island in a minivan as he brings in $40,000 a week gross for the gang. More
likely, however, a "multi-purpose vehicle" in this case is a
stolen luxury car.

Along with the move to larger-scale criminal enterprise
comes more advanced armament, from the old-fashioned gat
to the 9 mm semi-automatic pistol manufactured by Intratac
of Miami. Tec-9's at the time had threaded barrels that
allowed enterprising hoodlums to add illegal silencers, and
barrel extensions that suppressed muzzle flash, and they
could take high-capacity magazines. The gun was one of
nineteen named guns banned as assault weapons in 1994.
"Ch-ch, BLAOW" is an onomatopoetic cocking and firing of
the Tec-9 by the Wu-Tang Clan at anyone who might dis 'em.

Method Man (Clifford Smith) then raps the chorus:

> Cash rules everything around me
> C.R.E.A.M., get the money
> Dollar dollar bill, y'all

Inspectah Deck (Jason Hunter) raps the next verse, about his going to jail ("A man with a dream with plans to make C.R.E.A.M. / which failed"); but this is probably enough to suggest that the Wu-Tang Clan rapping "C.R.E.A.M." and Bing Crosby crooning "Brother, Can You Spare a Dime?" evoke different plays of emotion—as well as different practical measures—in response to financial adversity.

I am not sure that "C.R.E.A.M." will become, as "Brother, Can You Spare a Dime?" became, part of the popular song heritage that is usually referred to as the Great American Songbook. The Wu-Tang Clan's contempt for the society they sing about probably means they don't aspire to that particular kind of recognition. Nonetheless, "C.R.E.A.M." is a genre classic, which, as one enthusiast—a white twenty-year-old college student who prefers to be identified as "Methuselah"—told me,

> can't be picked apart as some minor ballad no one's ever heard. It's also got amazing longevity: it's going on 12 years old, which is ancient for a rap song, and it's still well-loved and quoted from. Furthermore, as Shaolin entered the rap lexicon, so has C.R.E.A.M., or cream: it's a standard synonym for "money" at this point, perhaps more accurately, a lot of money, used by rappers from all geographies and all ages.[4]

So at least in some sense, to compare "Brother, Can You Spare a Dime?" and "C.R.E.A.M." is to compare two well-known lyrics on similar themes, each representing a sensibility that large numbers of people found attractive despite some official hostility.

To my ear, almost all rap sounds belligerent and angry, but since I am not in Wu-Tang Clan's target audience, it is helpful to know how the song sounds to someone who is. Methuselah explains that "C.R.E.A.M." is "really not a celebration of an illegal lifestyle: it has a somber, melancholy beat, and, in my opinion, it can be argued that they advocate this only because impoverished ghetto children are given no other outlet." Somber and melancholy as it may be, "C.R.E.A.M." is a pure version of New Anger: anger that is proud of its angriness and eager to display its justifications

("Had second-hands, Moms bounced on old man"), its swelling self-conceit ("rollin' with this one / And that one / pullin' out gats for fun"), and its bristling menace ("Yo nigga, respect mine, or anger the Tec-9"). The reductive theme—"Cash rules everything around me"—is likewise a New Anger trope. Anger *can* be diffuse, but it usually likes to concentrate on a specific provocation. To admit that the world is ambiguous and full of complexity is to risk losing that precious anger.

Thus Methuselah is right. "C.R.E.A.M." doesn't sound like "a celebration of an illegal lifestyle." It sounds much more like anger trying to stay on message: "life is hell"; "I'm still depressed"; and "Niggas gots to do what they gotta do to get a bill."

Harburg's "Brother, Can You Spare a Dime?" aimed to wrench sympathy from the supposedly flinty-hearted who needed to be reminded of the sacrifices of the man who was down on his luck. That man once plowed the earth, built a railroad, worked in construction, and served in the army during the Great War. Now, in need, he presses his claims. The appeal worked, at least to the extent that the song gave some everyday emotional definition to the New Deal. The deep message of the song is that we should acknowledge the bonds of shared humanity. By contrast, the Wu-Tang Clan's "C.R.E.A.M." takes us into the world of grandiose self-pity and deep alienation, where the bonds of shared humanity seem absent. Method Man, Raekwon, and Inspectah Deck don't seem to enjoy life as urban predators. Perhaps they wish for something better, but they express no sympathy for their victims and no remorse. First-person accounts can, nonetheless, almost always wrench some scrap of sympathy (Methuselah: "impoverished ghetto children are given no other outlet"), but what "C.R.E.A.M." really begs is admiration. The Wu-Tang Clan says, in effect, "we deserve respect for our unapologetic thuggishness combined with our verbal dexterity."

And rather than appealing, ultimately, to common humanity, the Wu-Tang Clan is appealing to group identity.

Rap or hip-hop thus opens up a dimension of New Anger that I have not yet emphasized: its connection to our society's obsession with the kind of collective grievance that can be stylized down to a few rudimentary gestures. *My* group has suffered because of racism, sexism, or homophobia; *I* speak as a victim of group oppression and for my oppressed category. While New Anger serves many other grievances beyond my-group-is-oppressed grievances, it is very well suited to those particular grievances, because their scripts are well established and easy to perform. Hip-hop has become the sound track to a wide variety of identity politics.

And it is fairly well understood that way around the world. When some Maori in New Zealand embraced a version of ethnic separatism in the mid-1960s, they began almost immediately to tune in to the angry separatism of the Black Panthers and Malcolm X in the United States. And as the neotribalism of Maori activists grew, so did their emulation of African American styles. Today, Maori popular music is dominated by an imitation of hip-hop, which turns out to be a form of declaration almost perfectly suited to a rhetoric of self-righteous cultural resentment.

Do rappers have bees in their mouths? Interestingly, in Wu-Tang slang, the rappers identify themselves as "killa bees" or "killa beez." One of the spin-off Wu-Tang organizations is the Wu-Tang Killa Bees, with its own albums titled *Swarm* and *Sting*. The killa bee metaphor is extended to identify different hip-hop artists with various species of bees. Raekwon, Method Man, and Inspectah Deck, for example, belong to *Anthidium manicalcum,* an aggressively territorial bee species.

In choosing "C.R.E.A.M." to exemplify the anger in hip-hop, I pass over an abundance of rap songs with far angrier lyrics, droning with hatred of "queers" and "hos" and ricocheting rhymes about the glories of revenge. Eminem, for one, has adorned American music with a style that is essentially one long elaboration of self-obsessed hatred of the people and the world around him. Here is the opening of his rap "Just Don't Give a Fuck":

> Slim Shady, brain dead like Jan Brady
> I'm a M80, you Lil' like that Kim lady
> I'm buzzin, Dirty Dozen, naughty rotten rhymer
> Cursin at you players worse than Marty Schottenheimer
> You wacker than the motherfucker you bit your style from
> You ain't gonna sell two copies if you press a double album
> Admit it, fuck it, while we comin out in the open
> I'm doin acid, crack, smack, coke and smokin dope then
> My name is Marshall Mathers, I'm an alcoholic (Hi Marshall)
> I have a disease and they don't know what to call it
> Better hide your wallet 'cause I'm comin up quick to strip
> your cash
> Bought a ticket to your concert just to come and whip your
> ass
> Bitch, I'm comin out swingin, so fast it'll make your eyes spin
> You gettin knocked the fuck out like Mike Tyson
> The +Proof+ is in the puddin, just ask the Deshaun Holton
> I'll slit your motherfuckin throat worse than Ron Goldman

A little of this is perhaps all we need to be reminded that there are depths of mawkish self-pity disguised as anger beyond the Wu-Tang Clan.

But Eminem also offers a point of contact to another component of New Anger. In some of his songs, he positions himself as an anthem writer for the Angry Left. In "Mosh," for example, he begins with his usual self-pity ("A father who has grown up with a fatherless past") and obligatory boasts ("rap phenomenon [who has] mastered his craft") before getting down to business, which in this case is rousing Bush-hatred:

> Rebel with a rebel yell, raise hell we gonna let 'em know
> Stomp, push, shove, Fuck Bush, until they bring our troops
> home
> ....
> Let the president answer a higher anarchy
> Strap him with an AK-47, let him go, fight his own war
> Let him impress daddy that way
> No more blood for oil...

"No blood for oil." How did he ever think of that?

Hip-hop as a musical idiom can also be used to express sentiments other than anger, although when rap artists aim for other emotions, the idiom itself plays against them. In

her 2005 hit, "Hollaback Girl," Gwen Stefani is flirtatious and
the accompanying video is sassily humorous, but the lyrics
ostensibly depict an angry high school cheerleader calling
out a trash-talking rival for a fight:

> So that's right dude, meet me at the bleachers
> No principals, no student teachers

Hip-hop is thus not necessarily angry, but anger is its home
turf.

Defiance, Protest, and Lament

Music deserves a special place in any attempt to trace how
New Anger became established as an accepted mode of
behavior in American life. That's because, of all the arts,
music is the one that speaks most directly to our emotions.
Songs get into our heads and stay there. A few notes of a
once-familiar song and it is familiar all over again years—or
decades—later. People who never take the trouble con-
sciously to memorize anything remember tunes and lyrics,
especially when they capture a particular emotional nuance.
Songs constitute a school that teaches young people how to
flirt, how to romance, how to feel sorry, and how to hurt. The
accumulation of songs in memory and experience becomes
a kind of internal repertoire through which we can, in a very
subtle shorthand, evoke nuances of attitude. And we can
convey those nuances to others who share the repertoire. If
we want to experience physical grace, we can go to a pro basketball game or a ballet. If we wish to see beauty or cunning
visual artifice, we can go to the paintings in a museum. All
the arts have, of course, their own command of a range of
emotions, including anger. But music is the art that takes us
to emotion most directly, and popular music is America's
conversation with itself about the right ways to feel.

Hip-hop is now America's premier anger music, having
displaced in the 1990s several subcategories of rock, including punk, heavy metal, alternative rock and grunge. Rock 'n'
roll began in the 1950s as a rebellious but not an angry form
of music. It centered emotionally on the pleasures of escap-

ing convention and its acts of defiance were originally small-scale assaults against sexual taboos. Buddy Holly, Jerry Lee Lewis ("Whole Lotta Shakin' Goin' On"; "Great Balls of Fire"), Chuck Berry, and Elvis Presley play important parts in the story of how America lost its reticence, but neither their songs nor their performances communicated much anger.

Various songs about heartbreak and disappointment of the 1950s expressed the anger of broken romance, but the singer who captures the moment when a love has been betrayed is voicing anger only as part of the ordinary narrative of life: one emotion along the course of life familiar to almost all. The popular singer of the 1950s whose songs reached further into a darker corner of the soul was not a rock 'n' roller but the country singer Johnny Cash (1932–2003). Two lines from his 1956 hit, "Folsom Prison Blues," remain among the most chilling in American song:

> But I shot a man in Reno
> Just to watch him die

The power of the lyric, of course, is that the singer does not say he killed out of anger, but out of mere callousness, and his terse phrasing suggests that, even now as he languishes in prison, he remains unmoved by his cruelty. What bothers him is the idea of "rich folks eating / In a fancy dinin' car" on the train he can hear in the distance:

> Well, those people keep movin,'
> Goddammit, that's what tortures me.
> If they'd free me from this prison,
> If that railroad train was mine,
> You'd bet I'd move it on
> A little further down the line.

While Cash famously performed the song on a visit to Folsom Prison, no one mistook him for a prisoner serving a life sentence, and this too marks a key difference between genres.

Cash's "Folsom Prison Blues" connects not only with the blues tradition but with folk ballads extending back many centuries in which the singer portrays in first-person an actor in a violent episode. Rap lyrics may, in fact, employ the same license to invent characters and dramatize them. Eminem's "Slim Shady" is such an invention. But rap is also dominated by an autobiographical voice that emphasizes the singer's own experiences, which often involve crime and violence. Rappers speak of "keeping it real," which means living the life portrayed in the music—which often has led to tragic consequences. The shootings of Tupac Shakur and Notorious Big (Christopher Wallace) are the best-known examples, but over a dozen other rappers have been murdered: King Tubby (1989), Michael Menson (1989), MC Rock (1990), Brandon Mitchell (1990), Charizma (1993), Mr. Cee (1995). Seagram Miller (1996), Patrick Hawkins, known as Fat Pat (1998), Malcolm Howard (1999), Lamont Coleman, known as Big L (1999), MC Ant (1999), Raeneal Quann, known as Q-Don (2000), Bruce Mayfield (2000), Lloyd "Mooseman" Roberts (2001), Tonnie Sheppard (2001), Jam Master Jay (2002), and John Edward Hawkins (brother of Patrick Hawkins), known as Big Hawk (2006). Other rappers have been implicated in some of these murders. One rapper, Juston Potts, known as Kanyva, murdered his promoter (2004) after she criticized his work.[5]

The body count seems high enough to credit the hip-hop musicians with success in keeping the persona of an agitated, angry, and violent figure sufficiently "real." But when singers in other musical genres portray themselves as killers—or merely as angry—we need to attend more to the authenticity of artistic vision than to authenticity of street experience.

"Folsom Prison Blues" wasn't Cash's only song to brood about anger. The same year, he released "I Walk the Line," ostensibly a lyric about a man's determination to stay out of trouble because of his love for a woman. But the song evokes the man's tense efforts at self-control, and "the line" is another prison metaphor:

> I keep a close watch on this heart of mine;
> I keep my eyes wide open all the time.
> I keep the ends out for the tie that binds.
> Because you're mine, I walk the line.

His 1958 hits "Ring of Fire" and "Don't Take Your Guns to Town" likewise delve into emotions that threaten to consume. In the latter, a boy who wishes to believe "he had become a man" is laughed at by a stranger in a saloon. "Filled with rage," he reaches for his gun but is shot dead on the spot. It is a cautionary tale with a cold heart.

Cash sometimes made fun of his angry-man persona, as in his 1969 recording at San Quentin Prison of the Shel Silverstein lyric, "A Boy Named Sue." The boy meets up in a bar with the deadbeat father who gave him a girl's name:

> He was big and bent and gray and old
> And I looked at him and my blood ran cold,
> And I said, "My name is 'Sue!' How do you do! Now you
>   gonna die!"

Cash, who became known as "the man in black" for his usual attire, recorded a song by that title in 1971, in which he explained that he wore his "somber tone" for the downtrodden—the poor, the prisoners, those who haven't heard the Word of God, the sick, the old, and the drugged-out:

> But just so we're reminded of the ones who are held back,
> Up front there oughta be a Man in Black.

Thus his anger, in time, became identified with a certain kind of social protest.

In 1992, the Rock and Roll Hall of Fame inducted Cash, describing his early hits as "rockabilly." The recognition was partly a tribute to his having been one of the first singers to sign with the pioneering rock 'n' roll Sun Records (in 1955), and partly a matter of Cash's enduring popularity with other musicians.

If Johnny Cash represents the angriest inflection of hit music in the 1950s, he was expressing something very much in the vein of the old style of anger that struggled to keep its impulses under control. The characters he depicted were tough and unsentimental, but—apart from the boy named Sue—they did not parade their anger. Even the "Man in Black" persona, which could have been taken as ostentation, came across as more mournful than angry. The songs often worked by conveying the sense that a deep anger is unspoken. The words "I shot a man in Reno / Just to watch him die" dramatize anger by denying it.

Elsewhere in the musical scene of the late 1950s and early 1960s, anger was taking a different musical form. The folk revival created an avenue for singer-songwriters to engage in more direct political commentary, and Woody Guthrie's Depression-era ballads offered a model for leftists hoping to stir "the masses" to collective action. Pete Seeger (1919–) had been promoting folk-protest songs since the 1940s. He and Woody Guthrie organized a musical collective called the Almanac Singers in 1940, and he later formed his own group, the Weavers, which mostly performed standards such as "Goodnight Irene" and "On Top of Old Smoky." After he was called before the House Committee on Un-American Activities in 1955, Seeger was blacklisted. He left the Weavers in 1958 and joined the civil-rights movement, and Seeger's arrangement of the old spiritual "We Shall Overcome" became the movement's anthem. He also gave us "If I Had a Hammer," "Turn, Turn, Turn," and "Where Have All the Flowers Gone?" (written by Joe Hickerson).

Seeger was by far the most visible of the older folk singers when the music began to catch on in coffeehouses and on college campuses in the late 1950s, but he was also an avid cultivator of new talents, such as Bob Dylan, Phil Ochs, Peter, Paul & Mary, and Tom Paxton. His 1964 recording of Paxton's "Ramblin' Boy" helped propel the younger singer's career.

Folk music today is a relatively minor strand in American music. Most parts of the country, for example, have plenty of radio stations that specialize in rock and several that play hip-hop, but folk songs, like jazz and classical music, are broadcast only by a handful of usually amateur low-wattage college stations. But an account of anger music cannot completely bypass modern folk songs, both because they opened the modern era of anger music and because they launched the career of the most artistically important anger artist, Bob Dylan. Moreover, the folk protest song is not dead.

Tom Paxton, for example, is still churning out protest

songs, which more and more have the character of New Anger. Folk singers, more than musicians in any other genre, tend to preface and comment on their songs. Of his 2001 song "In Florida," Paxton writes:

> One of the things that attracted me to folk music so long ago was the huge number of songs about brigands, pirates, robbers and other socially inept types like that—both real and imaginary. There were songs about Captain Kidd, Pretty Boy Floyd, Robin Hood—hundreds of them. So, I formed an attachment for songs of great crimes, which is why all these years later I've written one about the election in Florida in 2000. I saw a pretty good bumper sticker that read: "Don't blame me. I voted with the majority."

The last verse of "In Florida" is a flat rendition of what has become leftist dogma about the 2000 presidential election in Florida, despite the finding by the *New York Times* and other disappointed observers that even if every disputed ballot in that state had been counted, Bush would still have won:

> The boys and girls in black robes met
> And held a tug of war.
> And when they cast their votes at last
> Bush won it, 5 to 4.
> Five judges selected the president—
> Five judges had their way—
> And I expect they'll all retire
> To Florida some day.

In songs like this, Paxton is not angry in the way that the Wu-Tang Clan's songs are angry—assuming that we can indeed call the blood-chilling tone and belligerence of Wu-Tang Clan's music a kind of performed anger. Rather, Paxton writes what he calls "short shelf-life songs" amounting to a kind of happy propaganda that sets politically correct clichés to music. The songs use satiric humor to stoke a fire that presumably is already burning, rather than throw any genuinely provocative sparks.

The angry songs of Bob Dylan, however, deserve altogether more serious attention. They provided the folkies with music that far outlasted the movement's short ascendancy to mass popularity and they eventually escaped the jejune leftist "social conscience" that turns most contemporary folk music into birthday party streamers for the languishing counterculture.

Circus Floor

Though he had already written a handful of protest songs ("Let Me Die in My Footsteps," "Hero Blues," "John Brown"), Bob Dylan's first great protest song was "Blowin' in the Wind" (1962), which concludes:

> How many years can a mountain exist
> Before it's washed to the sea?
> Yes, 'n' how many years can some people exist
> Before they're allowed to be free?
> Yes, 'n' how many times can a man turn his head,
> Pretending he just doesn't see?
> The answer, my friend, is blowin' in the wind,
> The answer is blowin' in the wind.[6]

The song seems angry at humanity's willingness to abide injustices in its midst, but the singer's anger is not directed at a particular, concrete instance of injustice. He seems to rail at a more fundamental condition and to imply an overwhelming but entirely vague consequence. Is the "answer" that's blowing in the wind socialist revolution, as a good many of Dylan's comrades in the early sixties hoped? Is it racial upheaval? Divine intervention? To name the possibilities seems to limit the song, which is one of those rare instances in which unspecified indignation actually works.

Dylan, in fact, is a bridge between old anger and New Anger. He rose to popularity initially by breathing new emotional life into old folk songs; then he found a new voice that, while exuberant and wide-ranging, seemed especially good at conveying scorn, contempt, and a whole sandpapery range of angry discontents. He helped teach a generation the imaginative possibilities of performed vexation. And yet, the Dylan songs that seem most to embody the qualities of New Anger came early in his career; his later songs frequently veer back into old anger's misgivings about itself. His 1968 song "I Dreamed I Saw St. Augustine" concludes:

> I dreamed I saw St. Augustine,
> Alive with fiery breath,
> And I dreamed I was amongst the ones
> That put him out to death.
> Oh, I awoke in anger,
> So alone and terrified,
> I put my fingers against the glass
> And bowed my head and cried.

Here, at least anger is isolating, not empowering; and the persona of the song is humbled. Songs such as this, however, still put Dylan's revelatory self in the foreground, which leaves plenty of room for New Anger to return—and it does. Still, for the purpose of seeing how anger unfolded in Dylan's music, the songs written between 1962 and 1968 are more illuminating.

After writing "Blowin' in the Wind" in 1962, Dylan wrote dozens of songs that either express direct contempt for those he judged responsible for social evils or angrily mock individuals he faulted for pride, hypocrisy, or other personal failings. His 1963 song "Masters of War" intriguingly turns up in 2004 as the top protest song of all time in the British music magazine *Mojo,* beating out Pete Seeger's (#2) "We Shall Overcome" and James Brown's (#3) "Say It Loud, I'm Black and I'm Proud"—and NWA's rap classic (#10) "Fuck the Police." The current popularity of "Masters of War" appears to be a case of New Anger searching the archives for its own precedents. The song, by itself, is among the weaker of Dylan's anger rants. It opens, "Come you master of war / You that build all the guns," and proceeds through sixty-four lines of simplistic accusations, ending:

> And I hope that you die
> And your death'll come soon
> I will follow your casket
> In the pale afternoon
> And I'll watch while you're lowered

Down to your deathbed
And I'll stand o'er your grave
'Til I'm sure that you're dead.

Most of the song is of a piece with this silly death-wish fantasy, but perhaps that is exactly what makes it a song for right *now*: "Masters of War" is really about the "I" that hopes the anonymous "masters" will die; that will follow the (inexplicably singular—what about all the other masters?) coffin; and that will stand around in the cemetery just in case a Buffy-style resurrection occurs. The song seems less about taking umbrage at gun builders and war profiteers than it is about Dylan asserting his own gigantic moral superiority to them. But a list of indictments is a pretty cheap form of argument, and the song registers a lot more self-satisfaction than it does revelation about the motives of Halliburton, Raytheon, Vice President Cheney or Secretary Rumsfeld—or their 1963 counterparts.

"Masters of War" seems a bit like what Michael Moore would say were he capable of anything more challenging than out-of-context quotations and misleading juxtapositions. Dylan's tone of self-righteous delight in the death of his declared adversaries, however, is a staple of New Anger today. At the January 2006 Senate Judiciary hearing, the wife of Supreme Court nominee Samuel Alito left the room in tears after hearing her husband bullied by senators who accused him of racism. Mrs. Alito's response was then mocked by contributors to a message board at the left-wing website, *The Daily Kos*. "Martha-Ann Alito is an idiot and a moron," said phoenixandrew; "What a whiny little b*tch. I'm GLAD she was reduced to tears," said Buzzer; "Cry, you cow," wrote Maine Atticus. And BTP, quoting from the cartoon *South Park* (and, indirectly, from the novel *Hannibal*), wrote, "YES! YESSS! Oh, let me taste your tears, Martha-Ann! Mmm, your tears are so yummy and sweet!"

It is probably not wise to look longer into this abyss in the American soul, but it is worth noting that phoenixandrew, Buzzer, Maine Atticus, and BTP are heirs of a sadistic and self-glorifying attitude that Dylan's "Masters of War" helped to promote on the left. Taking pleasure in the sorrows of one's adversary—what the German's call *schadenfreude*—is nothing new, but making such feelings central to one's self definition is rather new for Americans.

Another Dylan protest song enjoying a revival is "With God on Our Side," which is a collection of shallow anti-American ironies about the nation's wars ("you never ask questions / When God's on your side") culminating in the question whether "Judas Iscariot / Had God on his side." The answer? "If God's on our side / He'll stop the next war." Dylan's song "Only a Pawn in Their Game" opens with the assassination of Medgar Evers and moves through a series of dismissals. The assassin was "only a pawn in their game"; likewise the politicians who incited racial hatred, the cops who failed to enforce the law, and the poor whites who joined the Ku Klux Klan. "Only a Pawn in Their Game" is lyrically more telling than "Masters of War" and "With God on Our Side," but suffers from a similar strain of ideology. *Whose* game is Dylan talking about? *Who* exactly benefits from the murderous racism of the Jim Crow South? The implication, I suppose, is that the evil capitalists are once again pulling the strings (or pushing the pawns); but as soon as this idea is thrust into plain view, the song loses much of its force.

Dylan's most famous protest anthem, "The Times They Are a-Changin' "(1963), however, seems strangely absent from the left's current playlist. The song is every bit as angry and arrogant as "Masters of War." In it Dylan consigns all who stand in the way of the revolution to grim fates ("you'll sink like a stone"); orders politicians out of the way ("Don't stand in the doorway, / Don't block up the hall"); silences dissenting opinion ("And don't criticize / What you can't understand"); and rejects parental authority ("Your sons and your daughters / Are beyond your command"). The totalitarian impulse in the song is astonishing. Perhaps that is a hindrance to its revival, or perhaps it just sounds now like a premature declaration of victory.

Dylan's early-sixties protest songs now seem like a kind of

memo to the Newly Angry denizens of our decade: divide the world in two, between weak good guys and powerful creeps, but don't be too specific. The creeps are creepier if you assail them as shadowy exploiters. Implication is better than accusation.

In 1965, Dylan appeared at the Newport Folk Festival with the Paul Butterfield Blues Band, which used electrified instruments—an offense against the purist tastes of the folk revivalists, who famously booed their former favorite. Dylan replied to the catcalls by playing "Its All Over Now, Baby Blue," and then left the folk movement and propagandistic protest songs behind. But not the anger. In the decades that followed, he wrote and performed what amount to masterpieces of angry music: "Subterranean Homesick Blues," "Maggie's Farm," "It's Alright Ma (I'm Only Bleeding)," "Like a Rolling Stone," "Positively 4th Street"—

> You got a lotta nerve
> To say you are my friend
> When I was down
> You just stood there grinning

—among others, as well as songs *about* anger, such as "Too Much of Nothing" and "Tears of Rage"—

> Tears of rage, tears of grief,
> Why must I always be the thief?
> Come to me now, you know
> We're so alone
> And life is brief.

Such songs certainly helped to shape the emotional sensibilities of the generation that reached adulthood in the sixties and seventies. In some cases, we can point to actual artifacts of Dylan's influence—such as the title of *Rolling Stone* magazine and the name that the terrorist sect Weatherman adopted from "Subterranean Homesick Blues":

> You don't need a weather man
> To know which way the wind blows.

But he also taught that generation an angry acuteness about

falsities in human life. In "Temporary Like Achilles," he addresses a disdainful lover who ignores him:

> I watch upon your scorpion
> Who crawls across your circus floor.

Dylan's anger in such lyrics reaches a phantasmagoric clarity. The anger of the early social protest songs in only a few years transformed into a far more complicated inner landscape and the play between attraction and hostility. In "My Back Pages," he repudiated his earlier protest songs as simple-minded: "'Rip down all hate' I screamed / Lies that life is black and white." Dylan's emotional range continued to expand, but always with a deep edge of anger—at others or himself.

Smells Like Angry Music

Rock 'n' roll lyrics are not an especially fertile ground for tracing the history of anger in contemporary American music. Some varieties of rock *sound* angry, and some performers are famous for acting angry on stage, but rock as a whole is lyrically impoverished, and its anger music—with a few exceptions—especially so. When fans of rock 'n' roll speak of angry rock, the adjectives *loud* and *fast* are usually nearby. The group Babes in Toyland are interesting, says one writer, "because they are one of the first all-female bands to play the kind of loud, angry rock 'n' roll which typically has been claimed by male groups."[7] A reviewer praised another group, Dead by July, with the comment, "Every once in a while it's nice to hear a band just play loud, fast angry rock 'n' roll without worrying about record sales...."[8]

Writing *about* rock in fact contains a rich vocabulary of anger. News@Ultimate-Guitar.com praises the comeback album, *Contraband,* of Velvet Revolver by remarking, "Slash fires off an arsenal of metal riffs and serpentine solos. McKagan and Sorum lay down throbbing rhythms and Weiland sings in a voice that's equal parts rage and regret." DragStrip Riot likewise wins praise for keeping it angry:

> Rock 'n' roll, the devil's music was meant to be dangerous and
> DragStrip Riot aim to keep it that way. A stripped-down, angry,
> unadulterated, and unapologetic brand of rock 'n' roll that
> will make you want to drink, fight, and f__k.[9]

None of these are well-known rock bands, and while rock
enjoys a reputation as an expression of anger, it is hard to
find successful American bands that are known for producing
particularly angry music. Even the American version of punk
was noted more for its rebellious goofiness than for anger.
The Ramones' "Let's Go" and "Rock 'n' Roll High School"
are not angry songs.

Mojo's list of the top ten protest songs includes only one
rock 'n' roll number, and that by the original British punk
group, the Sex Pistols. Their 1977 song "God Save the Queen"
is surely angry:

> God save the queen, her fascist regime:
> It made you a moron a potential H bomb!
> ....
> God save the queen, she ain't no human being;
> There is no future in England's dreaming.

But this is anger for Her Majesty to deal with; to American
ears, it sounds sort of quaint. The Sex Pistols specialized in
angry songs, such as "Anarchy in the UK"—

> I wanna be an anarchist
> Oh what a name
> Get pissed, destroy!

—that revel in bad-boy behavior and that won an American
audience. But Americans seemed to respond more to the
flamboyance and insouciance of the act than to the actual
ill feeling. Punk music in the end had all the primal terror of
a smiley-face button.

The blues/rock guitar soloist Jimi Hendrix probably merits a mention in the discussion of anger. His August 17, 1969
performance at the Woodstock Festival included a rendition
of "The Star-Spangled Banner" ripped through with screech-
ing feedback. It is a kind of New Anger benchmark:
ostentatiously deconstructing and mocking the national

anthem. At the time, it was understood as a gesture of protest—against the Vietnam War? The Establishment? Racist *Amerika*? No one at Woodstock was really trying to draw such fine distinctions. Hendrix had other New Anger theatrics in his act. At a performance in London in March 1967, he set fire to his Stratocaster electric guitar, a stunt that he famously repeated at the Monterey Pop Festival three months later. The Monterey flaming guitar and the Woodstock "Star-Spangled Banner" performances were caught on film and eventually reached millions of viewers.[10]

By far the most lyrically sophisticated of the musicians that emerged in the late 1970s in connection with the punk version of rock 'n' roll was another British performer, Elvis Costello. He can sound convincingly angry, but Costello is also a chameleon who performs country, new wave, standards, chamber music, and almost anything else that comes to mind.

In the early 1970s, rock 'n' roll acquired the angry sound called heavy metal, which was indeed *loud* and usually *fast,* and it gave performers an opportunity to *look* furious. Perhaps it belongs in the narrative of New Anger in America simply because it provided a conspicuous model of people acting angry for no apparent reason and receiving mass adulation from adolescent boys for doing so. The original heavy metal bands were Led Zeppelin, Black Sabbath, and Deep Purple, with Black Sabbath—from Birmingham, England—widely regarded as exemplifying the genre. Its first album, *Black Sabbath*, appeared in 1969, and included the song "Black Sabbath," depicting a Satanic mass.

But was Black Sabbath or any of the heavy metal bands that followed actually angry, or was this music better understood as a kind of shockwave—a thrilling act of defiance for no particular purpose? "Metal's sound signature," write the music historians Michael Campbell and James Brody, "is distortion—extreme distortion."[11] They mention other conventions of the genre: "blues-derived pentatonic and modal scales, often unharmonized; power chords; extended, flamboyant solos; ear-splitting volume; scream-out, often

incomprehensible lyrics; and pounding rhythms, often performed at breakneck speed." The extreme distortion and
absence of harmony blot out the acoustical space where
other rock 'n' roll music employed the rhythm guitar, and
as Campbell and Brody see it, heavy metal's rejection of harmony contributes to the impression of sheer power:

> Progressions of chord generally imply movement toward a
> goal, even if it's the endlessly recycling one of "Earth Angel"
> and all of its clones. Movement toward a goal, in turn,
> implies tension...and release.... Like romance, harmony
> implies negotiation—will I get to the goal? Metal songs sel-
> dom negotiate; more often they slam from one key to the
> next [as in] Black Sabbath's *Sweet Leaf....* So, both for the
> image of power and because of the fact of power—the soni-
> cally overloaded power chord—metal songs often have little
> or no harmony.

All music expresses emotion, and the emotion at the
heart of heavy metal was the rage of self-assertion amplified
not just by the volume but by the frenzied mass audiences
that heavy metal bands attracted. Heavy metal hasn't gone
away entirely, and possibly can be considered part of the
soundtrack for some of the ostentatious I-can't-control-
myself forms of anger. But there is nothing much to say
about heavy metal lyrics. ("Your existence is a script.... Your
script will run short of ideas," as the band Death sings in
"Individual Thought Pattern." Or, "When we're in town,
speakers explode, we don't attract wimps because we're too
loud," as the British group Manowar used to sing.) In fact,
some of the heavy metal bands currently popular in the
United States are Dutch (Scavenger), Swedish (Dream Evil),
Finnish (Impaled Nazarene), and Icelandic (Down, Minus).
Primal screams are about the same in any language.

What language is that? "Death-metal vocalizing,"
according to Jim Fusilli, a reporter for the *Wall Street Journal,*
"is also known as Cookie Monster singing."[12] Death metal is
heavy metal music's final resting place, or its "extreme
branch" in the view of its fans. Cookie Monster, of course, is
the Muppet character from *Sesame Street* who speaks in a gut-

tural voice. Fusilli describes the death-metal vocals as "low, guttural and aggressive, with no subtlety, no melody and very little modulation.... [They] seem to come from a dark spot in a troubled soul." Monte Conner, vice president of Roadrunner Records, which produces death-metal recordings, has a more explicit aesthetic standard: "It should sound like they are gargling glass." The aim is to sound not just angry, but terrifying. Alas, says Conner, "the Cookie Monster school of death metal is dying." Musical fashions have moved on, interring bands like Sepultura, Suffocation, Carcass, and Obituary in the tomb of oldies-but-goodies.

Another version of angry rock that seems more self-consciously artful than actually angry is represented by "post-punk" or "new wave" bands such as the Talking Heads. In their 1977 song "Psycho Killer," the band's lead singer, David Byrne, presented some deranged lyrics with a blank stare and with such an emotional detachment that he seemed indeed ready to break into a murderous rage:

> I can't seem to face up to the fact
> I'm tense and nervous and I can't relax
> I can't sleep 'cause my bed's on fire
> Don't touch me
> I'm a real live wire
> Psycho killer
> Qu'est que c'est
> Fa fa fa fa fa fa fa fa fa far better
> Run run run run run away...

Byrne had other angry personae as well. In "The Big Country," he mocks American consumerism ("I wouldn't live there if you paid me"), but in the Talking Head's only top-ten single, "Burning Down the House" (1983), Byrne returns to the bizarrely affectless voice of a tightly wound man ready to go off the deep end:

> Cool babies
> Strange but not a stranger
> I'm an ordinary guy
> Burning down the house.

The song is a collection of phrases that only sporadically

make sense, and indeed a movie of one of the Talking Head's concerts was titled *Stop Making Sense,* after a line in another of the band's fractured but vaguely angry lyrics.

Rock has had one other access of anger: the rise at the beginning of the 1990s of grunge, a music that seemed to be invented to demonstrate the existence of levels of lyric inanity below that of the Sex Pistols and the Ramones. Grunge is described by one fan as "a brand of music combining deep riffs, with angry and sometimes depressing lyrics,…immensely popular among the youth at the time, as it seemed to resonate with their own feelings of insecurity and loneliness."[13] Perhaps the most famous song by the most famous grunge band is the 1991 "Smells Like Teen Spirit" by Nirvana:

> Load up your guns, bring your friends
> It's fun to lose, and to pretend
> She's over bored, and self assured
> Oh no. I know a dirty word
>
> ………………………
> Hello, hello, hello, how low?
> Hello, hello, hello, how low?
> Hello, hello, hello, how low?
> Hello, hello, hello

Or possibly the lyrics are:

> Load up on guns
> Bring your friends
> It's fun to lose
> And to pretend
> She's overboard
> Myself assured
> I know I know
> A dirty word
>
> …………
> Hello (x 16)

No one is quite sure. "Smells Like Teen Spirit" was sung by Nirvana's lyricist and lead singer, Kurt Cobain, whose enunciation challenged most listeners.

Cobain's song is the music of narcissistic ennui—the music, in other words, of the Columbine shootings. It is *too* self-absorbed and fascinated with its own fingernails to count as New Anger. New Anger involves a thirst for the attention of others. The Newly Angry are self-centered as well, in that their anger performances have a "look-at-me" quality. But even narcissism has degrees, and Cobain represents the nihilistic extreme. The seemingly motiveless kids who shoot up a school for the sake of making a name for themselves or the killers who sometimes walk into a McDonald's or a Wendy's just for the sake of killing are more or less in the spirit of "Smells Like Teen Spirit"—the spirit of anger as annihilated affect.

The song, however, touched some people who, perhaps, needed to touch some kind of bottom before they could begin to find any real motivation in life. In an essay published in the webzine *Salon* in 2002, Jamie Allen, a short-story writer, recollected the first time he heard "Smells Like Teen Spirit." In 1991, he was an unemployed college grad in Florida who spent his time listening to Bob Dylan and lamenting that he had not "been alive in the early 1960s." Even the Gulf War did not seem worth protesting. Dispirited and bored, he thought he might look for a job in sales. Then one day as he sat in his friend's pickup truck, that friend plunked the Nirvana CD into his high-end player:

> But halfway through *Teen Spirit,* I sat up in my seat. Clearly, the singer was pissed off, though I couldn't understand a word he was saying. But he was also reaching into the melodic stratosphere and coming back with a simple tune that made you want to do something, even if you were a washed-up ballplayer who thought you just wanted to drink beer.[14]

In long retrospect, Allen is able to explain a lot about the song, although it requires some unlikely familiarity with the short, sad life of Kurt Cobain, the Seattle singer who was twenty-four at the time. "Teen Spirit" was a deodorant worn by Tobi Vail, a former girlfriend of Cobain. Her roommate, Kathleen Hanna, once mocked Cobain by spray-painting "Kurt smells like Teen Spirit" on her apartment wall. Allen finds "genius" in Cobain's appropriation of the sentence. To him it means, "It smells like something fake. And the singer wants, above all, something real."

So the song's empty narcissism *can* be yoked to the core cliché in New Anger: an authentic self is an angry self. *I'm angry, therefore I am.*

Allen's admiration for "Teen Spirit" isn't diminished by his recognition that Cobain was covering old ground:

> But *Teen Spirit* is something like Dylan's *Blowin' in the Wind*. Old folksters will tell you that what Dylan said in that song wasn't revolutionary to those in the know in 1963; he just managed to capture the right words and feelings floating around Greenwich Village and present it in a package the whole world could buy. *Teen Spirit*, too, was one of those rare moments when a song was pulled from the air of a scene—Seattle and its spreading ethos of youthful malaise and artistic meanderings—and became greater than the sum of its parts.

Allen describes the song, plausibly enough, as "an acerbic rant against those who follow the herd," with Cobain singing the part of "the dupe." The music too participates in the irony. Cobain "hated those hair-metal riffs so popular in the late '80s," so he put one in. Allen unpacks other layers of irony in the song too, but I refer the reader to the original article for those. His general assessment is surely right not only for "Smells Like Teen Spirit" but for the whole genre of grunge music: "a general, angry disenchantment with (take your pick) the music industry, '80s greed that turned into '90s recession, TV-news patriotism, Republican politics, baby boomers and their self-centered view of their lives and history, etc."

In grunge, American rock 'n' roll appears at last to have found a way to express anger without simply being loud or requiring performers to agonize on stage. Ironic self-depre-cation coupled with cynical weariness, however, seems a fairly fragile artistic stance, and the grunge bands that con-tinued after Cobain's suicide in 1994, though popular, have never achieved quite the status of Nirvana. In a recent Inter-net poll asking people to name and rank the angriest songs, two of Nirvana's songs achieved honors: "Smells Like Teen Spirit" ranked ninth and "Territorial Pissings" ranked eighth. No other grunge songs made the list of the top forty-five.[15]

Culture Wars Soundtrack

While rock 'n' roll in its many subgenres remains the most popular music in the United States, country music is a not very distant second. In some ways, the lines between these two are not especially rigid. Music that sounds rock 'n' roll frequently makes the country charts and various country performers aim at "crossover" hits. Musically, a country song can sound a lot like an old-fashioned rock song. Both country and rock draw on the blues and both have strong connections to popular dance. But in a cultural sense, rock 'n' roll and country often seem to inhabit parallel universes.

The difference was especially evident the year after 9/11. As Stanley Kurtz observed in October 2002, MTV (which plays mostly rock and some hip-hop) at that point had no songs at all dealing with the terrorist attack or the U.S. response. But on Country Music Television (CMT), the war was "omnipresent"—

> A fan wins a chance to interview Reba McEntire and asks how 9/11 changed her life; countdown shows intersperse hits with shots of country music stars entertaining soldiers; and the phrase "Love Your Country" has become a popular network tag line.

Kurtz also mentions some of the videos on patriotic themes: Alan Jackson's "Where Were You (When the World Stopped Turning)?"; Aaron Tippen's "Where the Stars and Stripes and the Eagle Fly"; and Toby Keith's "Courtesy of the Red, White and Blue (The Angry American)." The salience of 9/11 and the war in Afghanistan, Kurtz remarked, was far from the only difference between MTV and CMT. "Most of real life is missing" from MTV, which concentrates on "primal screams of anger, lust, and alienation."

While Martina McBride over on CMT is singing about how

blessed she feels to have a wonderful family, System of a Down [on MTV] is singing about "the toxicity of our city." Now, of course, we'll be told that Martina McBride's "Blessed" is romantic pap, whereas "Toxicity" is edgy and more "realistic" about life. But I think they're both realistic: It would be silly to contend that love, faithfulness, hope, and gratitude aren't real or important elements in life.[16]

The differences between the musical fare on the two networks lie in both substance and style. Country music deals with the whole range of life's problems, from childhood to old age; MTV music deals almost exclusively with life from adolescence through the twenties. Country music insists on telling stories; MTV music occasionally tells a story but usually offers only a few narrative gestures or a suggestive situation. In the end, as Kurtz sees it, in the typical MTV video, "life outside a single person's anxiety, braggadocio, and sexual pleasure seems barely to exist." But in the typical country video, we are plunged into the complexity of ordinary life in both its funny and its heart-wrenching detail.

MTV and CMT in Kurtz's view are proxies of the culture war—although in that light it is worth noting that they are both owned by the same media conglomerate, Viacom. Perhaps Kurt Cobain could have made something of that.

Kurtz's analysis, in my view, is dead on. The cultural divergence between the two networks and the videos they display is another playing out of the divergence (and tensions) between red-state Republican and blue-state Democratic America; between Americans who view life from the lens of traditional religious faith and traditional family commitments on one hand, and Americans who view life through the lens of secularist and postmodernist assumptions. It is easy to overstate these polarities. Toby Keith, the author and singer of the quintessential angry 9/11 song—

This big dog will fight
When you rattle his cage
And you'll be sorry that you messed with the U.S. of A.
'Cause we'll put a boot in your ass
It's the American way

—is a registered Democrat, or as he puts it, "a conservative Democrat who is sometimes embarrassed for his party."[17] A handful of rock 'n' rollers place themselves somewhere on the right, such as gun enthusiast Ted Nugent. Rock has been appropriated as musical idiom by a substantial number of evangelical Christians. The actual political views of many performers are not clear and it is best to allow for the ambiguity and rethinking that are part of most people's lives, including musicians. But that said, the cultural polarity often seems to pull performers along even if they at first attempt to escape it.

Rock star Bruce Springsteen, famously close to his blue-collar roots and resistant to fashionable opinions, responded to 9/11 with an album in 2002, *The Rising,* that perched precariously on the fence between two emotional responses. In "Into the Fire," he prayed that the firefighters would inspire the nation: "May your strength give us strength; May your faith give us faith; May your hope give us hope; May your love give us love." But "Lonesome Day," "Counting on a Miracle," and other songs seemed strangely muted about the desire of ordinary people to assert themselves against the terrorists. The album has nothing to say about the war in Afghanistan or the heroism of soldiers taking the war back to the terrorists. It is silent on what most people would call love-of-country and patriotism. Kurtz suggested that this was because Springsteen was sensitive to the attacks from the left when Ronald Reagan used his song "Born in the USA" in his 1984 presidential campaign. Springsteen told the *London Times* after *The Rising* was released that he wasn't going to allow himself to be co-opted by "the political right.... That flag belongs to me...and I'm not gonna cede that image to any particular party or ideology."[18]

By 2003, however, Springsteen had added a "public service announcement" to his concerts warning about the "rollback" of civil liberties in the United States and had dropped the songs from *The Rising* from his performances.[19] And in August 2004, he announced that he had joined with other bands (including R.E.M., the Dixie Chicks, John Mellencamp, Pearl Jam, and Death Cab for Cutie) to give rock concerts in presidential campaign swing states to raise money for John Kerry and to urge voters to defeat the Bush reelection campaign. The concert series was promoted by the leftist anger group MoveOn.org.[20] Springsteen defended his decision to jump into partisan politics in an op-ed article in the *New York Times,* saying, "Our American government has strayed too far from American values."[21]

Springsteen didn't sound especially angry in his defense of the MoveOn.org tour. The rhetoric was more the toned-down we-should-demand-better-of-ourselves message of the Democratic National Convention. Indeed, Springsteen reproduced a collection of DNC clichés ("unnecessary war," "economic justice," "humane foreign policy") that sound more like the words of party flacks than those of a poetic songwriter. But beneath the clichés, the anger is clear. Springsteen found his way to a blanket acceptance of a "particular party" and its ideology after all.

Country Anger

Country is the least angry of the currently popular music genres in the United States. It has nothing of hip-hop's pervasive angry sound and vituperative lyrics, and unlike the rock 'n' roll supermarket with special angry sections in aisles four and six, country music has no subgenres that are devoted to alienation and anger. The closest it comes is a short-lived movement during the 1970s called "Outlaw," which began when singers Waylon Jennings (1937–2002) and Willie Nelson (1933–) rebelled against the Nashville establishment. They rejected the increasingly pop sound of Nashville and combined elements of rock with older folk traditions. They also adopted a lifestyle conspicuous for hard drinking and drug use. Sometimes an Outlaw song could be angry. Perhaps the best-known song of that sort was Johnny Paycheck's 1977 hit recording of David Allan Coe's "Take This Job and Shove It"—

Take this job and shove it,
I ain't workin' here no more.
My woman done left,
An' took all the reasons I was workin' for.
You better not try to stand in my way,
As I'm walkin' out the door.
Take this job and shove it,
I ain't workin' here no more.

Most Outlaw songs, however, were more rambunctious than angry, and while country music does have plenty of angry songs, they are dispersed through the larger list. They tend to present anger as a response to specific situations rather than as an avocation or an existential mode of being.

In "Concrete Angel," Reba McEntire mourns a little girl abused (and by song's end, killed) by her angry mother. The child goes to school:

Bearing the burden of a secret storm.
Sometimes she wishes she was never born.

Joe Nichols starts his song "If Nobody Believed in You" with a story of a boy playing Little League baseball who is berated by his angry father:

His father's voice was loud an' mean:
"You won't amount to anything."

"The Good Stuff," sung by Kenny Chesney, tells of a man going off to a bar after his first angry fight with his wife. The old barkeep, referring back to the richness of life with his now-deceased wife, sends him home:

He said: "When you get home, she'll start to cry.
When she says: 'I'm sorry,' say: 'So am I.'"

And examples like these can be multiplied—not angry songs, but songs *about* anger or in which anger is pictured as an obstacle that has to be surmounted.

Country songs that are actually angry usually deal with one of three themes: patriotic fervor, female wrath, or the condescension of the cultural elite. Some of the songs written in response to 9/11 take on the theme of anger directly.

Darryl Worley in "Have You Forgotten?" criticizes the liberal media for attempting to diffuse righteous fury:

> They took all the footage off my TV
> Said it's too disturbing for you and me
> It'll just breed anger that's what the experts say
> If it was up to me I'd show it every day
> Some say this country's just out looking for a fight
> After 9/11 man I'd have to say that's right.

Some of the country songs responding to 9/11 were too toughly worded even for CMT, which cancelled an appearance by Charlie Daniels at a benefit concert for the Salvation Army to help victims of the attacks. Daniels had wanted to sing "This Ain't No Rag, It's a Flag," which includes verses such as:

> You might have shot us in the back
> but now you have to face the fact
> that the big boy's in the game
> The lightning's been flashing
> And the thunder's been crashing
> And now it's getting ready to rain.

The song became a hit anyway.

Long before the crop of country songs commenting on 9/11, country singers wrote patriotic songs, some of them expressing anger toward America's foreign enemies, such as Charlie Daniels' 1980 hit, "In America." But not all country songs about war are angry. John Michael Montgomery's "Letters from Home" tells of a soldier who, in successive verses, receives letters from his mother, his sweetheart, and his father, with the refrain:

> I fold it up and put it in my shirt
> pick up my gun and get back to work
> and it keeps me drivin' on
> waitin' on letters from home.

The song mentions no enemies or reasons for war, expresses no anger, and depicts the soldiers not as furious revenge-minded warriors, but as men overcoming their fear ("like we ain't scared") to honor their obligations to their families and their country. Likewise, the female trio SHeDaisy in "Come

Home Soon" never mention the war directly, but the song is a prayer for the safe return of the troops:

> I wonder, I pray
> I sleep alone, I cry alone
> And it's so hard living here on my own
> So please come home soon.

The video for "Come Home Soon" depicts a candlelight prayer service attended by the wives and girlfriends of servicemen, and ends with a dedication across the screen, "For all our heroes here at home."

Anger in the female wrath songs of country music focuses on errant boyfriends and abusive husbands. Country also has lots of brokenhearted songs by male singers, but they rarely touch the anger chord the way many of the women singers do. In "Fist City," Loretta Lynn threatens to beat up a woman who has been "a-lovin' with my man"—

> You'd better close your face and stay out of my way
> If you don't want to go to Fist City.

Rachel Proctor in "Me and Emily" sings about fleeing with her daughter from a man who has turned violent. "It would kill me if he ever raised his hand to her," she says. The song implies a great deal of anger but overtly emphasizes the singer's determination to protect her child, and it ends:

> At least there's one good thing he gave to me
> And she's starting to wake up.

In Martina McBride's song "Independence Day," a woman recalls the day when she was eight years old that her mother struck back at her abusive husband by burning down the house, presumably with that "dangerous man" in it:

> Let the weak be strong, let the right be wrong
> Roll the stone away, let the guilty pay
> It's Independence Day.

The Dixie Chicks in "Sin Wagon" sing of acting out female wrath in a different way:

> Praise the Lord and pass the ammunition
> Need a little bit more

of what I've been missin'
I don't know where I'll be crashin'
But I'm arrivin' on a sin wagon.

And the Dixie Chicks in their notorious "Goodbye Earl" sing of Wanda and her best friend Mary Anne poisoning Wanda's abusive husband Earl and then disposing of his body in a lake. The music is jaunty and the video depicts the murder as a sweet victory for all put-upon women:

So the girls bought some land
And a roadside stand
Out on highway 109
They sell Tennessee ham
And strawberry jam
And they don't lose any sleep at night 'cause
Earl had to die.

Of course, the Dixie Chicks have courted controversy in other ways too. In March 2003, lead singer Natalie Maines told an audience in London, "Just so you know, we are ashamed the president of the United States is from Texas." When the story broke in the British newspaper *The Guardian*, it described them as "the good-time girls the country establishment loves to hate."[22] Maines' criticism led to a temporary boycott of their music by some radio stations—and to a great deal of hyperventilating on both sides of the culture divide. *New York Times* columnist Paul Krugman, for example, compared the boycotters (with coy ellipsis) to Nazi book burners: "To those familiar with 20th-century European history it seemed eerily reminiscent of.... But as Sinclair Lewis said, it can't happen here." Then he conjured a theory that the radio chain Clear Channel was engaged in a dark conspiracy with the Bush administration to silence political critics.[23]

The third common way for anger to show up in country songs is in expressions of resentment against the cultural elite. Garth Brooks' exuberant "Friends in Low Places" tells a story of a country fellow showing up at a girlfriend's black-tie party and recognizing that he doesn't belong. The first two lines of the song immediately establish the cultural mismatch:

> Blame it all on my roots
> I showed up in boots.

"Roots," of course, is a word rich with significance in the culture wars. Country folk, who are close to their roots, are used to having the elite sneer both at their supposed backwardness and at the cultural pathologies that the left sees in "American roots," such as love of guns, excessive patriotism, sexism, and racism. "Blame it all on my roots" sings Brooks, without having to add, "because I know that's what you'll do anyway."

Having discovered his mistake, the singer says, "we may be through / But you'll never hear me complain," and then launches into his explanation:

> 'Cause I've got friends in low places
> Where the whiskey drowns
> And the beer chases my blues away
> And I'll be okay
> I'm not big on social graces
> Think I'll slip on down to the Oasis
> Oh, I've got friends in low places.

The song thus becomes a celebration of the conviviality among the folks excluded from the upper-crust world of the former girlfriend, "that ivory tower / That you're livin' in."

"Friends in Low Places" is much too buoyant a song for anyone to call it angry, but its emotional lift comes from the unspoken anger the singer feels at the condescension of the people at the party. And this is the key to almost all country songs expressing anger at the cultural elite. The CMT crowd, the "red states" audiences, and traditionalist Americans everywhere fully recognize that they and their cultural preferences are looked down upon by the university professors and newspaper columnists. And sometimes, in country music, they reply. Gretchen Wilson in "Redneck Woman" avows:

> No, I can't swig that sweet Champagne, I'd rather drink beer
>   all night
> In a tavern or in a honky-tonk or on a four-wheel drive
>   tailgate.

She recognizes the social standing that her tastes give her ("Some people look down on me, but I don't give a rip") and she takes pride in living well by a different set of expectations:

> Victoria's Secret, well their stuff's real nice
> Oh but I can buy the same damn thing on a Wal-Mart shelf
>   half price
> And still look sexy, just as sexy as those models on TV;
> No, I don't need no designer tag to make my man want me.
> Well, you might think I'm trashy, a little too hardcore
> But get in my neck of the woods, I'm just the girl next door.

As with "Friends in Low Places," the anger in "Redneck Woman" is a little below the surface. The song sounds proud and high-spirited, but in almost every line the singer is repudiating the scorn of those who consider themselves her social betters. "Redneck Woman" also contains a line that perfectly echoes the sarcastic opening, "Blame it all on my roots," in Brooks' song. Wilson sings, "I ain't no high-class broad / I'm just a product of my raising."

Brooks' reference to his roots and Wilson's reference to her being a "product of her raising" offer a slight whiff of cultural relativism, as if the country folks wouldn't mind the condescension if the cultural elites just left them alone. But this shouldn't be taken at face value. What's really happening is that the country songs are mocking the hypocrisy of an elite that proudly proclaims its open-mindedness while simultaneously expressing contempt for traditional values. Country musicians pick up on the posturing of those who say they are for "the people" while condescending to them.

Country's ironic attack on cultural relativism is especially clear in the group Montgomery Gentry's song "You Do Your Thing." The singer says he likes the backwoods, fishing, and camping; and to someone who presumably doesn't, he says, "You do your thing, I'll do mine." That invitation bites deeper as the song progresses:

> I ain't tradin' in my family's safety
> Just to save a little gas
> And I'll pray to God any place, any time

And you can bet I'll pick up the phone if Uncle Sam calls
   me up.
You do your thing, I'll do mine.

The small-car-driving, secularist war opponent is now the target of the singer's ire, but is still invited to go his own way. The singer proceeds to defend traditional child rearing ("A broken rule, a consequence"), hard work, and self-reliance ("If I don't get my fill on life I ain't gonna blame no one but me"). All this could be heard as a strained defense of the singer's loyalties, characterized as just a matter of lifestyle choice, with the corollary that the secular advocate of the liberal welfare state whom he addresses has merely opted for a different choice. But the song ends:

You ain't gonna be my judge
Cuz my judge will judge us all one day
You do your thing, I'll do mine.

The toleration turns out not to be based on the secularist's relativism, but on faith in a God who enforces universal justice.

The duo Montgomery Gentry (Eddie Montgomery and Troy Gentry) is sometimes described as a return to the Outlaw movement in country music. One writer noted the "snarling tone" of their song "Hillbilly Shoes," which includes the lyric:

Ain't too much these boots can't do
Might even kick a little sense into you.

But the same writer observes that in person the singers Eddie Montgomery and Troy Gentry are imposing but well mannered and don't aim for surly or distant personae.[24] The threat to "kick a little sense into you" may sound gruff, but it's hardly in the same league as Eminem's expostulation of the random mayhem he would like to commit:

Bitch, I'm comin out swingin, so fast it'll make your eyes spin
You gettin knocked the fuck out like Mike Tyson.

While country music is not pervasively angry, it is a medium of expression broad enough to convey anger in situations that warrant it and to calibrate that anger very precisely. None of these songs is explosively angry or turns anger into something that the singer revels in as glorious and empowering. The closest thing to New Anger in country music may be some of the songs by the Dixie Chicks, but even those are restrained by a narrative framework and a good deal of irony. Rather, what country music provides is a sustained glimpse into the world of "old anger," where anger was one emotion among many, and one that called for self-control rather than abandonment to the pleasures of wrath.

Country music is, not coincidentally, linked to the side of the culture war that attempts to sustain older American values against the tide of expressive individualism that welled up in the 1960s and that provides the underlying force for New Anger today. People have always gotten angry, and anger is not inherently a pathology. Anger is an element that must be integrated with other feelings to allow us to live full and responsible lives. In that sense, country music is the most adult music available to most Americans. Though it is frequently sentimental and sometimes cloying, country music as a whole expresses more of the range of human experience than hip-hop, folk, or rock. Its songs, for example, frequently operate on a much larger time scale: not just what's happening "right now" or, as in hip-hop, how rough I had it growing up, but in a time scale of generations. In his song "There Goes My Life," Kenny Chesney tells the story of a teenager who sees his "dreams going up in smoke" when he learns he has gotten his girlfriend pregnant. By the end of the song, we are twenty years down the road as the boy, grown into a mature and proud father, watches his daughter head off in her Honda for the West Coast, and the refrain "There goes my life" has completely reversed its meaning.

The techniques of country music may be musically simple, but no simpler than the other popular genres. Its level of emotional complexity, however, is much greater, and it can stand as a measure of how New Anger has impoverished other forms of music. I suspect that what is true in music is true in other artistic media as well. When anger is given free license, it dominates other emotions, which, if they are expressed at all, lose their own vibrancy. Angry paintings, angry movies, angry theater, and angry art generally head down this path. For the sake of brevity in this book, I'll leave popular music as the primary example. But lest we lose track of just how angry—and ugly—much of that music is, let's recall what the rappers are offering.

All the Rage

One of the common motifs of rap is trading angry insults with other rappers. Sometimes this turns into deadly violence, but usually it is merely verbal. In "Hey Fuck You," the Beastie Boys insult fellow rapper Eminem:

> MC's are like clay pigeons and I'm shootn' skeet
> I just yell pull and Eminem drops the beat
> You people call yourselves MC's but your garbage men
> Takin' out the trash when you pull out the pen
> And if you don't like them hey fuck you!

Rapper 50 Cent in "Cutmaster C Shit" threatens other rappers with his .44 caliber magnum revolver:

> I walk around with a big four four
> You front on me, I'm gonna get at you dog
> I be right at your crib, waitin' at your door
> What up bitches.

But enough. Anyone who wants to take the time to listen to hip-hop or to read transcriptions of the lyrics can pretty quickly size up a world that is about ego, resentment, intimidating rivals, celebrating criminality, demeaning women, consuming and selling drugs, boasting of wealth and luxury, spending time in prison, and demonstrating verbal dexterity. The verbal dexterity is sometimes real and can be impressive if you can get past the self-barricaded spiritual and moral wasteland of everything else. This is not a world of sustained human relationships or recognition of the complicated interdependencies that make life both difficult and worth living. It is life reduced to existential urgencies and appetites.

No doubt that accounts for its appeal to nihilistic white teenagers who like to imagine, from positions of cocooned safety, what life on the edge is really like. Anger is indeed a primal emotion and the artifices of anger, so long as they look realistic, beckon with a sense of authenticity that is all too often missing in lives that have been stripped of the context of enduring traditions. New Anger, however, is never really authentic. It is just a performance, and hip-hop is one more form of staged rage. This kind of anger can only feed on itself, enjoying its momentary sense of empowerment, since ultimately it leads nowhere at all. Brother, can you spare a dime?

SIX

IN THE BEE HIVE

How Americans Explain and Justify Anger

Coco Henson Scales recently published the lead article in the *New York Times* "Sunday Styles" section, describing her experiences as a hostess at Hue, a trendy Vietnamese restaurant in the West Village section of New York City.[1] Ms. Scales did not entertain a very high opinion of the customers and she seems to have had no compunction about sharing her attitude with the larger world:

> Celebrities and models are my least favorite customers. They never want to pay and they demand constant attention. The models wear jeans or a jean skirt with heels and a white T-shirt. Drunken skeletons, they stand outside smoking and talking in foreign accents. They don't tip, but if they aren't here, the men who do tip won't stay, so we cater to models.

Drunken skeletons aside, Ms. Scales says she liked working in a restaurant, although she did have to overcome a problem: "Initially, I am too nice." She sympathized with customers' complaints. The manager insisted, "Stop apologizing so much." Over time, she learned her lessons and, by developing the appropriate level of contempt toward the clientele, bonded with her sarcastic coworkers. At the end of a year, when she told her boss she was quitting, he replied, "But you just learned how to do your job."

Every occupation probably has its own jaundiced-insider perspective. A physician I know refers to motorcycles with a certain wry optimism as "donor-cycles," as though every easy rider were roaring to a future as a source of organ transplants. But the *public* parading of contempt for the customer, once fairly rare, has become a staple of the angri-culture. Ms. Scales wishes us to see her as inwardly standing above the haughty fashion models and pushy celebrities that she catered to on the job. It isn't hard to sympathize with her anger—up to a point. We see the customers, through her eyes, as either rude or gullible. But we also get to see something rather unattractive about Ms. Scales herself, who stars in her own story about her disdain for the vulgar rich and the people who serve them.

Anger—plain old anger—often tempts people in the heat of the moment to say more than they ought to. New Anger, by contrast, tempts people to make a spectacle of their resentments. Sometimes that spectacle is humorous, but it is seldom attractive.

Living in the United States has become a matter of dealing with angry people almost all the time—or at least a lot more frequently than we would like. Way too many of the people we live and work with have bees in their mouths; it is as though the hive had emptied out into the nation's coffee cups and had been sipped up with the morning paper. Visitors from abroad, once impressed with the friendliness of Americans, have begun to remark instead our surliness. A thirteen-year-old Colombian girl visiting the United States told Marcela Sanchez, a writer for the *Washington Post,* that everyone in America seemed angry. This prompted Sanchez to tally up her own encounters with the angri-culture that morning: the rude clerk at the airline ticket counter, the irate cashier at the juice store, and the hyperefficient waiter who was "fast but furious."[2]

Sanchez reflects on the possible causes of this anger: lots of stress, anger about Iraq, and political divisiveness come to mind. She suggests that "values debates" are "more acrimonious than essential," and lodges specific blame at President Bush for pushing a constitutional amendment to ban gay marriage as the most heated of nonessential "values debates." Such debates are "unconstructive in the long term" and make people "feel less content with their everyday lives."

Somehow I don't think being forced to decide on gay marriage directly explains the nasty-tempered juice seller or the angrily frenetic waiter. Maybe they went to the same school as Ms. Scales.

As more and more people notice the overt expressions of anger—and some begin to notice the more subtle expressions of the angri-culture—we encounter more and more ad hoc explanations like those of Ms. Sanchez. Such explanations are certainly not entirely wrong. In Ms. Sanchez's case, her intuition that "values debates" have *something* to do with the swarm of anger around her is right. But the connection between a debate over gay marriage (or gun control, prayer in schools, stem cell research, etc.) and angry juice sellers isn't "stress" or even the general level of irritability in society. It is, rather, two things: the urgency of the idea that anger is good and that expressing it is even better; and the reorganization of personalities and psychological dispositions among Americans as we have incorporated this new ideal.

Anger as an ideal cannot be sustained without people who embody the ideal. It has taken several generations of cultural redirection, however, to produce a population in which large numbers of people find the satisfactions of anger to be more fulfilling than those of self-control.

Grrrls Just Wanna Be Fierce

As a graduate student in anthropology at the University of Rochester in the late 1970s, I studied under an austere woman, a professor of anthropology named Grace Harris. Professor Harris spoke in full and precise sentences; she seemed to be in cold self-control. We graduate students lived in some fear of her anger, which we knew would freeze us in our tracks if we should ever provoke it. But if Professor Harris was angry at all, it must have been a very old-fashioned anger. I never heard her raise her voice or speak crossly to a student. She commanded attention without the aid of today's expressive anger.

Professor Harris's major contribution to anthropology was a book titled *Casting Out Anger,* about a warmhearted people in warmhearted Kenya, the Taita.[3] The title of her book refers to a small ritual called *kutasa* performed by the Taita and many other East Africans. An individual takes a mouthful of liquid and sprays it out with a prayer announcing that with the liquid goes all the secret and festering grievances that the man or woman holds, usually against members of his or her family. Harris observed:

> *Kutasa* was usually performed in a squatting position with the arms held loosely across the knees, one hand holding a container of sugar cane beer, unfermented cane juice or water. Spraying out mouthfuls of liquid, the performer uttered phrases, exhorting or supplicating a mystical agent or agents and calling down blessings on one or more living humans and on what pertained to their welfare. At some point the utterances explicitly or implicitly rejected the angry feelings of the performer himself.

For *kutasa* to work, according to Taita belief, the supplicant had to have "a heart 'clean' and 'cool', freed from anger and resentment." One cannot cast out anger while in its grip.

Bees in the mouth? Beer out of the mouth. Consider this my contribution to the self-help-through-ancient-tribal-wisdom movement. I have been told by other anthropologists who work in East Africa that versions of *kutasa* are found throughout the region.

Across the world in all cultures and throughout history, the most common sort of anger is displeasure with relatives. The family is the school of emotions as well as the place where we wrestle with our most complex relationships. Ask people about anger almost anywhere and you generally will hear stories about parents, siblings, spouses, sons, and daughters.

Fred Myers, an anthropologist who studied the Pintupi aborigines of the Australian Western Desert, observed that Pintupi get angry (*rarru*) when a relative does not offer them food, which is interpreted as a basic rejection of reciprocity. In the early 1980s, a band of nine Pintupi who had had no previous contact with European civilization came out of the desert and reestablished contact with their relatives living near European settlements. Myers witnessed one of the reunions, in which two brothers from the desert band encountered their sister, Topsy, who had been left behind twenty years earlier: "On first sight of her in their mother's camp, her youngest brother's face turned dark with rage; immediately he grabbed a fighting stick and attempted to strike her." The other brother, arriving moments later, threw boomerangs at Topsy and had to be restrained by other relatives as he hoisted a spear. They were angry, it turned out, because Topsy had not searched for them as a caring sister should.[4]

But if anger is common in families in every culture, so are rules for preventing anger; separate rules for controlling it when prevention fails; and still more rules for making up afterwards. Human societies would not last without such rules. The family is too important to allow it to descend into a free-for-all of resentments, accusations, and spite. The Taita ritual of *kutasa,* "casting out anger," is one of the myriad ways that cultures have devised to deal with the problem.[5]

Americans are no exception. We may not rinse and spit out anger, but for most of our history, the family has sought ways to teach children to control their anger and we brought considerable pressure on husbands and wives to control their tempers too.[6] The current profusion of self-help books and anger management classes testifies that these goals remain valid to many Americans. Some of our efforts to control anger, however, have taken a decisive turn away from the old judgments that anger is either a moral infraction or a personal weakness.

One major departure is the advent of articles and books urging women to use anger to empower themselves both inside and outside the family.

For example, in their recent book, *The Anger Advantage: The Surprising Benefits of Anger and How It Can Change a*

Woman's Life, Deborah Cox, Karin Bruckner, and Sally Stabb set out to debunk what they see as myths that stand "in the way of our connection with [our] goals and dreams." They had been taught as "little girls" that "we were selfish for feeling angry," and they were scared when their parents were angry. On the whole, they had been trained by their families and schools "to put others' emotional needs ahead of our own."[7] Pooling their talents, the three authors created what they call the Women's Anger Project, of which their book is a consequence. Their thesis is plain: "When women attempt to *get around* their anger without fully acknowledging it, they lose a lot of valuable information and experiences that help them evolve into their full selves."

The Anger Advantage is chock-full of interesting arguments and examples in support of this idea. For example, the three authors identify "seven anger myths, including "anger is destructive and naughty," "anger ruins relationships," and "anger is avoidable." And they list "Ten Anger Traps to Avoid," including "Trap #2: Thinking you must justify your position if you're angry; assuming that you must make logical sense to yourself or someone else"; and "Trap #10: Trying to force yourself to forgive and forget." The book ends with a section titled "Weaving Your Anger Tapestry":

> Imagine your anger as a bright and glowing sun-yellow thread. At the core of the experience of anger, these glowing threads are woven together to form a basic pattern of pure anger. This is the raw emotion that you were born with, that our species developed out of thousands of years of successful evolution. This is the fiber of a true acknowledgement of anger to the self. The sun-yellow thread represents all the adaptive power of anger; to clarify who you are, to set your boundaries with others, to motivate change, to strive for connection, to cue you when it's time to shift into a new gear, to make a difference in the world.

Cox, Bruckner, and Stabb provide an account of anger, in other words, that is essentially the complete inversion of traditional accounts. Anger in their view is a power to be tapped to make a woman a better mother, wife, lover, and friend, and more successful on the job as well. Anger used astutely enhances both intimate relationships and worldly pursuits. They advise a woman to "Revel in it. Wrap yourself up in it. Claim it. Flaunt it. Dream with it. Go forward with it."

Patti Brietman, one of the feminists who endorsed *The Anger Advantage,* pronounced that "There are countless legitimate reasons for women to be angry today." Just today? No doubt women (and men) have always had "countless reasons" to be angry. Life is hard and frequently unfair, but it used to be a lot harder and vastly less fair. Back in the day, people struggled against anger partly because they understood that anger usually made bad matters worse. Now we have cultural theorists to tell us that (at least for women) anger is "legitimate" and the smart player learns how to use it.

Cox, Bruckner, and Stabb are by no means alone in extolling the empowering aspects of anger, though some of the self-help authors offer more temperate versions of the idea. In *Make Anger Your Ally* (1990), Neil Clark Warren advises readers of both sexes to control "explosive anger" but make use of the underlying emotion, since "When we are angry, we have enormous power available."[8] In *The Dance of Anger: A Woman's Guide to Changing the Patterns of Intimate Relationships,* Harriet Lerner observes that women, "rather than using our anger as a challenge to think more clearly about the 'I' in our relationships, ... may, when angry, actually blur what personal clarity we *do* have." Lerner hopes to teach her readers "to use our anger effectively."[9]

In 1988, two scholars, Francesca Cancian and Steven Gordon, published a study in which they systematically reviewed the advice on "love and anger" in American women's magazines from 1900 to 1979. They found a "zigzag pattern" of change between advice that extolled traditional values (such as patience and self-sacrifice) and what they chose to call "modern" attitudes, which included self-expression, individuality, acting on impulse, expressing anger, and confronting marital problems directly. According to Cancian and Gordon, articles advising women to express anger in their marriages were scarce from 1900 to 1949, but then started to take off in the 1950s, and by the 1970s outnumbered articles advising "avoidance."[10] The number of articles on either side is surprisingly small, but the trends are clear. Cancian and Gordon make no mystery of their own stake in this matter. They view magazine articles that aimed at "suppression of anger and love as self-sacrifice" as reinforcing women's "powerlessness," which is a slightly roundabout version of Cox, Bruckner, and Stabb's thesis that women's anger equals power. By labeling articles that counseled *self-control* as urging women to "avoid conflict," they distort the substance of at least some of that advice. Controlling one's anger might well be seen as a way of mastering, not avoiding conflict. But Cancian and Gordon's tabulation does nicely illustrate the continuation of older ideals even as newer ones gained ground.

	Number of articles in women's magazines urging women to avoid anger and disagreements	Number of articles in women's magazines urging women to express anger and disagreements
1900–1909	1	1
1910–1919	2	0
1920–1929	3	2
1930–1939	6	2
1940–1949	4	0
1950–1959	6	3
1960–1969	6	4
1970–1979	4	9

Self-help books and articles show one face of the new ideal of anger. Another is the mythologizing of anger. *Women Who Run with the Wolves* (1992) by Jungian analyst Clarissa Pinkola Estés was a bestseller in its time. Estés writes as a promoter of the "Wild Woman," a type she fears is vanishing. The book begins, "Wildlife and the Wild Woman are both endangered species," a proposition that seems remarkably inaccurate on both counts. One of Estés' chapters is titled "Marking Territory: The Boundaries of Rage and Forgiveness." The Wild Woman's "tutelage," as Estés refers to the self-conscious act of tuning in to an archetype, helps women "reclaim the ancient, the intuitive, and the passionate," which has all sorts of benefits, such as helping women make their "ideas manifest in the world" and teaching "receptive mates about wildish rhythms." But to get to these benefits, Wild Women have to learn to "release" their "women's rage."[11]

In other words, Estés offers yet another version of the argument that "repressing" anger is bad. ("Like trying to put fire in a burlap bag.") Estés' specialty as a writer is folk-sounding metaphors that are meant to testify to the ancient sources of her insights. In this case, we learn our lesson via a Japanese tale about "Crescent Moon Bear" in which a woman faces ursine rage in order to learn how to deal with her distempered husband. Estés teases several meanings out of the story, but they can probably be summed up in her two declarations, "We want to use anger as a creative force" and "We want something to show for feeling angry." Like almost every other writer on the topic, Estés ends up counseling some kind of moderation—advising women, in effect, to use anger intelligently rather than waste it in useless outbursts.

She also comes out on the side of forgiveness. To be stuck in outdated rage, she observes, "means to be tired all the time, to have a thick layer of cynicism, to dash the hopeful, the tender, [and] the promising.... It means bilious entrenched silences. It means feeling helpless." Her answer to this sort of chronic, deadening anger is for the angry woman to summon her "creative" energies to "forego, forebear, and forgive." No need to glance back: Estés is counseling women to embrace what Cox, Bruckner, and Stabb call "Trap #10." The disagreement, however, is probably superficial. All of these writers agree that for anger to become empowering, it must be acted on. A bottled-up anger just grows stale and vinegary.

In 2002, Cathi Hanauer, a novelist and former advice columnist for the magazine *Seventeen,* published a collection of essays by twenty-six women under the title *The Bitch in the House.* Hanauer's original project was to explain the "seeming epidemic of female rage," and she declares, "This book was born out of anger—especially, my own domestic anger, which stemmed from a combination of guilt, resentment, exhaustion, naïveté, and the chaos of my life at the time. But ultimately, it is not an angry book." Some might dispute that, but it is true, as Hanauer says later, that many of the contributing women "weren't enraged." *The Bitch in the House* is indeed not so much about rage as about emotional calculation.[12]

Among the contributors, E. S. Maduro in "Excuse Me While I Explode" wonders at the age of twenty-four how "to figure things out; to try to learn how to feel pride and even power without running myself ragged; to be with a man without being angry for the rest of my life." Jen Marshall in "Crossing to Safety" extols the virtues of living at a substantial distance from a boyfriend and finds it "infuriating how people expected me to radically amend and truncate my life so it would fit comfortably into his." In "Moving In, Moving Out, Moving On," Sarah Miller writes about being "completely disgusted" with herself for her job writing a sex column for a men's magazine and the "miserable human experiment" of living with a man out of "fear of being alone." Almost all the essays take similar forms of self-recriminating autobiography woven together with a more diffuse and pervasive anger at the myriad difficulties of getting along with the opposite sex.

The Anger Advantage and *Women Who Run with the Wolves* are examples of the explicit idealization of anger. *The Bitch in the House* portrays the lives of women who have grown up taking that message seriously. But the idealization of women's anger is evident in other cultural forms as well. In fact, we now have a phrase, "girl power"—or "grrrl power"— that evokes the praiseworthiness of anger in females who are not quite old enough to run with the wolves.

The term "grrrl power" has been around since about 1990. The earliest newspaper reference I have traced is to a story in 1994 about the "Lesbian Festival" in Northampton, Massachusetts, which featured a two-day, ten-band concert under the rubric "GRRL Power" and included groups such as

Lunachicks, Cheesecake, and Sexpod.[13] The term soon gained wider currency, though by 1999 journalists who used it still felt the need to offer an explanation. A writer for *Cannabis Culture* magazine that year, for example, wished to celebrate seventeen-year-old Sarah Gack's successful challenge to the drug policy of her high school in Nevada City, California, saying:

> Sarah Gack is typical of a new subculture of adolescent females, whose collective look, ideology and style has been called "grrrl power," by media pundits. The "grrr" part of the moniker denotes the fact that these girls are not demure, not passive, not polishing their nails, worried about boys or dressing in pink....
>
> Instead, they come across as hybrids of defiant male and female traits. They have quirky fashion sense, cut their hair short, work hard at whatever interests them, engage in extreme sports and reckless adventure. They want independence, a better world, freedom from rape and sexism. They don't take shit from anybody. It's like the bumper sticker says: Grrrl Power rules![14]

Grrrl power is an interesting twist on feminism, insisting simultaneously on power and a certain kind of femininity, as expressed in a word—"girl"—that feminists had once tried to chase into oblivion. But the *grrr* in grrrl power is a growl of power that roots itself in anger—and, like all forms of New Anger, is meant to be seen and admired. Grrrl power is performed anger that comes with its own fashions, coiffures, and lifestyles.

> Chanel-sneakered girls in pearls and denim,
> Innocence lacquered in female venom

So begins a verse review, by John Seabrook in the *New Yorker,* of a spring 2001 fashion show in which Karl Lagerfeld's grrrl-ish athletic wear was on display. The show was in Paris, but the style was surely American.[15]

The nonce-word "grrrl" has also gained its own chronicler. *Everything You Need to Know about the Riot Grrrl Movement: The Feminism of a New Generation* by Cherie Turner, for example, is a 64-page booklet aimed at six- to ten-year-olds.[16]

I guess six-year-old girls these days must be curious about Riot Grrrls. *School Library Journal* offers this comment on Turner's book:

> The Riot Grrrl Movement had its roots in the 1970s punk scene in which young women were welcomed and encouraged "to be nasty, aggressive, vitriolic, and outraged, to howl and roar and raise a ruckus." By the 1980s, women had been relegated to the margins of punk. Riot Grrrl was an early 1990s offshoot of its revival founded by feminist musicians, writers, and their friends in Olympia, Washington.

The term "girl power" (in more traditional spelling), however, somehow manages to keep its angry edge just far enough below the surface to sound innocent. In plain dress it shows up in all sorts of places. A *National Geographic* special on species in which "females call the shots" is titled "Girl Power." A newspaper article about the appeal of Pokémon and Japanese comics to American girls runs under the headline "Girl Power." And the U.S. Department of Health and Human Services under President Bush runs a program called "Girl Power" for girls age nine to thirteen. HHS's website includes a section on "Girls' Thoughts on Girl Power."

Grrrl power also has its own comic strip, drawn by Lela Lee and gathered in a book titled *Angry Little Girls* (2005). Lee introduces her characters, including:

> Kim the angry little Asian girl is true to her moniker. She is one short-tempered little girl. Grrr!!! Grrr!!! Grrr!!!

> Deborah the disenchanted princess. She's a girl who has it all—beauty, money, cute clothes, great hair—but she's NEVER happy! Sigh...

Kim and Deborah, along with Maria "the crazy little Latina," Wanda "the fresh little soul sistah," and Xyla "the gloomy girl" deal with life's problems. In "Motherly Love," Kim tells her mother, "Mother, I have no friends." Mother replies, "You ugly. That why you have no friend." Lee's comic insight doesn't get much beyond this, but her book was published by a major press and I have seen it displayed in the major bookstore chains.

It is a close question whether such mainstreaming draws

the venom out of an idea or merely habituates us to the underlying assumption. Somewhere in the back of even the more innocuous pronouncements of girl power lies the notion that a young woman's power comes from her ability to summon and deploy anger.

And that's a very long way from those warmhearted people in warmhearted Kenya doing their best to cast anger out, lest it overwhelm the relationships on which family life depends. Maybe "the anger advantage" extolled by Cox, Bruckner, and Stabb wins the tennis match. Maybe the women running with wolves and consorting with Crescent Moon Bear are better at manifesting ideas and getting into wildish rhythms with their mates. Maybe Sarah Gack, digging deep into her adolescent clichés, struck a blow for civil liberties. But almost certainly we are witnessing the celebration of a new cultural ideal that, in these expressions, is strongly opposed to older ideals of overcoming anger both for the sake of others and for one's own ultimate good.

The new ideal didn't emerge out of thin air. Like most forms of New Anger, it was planted a generation earlier in the 1960s and 1970s. Among its original advocates are figures such as Robin Morgan, who included in her 1970 book, *Sisterhood Is Powerful,* her free-verse "Letter to a Sister Underground," in which she explained the diabolical stratagems of men:

> The Conquerors.
> They're always watching,
> invisibly electroded in our brains,
> to be certain we implode our rage against each other
> and not explode it against them.

And warned:

> Don't accept rides from strange men,
> And remember that all men are strange as hell.[17]

Morgan and other radical feminists of that time exhorted women to rid themselves of the restraints on anger supposedly inculcated in them by patriarchy.

The idea that women ought to express anger more

openly was not solely a conceit of radical feminists. It was quickly establishing itself in mainstream culture. As early as 1972, the pop psychologist Dr. Joyce Brothers advised readers of *Good Housekeeping* in an article on how to keep their marriages vibrant, "Anger repressed can poison a relationship as surely as the cruelest words."[18] Novelists with a feminist agenda were also popularizing the notion that women who restrained their anger only paid for it down the road. In Marilyn French's 1977 novel, *The Women's Room,* for example, the heroine reflects on her situation in a manner that almost suggests she has been reading a back issue of *Good Housekeeping:* " 'Love,' she muttered to herself. It makes you, she felt, hide your own anger from yourself, out of fear, so that by the time it does come out, it is poisonous."[19]

In the 1970s, these were daring new thoughts. American women were, in effect, being challenged, cajoled, and sometimes shamed by the feminist cultural elite into relinquishing older ideals about the importance of repressing anger. By the 1990s and the present decade, the older ideals have more or less succumbed to the newer standard. American women, of course, have not all suddenly become wolf-running Riot Grrrls. Cultural change is always a complex stitching and restitching of *competing* ideals. But it is unmistakable that the temper of relations between the sexes in America has been deeply altered by an ethic taught to girls at a very early age that encourages confrontational expression of anger within their personal relationships.

Mean Macaws

Relinquishing anger was never very easy, but the new idealization of anger makes the effort to control it much harder. On June 12, 2004, Judge Susanne Shaw of Orange County Superior Court sentenced Anthony James Ellis, fifty-three, to 120 days of community service and fined him $3,577.26 for punching his pet macaw, Johnny. Mr. Ellis lost his temper after Johnny bit his arm. Judge Shaw also ordered Mr. Ellis to take anger management classes.[20]

Only a few of us have been assaulted by mean-spirited macaws. Yet many of us seem to feel entitled to strike back verbally and sometimes physically at a world that nips us. In searching for an explanation of this widespread anger, many observers offer rationales not so very different from Mr. Ellis's: they blame the macaws.

A news producer at a TV station in Florida, for example, told me that the constant barrage of blood-splattered and smoke-darkened news drives American anger. The subtext of such news is that we are helpless in a violent and unjust world. Television news needs to stimulate viewers, and arousing their often-undirected anger agitates people enough that they keep watching. At one level, anger is caused by the gruesome footage itself; and at another level, the TV executives who manipulate the viewers' emotions for commercial gain are the media macaws nipping subliminally at our arms every day.

A woman in New York City who counsels young people told me that she sees anger flooding into teenagers who are drained of self-respect by their own promiscuity. Aimless sexuality, the "sex in the city" of one shallow encounter after another, creates the sense of worthlessness that underlies the stubborn resentments of our age. The causes of anger, in her view, are the secularists who undermine the moral strictures these adolescents need in the midst of a vulgar and sexualized culture.

A public relations manager told me that taboos against saying politically incorrect things build frustration in ordinary people—a frustration that bursts out on talk radio and occasionally boils over into even angrier displays. The stigmatizing of ordinary and often-valid social observations as "hate speech" does not, in his view, draw us closer to a civil society. To the contrary, the new impediments to free expression of everyday complaints create a reservoir of ill feeling, and this explains the grim anger of so many people on the Internet and other places where the victims of liberal censoriousness can find opportunities to speak.

The TV producer, the youth counselor, and the PR

manager offer what I take to be genuine insights, not unlike Ms. Sanchez's reflections on the anger that her thirteen-year-old visitor from Colombia noticed. Stress, political divisiveness, and "values debates" are macaws too—forces outside ourselves that can be blamed for "making" us angry. These forces I take to be real—just as real as Johnny, who suffered a broken beak when Mr. Ellis punched him. But, both individually and in combination, they are too narrow to explain the comprehensive quality of New Anger. If-it-bleeds-it-leads news footage, teenage promiscuity, and rebels against the enforcers of PC are pretty disparate sources of anger. "Stress" is a concept so vague that it can be applied to virtually anything. Al-Qaeda causes stress, but so does the ordinary morning commute. A word that expansive explains nothing. Political division is inherent in most systems of government and has been endemic to the United States for centuries. Values debates are always at the center of self-governance in a democratic republic. Any and all of these factors can be wrapped into the anger that pervades our culture right now, but that anger has a distinct character of its own, apart from the aggravations that seem to trigger it.

The difference is that, in contrast to the old culture's primary emphasis on self-control, our culture now rewards and celebrates anger. The premise that "anger is good"—that it is liberating, wholesome, creative, and empowering—transforms the myriad possible aggravations into *welcome opportunities*. To get angry, we don't need Johnny to take a nip at our arm. We are already primed for anger and are, much of the time, simply waiting for Johnny or any other macaw to "give us a reason."

In 1984, Willard Gaylin, a New York psychoanalyst, published *The Rage Within: Anger in Modern Life*, in which he argued that anger is an obsolete emotion, left over from our evolutionary past when we needed to respond quickly to physical dangers. In civilized societies, according to Gaylin, these biological responses "diminish rather than enhance our chances for survival," and he calls on us to "modify our culture" to replace "frustration and despair" with hope and trust.[21]

Gaylin's book today reads like a strangely antique document. He fretted that anger "particularly in the urban centers" had grown to monstrous proportions; that anger and fear together coarsened and desensitized us and that this process—"the inevitable and dangerous intensification of fear and anger in everyday life"—was destined to continue. Gaylin imagined that what had happened in Mayor Ed Koch's New York City—which was indeed pretty grim—was bound to happen in other cities and to creep into the smaller towns, the "Springfields," as well. But what came to Gaylin's mind when he wrote about this urban "anger" was street muggings, racial assaults, rapes, and murders. He considered bigotry and scapegoating to be among the prime causes of anger. And he was full of remorse when, taunted by three teenage boys and assaulted by one of them: "I wheeled and with all the pent up rage contained within me grabbed him by the shirt, pulled him nose to nose and, spitting into his face, told him if he so much as touched me one more time I would beat him into the ground." Gaylin's turning on his tormentors would appear to many of us urbanites as smart and effective anger, but Gaylin, to the contrary, continued: "My expression of rage was a stupid and foolish action; a vestige from boyhood.... In retrospect I was shaken and upset by my lack of control."

Clearly, when he was writing in the 1980s, Gaylin had had no epiphanies about the liberating quality of New Anger. His half-boastful shame, however, does suggest that the strictures of old anger weren't working for him either. He seemed to be in the twilight between the world of manly self-defense, where controlled anger could be deployed for legitimate reasons, and the narcissist's love of posturing. And so Gaylin is best seen as a transitional figure—a man on the cusp of New Anger.

Among Gaylin's more peculiar responses to the threatening world of pre-Giuliani New York City was his declaration that "We must protect our ordinary citizens from the sociology of their anger." In my experience, most people know how to defend themselves against all forms of sociology: they ignore it. But what Gaylin really meant was that we needed to attend to the social pathologies that he believed were driving anger, and the way to do that, in his view, was to expand liberal social welfare programs. The possibility that a vigorous mayor and community policing could dramatically cut the crime rate and end the reign of intimidation by the street thugs, as Rudy Giuliani did, never crossed Gaylin's mind. He did, however, worry that the first President Bush had won the election by having "shamelessly exploited the cycle of fear, anger, humiliation, and frustration" while "health, education, and urban decay were trivialized." And Gaylin feared that frustration and anger would lead to "false solutions; to a rise in bigotry and prejudice and ultimately to the fragmentation of our society into hostile and distrustful paranoid camps."

Gaylin mistook a temporary period of poor civic leadership in New York for a near-cosmic and "inevitable" condition of social collapse. He encountered criminality and misinterpreted it as rage. He defended himself against street toughs and then surrendered to self-recrimination. And he feared a surge of racial and ethnic "bigotry and prejudice" that proved imaginary, although his imagination marched in step with the left's increasing use of accusations of racism as a way of stigmatizing its opponents.

As the left pivoted in the 1980s from anti–Cold War rhetoric to the promotion of "diversity" in the form of racial preferences, it increasingly evoked imagery of an explosively angry urban underclass composed, seemingly, mostly of African American and Hispanic males. The Los Angeles riots that began on April 29, 1992, following the acquittal of the four police officers tried for beating Rodney King, seemed to give some credibility to prophecies such as Gaylin's—but only for a moment. The lasting image of the riots wasn't one of an angry underclass demanding justice. It was the film taken by a helicopter cameraman showing Reginald Denny, an innocent motorist, being pulled from his truck and beaten within an inch of his life. One of the attackers concluded by smashing a cinder block on Denny's body and then flashing a gang sign to the photographer overhead.

The worldview on display in *The Rage Within* is probably not extinct, but it is now rare. For Gaylin, anger was terrifying; for supporters of grrrl power, MoveOn.org, Hip-Hop Summit, anger is revitalizing. For Gaylin, the primary image of anger twenty years ago was the anonymous street criminal; for Americans now it is Howard Dean, Al Gore, or a millionaire rapper. Arguing from liberal-left premises, Gaylin imagined the ideal society as one in which anger has vanished. But the left now is enraptured with grievance politics and extravagant expressions of anger. Gaylin worried about anger triggering social fragmentation. Today, anger is a badge of authenticity among social groups that vaunt their own histories of victimization, and we have learned to praise "diversity" (i.e. fragmentation) as one of our signal strengths.

How could a serious analyst writing in the 1980s paint a picture of anger that misses the culture of self-enraptured grievance? In retrospect, New Anger had been formulating itself as far back as Bob Dylan's early-sixties protest songs, and it had made itself spectacularly visible at the 1968 Democratic National Convention. Yet in the 1980s it was somehow hidden. Even though the idealization of anger was well under way as Gaylin wrote; he simply couldn't see it. His picture of anger in America in the 1980s was that the culture had left the self-glorifying protests of the 1960s and the narcissism of the 1970s behind. He wrote, "If the dominant pathology of the moment is anything, it is not self-involvement, it is alienation and distrust." Under these terms, in a chapter titled "Angry All the Time," he gathered a whole flock of aggravating macaws: muggers, brutal husbands, battering parents, diminished self-esteem, the sense of deprivation people feel when they see others with more and bigger pieces of the pie ("relative deprivation"), injustices, the middle-class sense of betrayal, adolescent frustrations, racial humiliations, and the despair of dispossessed minorities.

The list mixes up many different kinds of and occasions for anger. The macaws fly every which way, while Gaylin manages not to see the great blimp New Anger as it appears on the horizon.

Angry Young Men

Feminists in the 1960s and 1970s theorized a variety of reasons why women should get angry: that anger was a path of liberation from internalized oppression; that anger was a tool for promoting social justice; and that women's anger was empowering. Along with this came a frequent subtext: that men's anger was cruder than women's anger and inherently dangerous for women and the world at large.

No comparable sex-specific theoretical valorization of men's anger was put forward at that time, although in the 1980s a self-styled primitivist "men's movement" emerged, beating drums and extolling a kind of uninhibited expression of emotions among men. The men's movement, however, was a fringe affair and had nothing like the mainstream follow-ons of the feminist exalting of anger as inherently valuable. We have "grrrl power" endorsed by Health and Human Services, but no special effort to enhance "boy power."

Does this difference matter? For all the promptings to anger aimed at them, most contemporary American women do not seem especially angry. For the majority, the inhibitions to anger may have relaxed a few degrees, but human temperament has not changed. What has changed is that a substantial minority of women *do* strongly identify with the idea that anger is empowering. This feminist minority is a significant force in what I have called the angri-culture, supplying some of its most successful appeals.

If we look for instances of New Anger, however, it is at least as prevalent among men as among women. It just lacks the kind of gender-specific cheerleading that some feminists supplied for women's anger. The contemporary lack of justifications for male anger is, from a longer perspective, quite unusual. For most of their history, the Western societies upheld codes of honor that authorized male anger in certain situations. A husband was right to be angrily offended at another man's attention to his wife; insults to a wife ought to be answered; defamation of his own character might likewise deserve angry rebuke. While these strictures have not completely vanished, they have dwindled in significance. Codes of male honor now are more conspicuous in criminal gangs than in, say, the halls of Congress.

This wasn't always so. On the floor of the House in 1798, Congressman Roger Griswold, a Federalist from Connecticut, insulted Matthew Lyon, a Republican from Vermont, by referring to Lyon's having once been an indentured servant who had been traded by his master for livestock. As John Ferling recounts in *Adams vs. Jefferson: The Tumultuous Election of 1800*:

> Lyon retaliated by spitting in Griswold's face, and Griswold in turn thrashed the Vermonter with a cane. Lyon fought back with fire tongs. The brawl ended only when colleagues separated the gladiators, who by then were punching and kicking each other as they rolled about the chamber floor.[22]

Even in an epoch that attempted to inculcate the importance of dignity and self-control, the wrong word or the wrong tone could escalate into a street fight. Today, of course, with the television cameras recording proceedings in the House and the fire tongs safely out of reach, nothing like this could happen.

The last time male anger received some serious public recognition verging on grudging respect was a literary movement in England in the 1950s, which reveled for a while under the rubric "the Angry Young Men." These were writers who, having risen from the working class to university educations, found themselves thwarted by the snobbery of the British class system. That snobbery is perhaps evident in a reference work written after the movement faded:

> **Angry young man.** Term indiscriminately applied to a number of British writers in the mid 1950s, some of whom were remarkable for stupidity rather than anger. Writers saddled with the label have included Kingsley Amis, John Osborne, and Colin Wilson. The paradigm of the angry young man is Jimmy Porter, in Osborne's play *Look Back in Anger* (1956): confused in the process of violently rejecting establishment values, but frustrated by ignorance and the lack of alternative values to which to enslave himself. Invention of the phrase in this connection has been authoritatively attributed

to the Irish writer, the late Leslie Paul, whose autobiographical *Angry Young Man* appeared in 1951. But he was then 46; and was over 50 when he wistfully drew attention to his choice of title in a letter to the press.[23]

This would hardly encourage anyone to say, yes, I should like to be an Angry Young Man too. On the other hand, the myriads of American young men, mostly middle-class and white, who devote themselves to violently misogynistic rap or who don images of the homicidal sadist Che Guevara suggest that the allure of being seen as an Angry Young Man isn't entirely gone. It has simply been reduced to an off-the-shelf, mass-marketed brand that says next to nothing about the individual's particular life experience or encounters with deep-rooted social barriers.

In 1976, the singer/songwriter Billy Joel released a song titled "Prelude/Angry Young Man." He performed it again in a "millennium concert" in 2000, where its condescending tone toward the proud but clueless kid with an attitude became even more piquant:

> There's a place in the world for the angry young man
> With his working-class ties and his radical plans.

That place, however, doesn't look like it would be worth visiting:

> There's always a place for the angry young man
> With his fist in the air and his head in the sand.

Joel, who has made a long career out of strenuous banality, is perhaps the perfect epitaph writer for this particular form of self-conscious rage.

Anger Rules

The surge of anger in contemporary American life is the result of a new way of looking at the world, not the outcome of a converging list of grievances. Muggers, brutal husbands, battering parents, and most of the other sources of anger that caught Gaylin's eye back in the 1980s were not new phenomena then; nor do we have much evidence that such conditions are worse than usual now. In fact, by objective measures, some of these crimes have decreased. The TV producer, the youth counselor, and the PR manager at least offer a connection between the increase in anger and real changes in our social world. But their explanations are too small. The swell of New Anger doesn't really depend on 24/7 mayhem on the news, adolescents who have lost their self-esteem through casual sex, or talk radio rebels. It rises instead on the shared sense that anger is somehow good.

Somehow is not a very specific qualifier, but that's because it represents a moment that is still unfolding. I don't think Americans can say with much precision why anger has escaped the moral box we used to keep it in. If we could put the idea out on the table for specific examination, it might well lose some of its glowering appeal. But if such a definitive dissection is not possible, popular culture does at least supply some hints.

In 1983, George Lucas released the third of his *Star Wars* movies, *Return of the Jedi,* the climax of which must be among the most familiar scenes in the history of Hollywood movies. The Emperor attempts to lure Luke Skywalker to the "dark side," first by offering him his lightsaber:

> "You want this, don't you? The hate is swelling in you, now. Very good, take your Jedi weapon. Use it. Strike me down with it. Give in to your anger. With each passing moment you make yourself more my servant."

Luke, of course, after partially giving in to the temptation, renounces it rather than kill his father, Darth Vader. But even as Luke escapes, the idea of anger as a deep source of power is registered with cartoon clarity. The overt moral lesson in Star Wars seems thoroughly traditional: anger is actually a lack of self-control that leaves the angry person as an object to be manipulated by others; and the power that comes with anger is, after all, the power of the "dark side."

Another movie that contributed to contemporary ideas about anger was seen by far fewer people, but I found that it was mentioned again and again by people I talked to while working on this book: the 1970 movie *Five Easy Pieces.* The movie depicts a trip home to his dying father by Bobby Dupea, a scruffy, disaffected oil rig worker who had been a child prodigy on the piano. Dupea, played by Jack Nicholson, gets angry at a waitress in a diner who refuses his order for an omelet with tomatoes instead of potatoes, and toast on the side. "No substitutions," says the waitress, but Dupea proceeds to chart his own menu:

> *Waitress:* I don't make the rules.
> *Dupea:* OK, I'll make it as easy for you as I can. I'd like an omelet, plain, and a chicken salad sandwich on wheat toast, no mayonnaise, no butter, no lettuce. And a cup of coffee.
> *Waitress:* A number two, chicken salad sandwich. Hold the butter, the lettuce and the mayonnaise. And a cup of coffee. Anything else?
> *Dupea:* Yeah. Now all you have to do is hold the chicken, bring me the toast, give me a check for the chicken salad sandwich, and you haven't broken any rules.
> *Waitress* (spitefully): You want me to *hold* the chicken, huh?
> *Dupea:* I want you to hold it between your knees.

The waitress then asks Dupea to leave ("I'm not taking any more of your smartness and sarcasm") and Dupea dumps the table, water glasses and all.

The movie offers this scene semi-seriously as a battle between an uptight, rule-bound waitress and a man who has no patience for arbitrary rules. Dupea is not an attractive character, but we are meant to see his anger at the waitress in a light similar to the frustration that the '60s generation felt with the meaningless strictures of "the system." Alienated from American society ("I move around a lot. Not because I'm looking for anything really, but 'cause I'm getting away from things that get bad if I stay."), Dupea seems to be granted a license by the movie to behave outrageously toward the waitress because of her unaccommodating attitude.

The scene became famous as a showpiece for Nicholson, who is himself famous for his bursts of destructive anger, but it has also become a cultural touchstone. For some, it is "the best waitress scene ever," a memorable putdown of annoying waitresses. Nearly a thousand websites cast it in such approving terms. But when people brought it up in conversations with me about anger, the sentiment was the reverse. One woman told me that her sympathies were entirely with the waitress, who is humiliated while just trying to do her job. A male film critic mentioned the scene as the point where American movies began to celebrate gratuitous anger. Another woman brought it up saying she was appalled when she first saw the scene and remains puzzled that people think it humorous.

This scene is generally remembered more than the rest of the movie. In context, however, it is even more telling. Dupea isn't really a working-class guy. He was born to wealth and was successful as a concert pianist, and his work as an oil rigger is just his personal quest for authenticity. The waitress, however, is the real thing: a woman with few other options trying to make a living at a tough job. So the restaurant scene really offers a privileged elitist who has the freedom to float among whatever social roles he pleases, raging against someone he regards as beneath him because she is so bound to the conventions of her job. She is a resident of the working class; he is merely a truculent visitor. But the movie essentially invites us to see things his way. We, the sophisticated audience, are asked to share in Dupea's contempt for meaningless conventions, even if we squirm a little at his cruelty to the waitress.

The Return of the Jedi and *Five Easy Pieces* are movies from disparate realms of Hollywood sensibility: a fantasy science fiction aimed mainly at children, and a serious adult drama. But the cultural revaluation of anger is not just glimpsed in both—it forms the theme of their most memorable scenes. *The Return of the Jedi* offers the fascination of anger as a source of immense power and *Five Easy Pieces* gives us an early version of anger as an egotistic performance of the liberated individual displaying his superiority to the dumb conformists who are aggravating props in his drama. Both movies look with seeming disapproval on the anger they portray, but make that anger taste delicious.

But popular culture is not the only place to look for insights on New Anger. Revealing comments often turn up when people begin to reflect on their personal experiences. Here is the late Caroline Knapp (author of *Drinking: A Love Story* and *Appetites: Why Women Want*) as she starts to contrast male and female styles of anger:

> Why can choppy waters—an inevitable feature of any close relationship—be so monumentally hard for women to navigate? Sometimes, when one of us has her back up about something, Grace and I talk about "the male blow-off valve," a reference to the blithe, no-big-deal style of male conflict resolution. Exhibit A: Several summers ago Grace and I spent a weekend together in New Hampshire, accompanied by a mutual friend named Tom, who's a real guy's guy. Our first morning, Tom borrowed Grace's sports watch when he went out for a run and promptly lost it. Grace blew up at him briefly ("Oh, you idiot, I knew you'd lose it!"); he huffed back ("C'mon, it's no big deal, I'll buy you a new one."); one $20 Timex later, the incident was forgotten.[24]

Well, at least by Tom. Grace, maybe. Caroline, however, clearly treasured it.

This is a wonderful counterpoint to Cox, Bruckner, and Stabb's *The Anger Advantage* and Estés' *Women Who Run with the Wolves*. Knapp and her friend Grace resent—and envy—a male ability to avoid turning a moment of anger into a prolonged and complicated dance of mutual resentments. According to Knapp, anger, far from empowering women, leads them into an emotional cul-de-sac. She goes on to describe how complicated the mutual recriminations can be after a trivial tiff before she and her friend can get over it. No Darth Vader here, nor any "I don't make the rules." Knapp picked something else out of the zeitgeist—the "no-big-deal style of male conflict resolution" and its female opposite.

The no-big-deal style is a way of diffusing emotions in a culture that has misplaced its sense of how to keep anger in check. Where every disagreement, no matter how trivial, has the potential to flame up into intemperate display and an opportunity to spelunk in the deeper recesses of one another's subconscious motives, no-big-deal minimization offers a way out. It is not just the "male blow-off valve." It is the necessary complement to New Anger, which does not leave much room for a middle ground between affected indifference and compounding complication. Knapp's observation about the male and female preferences in expressing anger, however, is surely right. Despite the drum-beating male consciousness-raising of the 1980s, and the male-bashing that was the other side of this coin, American men do not generally find themselves called to pursue the labyrinthine anger that feminism has brought to the lives of many American women.

Dreaming of Anger in the Northeast Kingdom

Not every man is equipped like Caroline Knapp's friend Tom with the male "blow-off valve." Garret Keizer is an Episcopal minister in a small village in Vermont's "Northeast Kingdom"—the three most snowshoe- and backpack-invested counties of a state crowded with wilderness. Confessing to his own lifelong struggle with anger, Keizer has written perhaps the best and certainly the most deeply reflective book on anger in recent times, *The Enigma of Anger: Essays on a Sometimes Deadly Sin* (2002). Some of the enigma of the title might be found in Keizer's strange combination of penetrating insights and oblivious banalities. Sometimes he presents anger with breathtaking clarity and a page later clings to obtuseness as though it were a tow line hauling him up to the summit of spiritual insight.

Although *The Enigma of Anger* does not specifically set out to examine the angri-culture, Keizer recognizes that anger has become "a mentality" and in some contexts "a privilege." He observes, for example, that many forms of anger involve false assumptions about what other people may be thinking. Anger in this sense amounts to "storms brewing in our heads over grievances that are also, to a large degree, brewed in our heads." He wonders if television is partly to blame, not for its content but for making people around us "less real to us and we to them than the phantoms occupying our attention." Exactly counter to Willard Gaylin's notion that modern anger is driven by the real violence in our society, Keizer suggests that we are inclined to exaggerate "the dangers of our neighborhood" as part of a fantasy life that "expresses itself in daydreams of revenge and self-defense." Road rage, according to Keizer, is an aspect of this fantasy. "Driving, after all, is an experience not unlike watching television, with a windshield for a screen." This leads to a moral caution: "We need to be on guard against confusing the motives of our adversaries with the vulnerabilities of our own minds."[25]

Keizer is also perceptive about the role of anger in identity politics. One form of "privileged anger," he notes, "amounts to saying that you get mad because that's who you are, or at least a big part of who you are. Anger is what you are known for, your trademark, and it ought to be respected as such." Another form of privileged anger is to use one's emotions "as cut-rate substitutes for what used to be called character. If I am known for displaying a certain emotion, it saves me the trouble of knowing what I actually feel."

But Keizer is more concerned to anchor these insights in his personal life and in stories from the Bible, classical mythology, and literature than in the hum of contemporary American life. Thus it is not quite clear who he has in mind as taking anger for a trademark or which figures in our national life exemplify using emotions as cut-rate substitutes for character. Keizer seems to see that there is something different about anger today, but he is more concerned with looking at the anger he feels and sees with the eye of eternity: "When those afflicted by sloth and avarice can become most angry is when someone or something—like a dissatisfied spouse—disturbs the tranquility of their chosen sarcophagus." In this long perspective, anger is as old as human nature, and Keizer's starting point is appropriately theological. Anger is a sin that keeps company with all the other sins: "with the false proportions of envy and pride, the false sensuality of gluttony and lust, the false opposition of avarice and sloth." These are not stale categories in Keizer's thought, but points of entry into the forest of emotions: "We can also make an idol of our own conscientiousness. We grow angry when it fails to stand up against every obstacle, and we may also grow angry when others fail to bow down before it." This seems to me a neat description of one kind of political anger, but as usual with Keizer, the deft abstraction is left unmoored to any particular person.

But when Keizer does turn to the contemporary world, he turns out—appallingly—to be a full-fledged citizen of the Republic of New Anger. He writes near the end of *The Enigma of Anger,* for instance, that "one grace of our era is the chance to achieve personal honesty at a fairly sophisticated level." This sounds like the floodwaters of "authenticity" about to burst the dam of traditional self-control. And indeed, a moment later he is proudly telling us about his sending a note to a school principal, encouraging him to hold fast in the face of criticism. The good minister offers this solace from Andrea Dworkin: "On one level I suffer terribly from the disdain that much of my work has met. On another, deeper level, I don't give a fuck."

Keizer also finds that "the grace of our era is made flesh in the struggles of a particular group." Gay and lesbian "coming out" is yet to be reckoned, he says, for how "courageous and how political an act this is." Keizer joined in the political fight over gay "civil unions" in Vermont, and by his own account compared the opposition's slogan "Take Back Vermont" to the Nazi *"Nicht Juden"* signs. Having written an attack on the Take Back Vermonters, he says he "felt nothing but a dreadful sense of compassion, not just for the victims of bigotry this time, but for the bigots too."

So, in the end, Keizer turns out to be another leftist partisan who cannot imagine any reasoned argument on the other side of the "civil unions" debate, or attribute any integrity to his opponents, who are allowed only the sliver of humanity that resides in the epithet "bigots." In fact, I don't know of any prominent critic of civil unions or gay marriages who fails to take seriously the civil-rights claims put forward by those who advocate these innovations. The critics, however, also insist on the importance of the traditional claims of heterosexuality and of marriage as an institution reserved for the union of man and woman. The left's chosen tactic, as Keizer shows, has been to stigmatize any criticism of civil unions or gay marriage as bigotry—a tactic that removes the very possibility of informed debate and incites anger on all sides.

Keizer's decision to close his book on this note is unsettling, and it offers strong evidence of how much the culture war really costs. After many a thoughtful, introspective chapter on the nature of wrath and our efforts not to cede our lives to it, Keizer turns at last into an illustration of the boastful shallowness that is at the very center of New Anger.

SEVEN

SELF-STORAGE

How Americans Made Room in Themselves for Anger

On August 13, 2004, some kids in Santa Ana, California, got a cool idea: throw rocks at a nest that bees had built on the wall of a two-story apartment building. The bees issued forth in a giant swarm that forced firefighters to quarantine a four-block area. News reporters and a TV cameraman were stung; two people were hospitalized; but an exterminator finally fogged the hive—a 500-pound, 120,000-inhabitant bee metropolis.[1]

A bee in the mouth is always bad, but a rock in the hive is possibly worse.

The notion that anger is good—that it empowers the oppressed, inspires the timid, and unleashes creativity—compels a lot of contemporary Americans who have turned to anger politics and anger music with zest, opted for grrrl power on the playground and in their romantic endeavors, and joined the culture war as improv performers of rage. The angri-culture was built, one cartridge belt by one eyebrow safety pin at a time, with romanticized images of anger. But how exactly did these images achieve their appeal? How did the idealization of anger beat down the older, durable idea that anger is something to resist?

New Anger prevailed in large part because Americans changed themselves to make room for it. We have, over the course of several decades, made ourselves into people who welcome and in some ways *need* to be angry in order to feel right with ourselves. The normative American personalities have changed, from men and women who found deep satisfaction in controlling anger and channeling it away from both their public personae and their private relations, to a new breed of self-seekers for whom feeling angry and expressing it are crucial to feeling alive.

The prevalence of anger in America today is not the result of unprecedented provocations or unbearable stress. To the contrary, anger thrives because we are a people who are now profoundly primed for anger.

The priming had two parts: a quasi-intellectual rationalization of anger as a force to overcome the supposedly hypocritical custodians of the old culture, and an infatuation with figures who embodied the new spirit of angry freedom. The theorists of New Anger played their part, but the individuals who exemplified New Anger carried the message home. Some of the early exemplars remain familiar in today's angri-cultural pantheon: Allen Ginsberg, Gloria Steinem, Abbie Hoffman, Bob Dylan, and Malcolm X. Others have largely faded into the groups they were part of: the Black Panthers, the Students for a Democratic Society, the National Organization for Women. But perhaps the largest portion of the exemplars were never widely known. They were just those individuals who, in a particular moment and a particular setting, burned with incandescent anger in the admiring eyes of those a little younger and a little less formed.

They were the kids who climbed atop police cruisers to shout callow slogans at cops, who threw away someone else's war medals in well-choreographed protest, or hurled rocks at hornets' nests.

Anger broke though the generations-old habits of self-restraint and even older traditions of moral censure as part of the larger cultural transformation that began in the fifties and reached its decisive moment in the sixties. New Anger is built on the ruins of an older, now largely invisible culture of refusing to be provoked easily. It was not a culture of timidity. Teddy Roosevelt's favorite adage, "Speak softly and carry a big stick," was a counsel for those who honed their judgment about when to keep on walking and when to fight. In fact, folklorists have traced over a hundred American adages that offered similar prudential advice, such as:

> Anger and folly walk cheek by jowl.
> Beware the anger of the patient man.
> Don't get angry, get even.
> An angry man opens his mouth and shuts his eyes.
> Kill your anger while it's hot.
> Anger is a wind that blows out the light of the mind.
> He is a fool who cannot be angry; a wise man who will not.

Not to neglect, "Anger is a stone cast at a wasp's nest."[2]

A people who coined such phrases were obviously familiar with what happened when family members, friends, and they themselves failed to keep their tempers in check. A personality shaped by efforts at self-restraint wasn't then and isn't now immune to anger. The person who cultivated patience, listening, forgiveness, and self-control, however, developed a character that contrasts sharply with the emotionally expressive individualist who dominates the scene today. At the heart of this contrast are differences in the sense of self.

Americans, of course, have never had just one, entirely unified, sense of self. At any historical moment at which we choose to look carefully, we are sure to find competing claims, rooted in religion, region, ethnic tradition, and more. George Washington's sense of self seems very different from fellow Virginian Thomas Jefferson. Dolly Madison and Emily Dickinson would seem to be not just positioned in different stations in life, but moved by inner forces each unknown to the other. Emerson and Poe are cut from different cloths, as are Stonewall Jackson and William Tecumseh Sherman. George Washington Carver and W. E. B. Du Bois had not only competing visions of the future of African Americans, but radically incompatible conceptions of their inner selves.

Within this robust variety of American personalities, however, we can still discern some common conceptions— among them an ideal of self-mastery and reserve. In this vein, anger is something that Americans long regarded as a force to be kept at bay as long as possible. American English testifies to this attitude. Every generation seems to have expanded our vocabulary for anger with words and phrases that characterize the angry person as broken or out of control. The word "ornery" came into American speech around 1800 as a variant of "ordinary," meaning poor and mean, and soon was a way of saying that someone was bad-tempered and crotchety. Here are some other expressions with their approximate dates:

Ornery—1800	Have it out—1889
Mad as a wet hen—1821	Grouch—1896
Riled up—1825	See red—1897
Fly off the handle—1825	Have kittens—1900
Wrathy—1828	Old rip—1904
Cussedness—1830s	Get one's goat—1904
In a huff—1830s	Mad as a rattler—1908
Get by the ear—1831	Hot under the collar—1910
Miffed—1832	Peeved—1915
Conniption fit—1833	Get under his skin—1915
Meat-ax disposition—1834	Put on fireworks—1923
Crusty—1834	Steamed up—1923
Hopping mad—1834	Go up in flames—1924
Flare up—1839	Fit to be tied—1924
Swear like a trooper—1839	Blow one's top—1929
Get a rise out of—1843	Pissed off—1930s, possibly earlier
Look daggers—1845	Get one's dander up—1930s
Blow one's stack—1847	Have a hemorrhage—1932
Short as a piecrust—1849	Has a chip on his shoulder—1934
Shirty—1850	Boiling mad—1937
Get into one's hair—1880	Ticked off, t'd off—1940s
Hit the roof—1882	Blow one's fuse—1945
Get out on the wrong side of the bed—1885	Mad as blazes—1947
Sore—1886	Blow a gasket—1953

Many of these are expressions that poke fun at someone who is angry or prone to anger, or that might be used to extenuate one's own angry outburst.[3] None of them suggests that expressing anger or being quick to anger is praiseworthy.

Common vocabulary is one line of evidence about our formerly common appraisal of anger as personal weakness. Another line of evidence is literary. Poets as different in temperament as Herman Melville and Marianne Moore, for example, touch a common chord. Melville, in "The Eagle of the Blue," looks on a live eagle kept by Union troops engaged in a Civil War battle:

> Austere, he crowns the swaying perch,
> Flapped by the angry flag;
> The hurricane from the battery sings,
> But his claw has known the crag.
> ....
> The pride of quenchless strength is his—
> Strength which, though chained, avails;
> The very rebel looks and thrills—
> The anchored Emblem hails.[4]

The eagle thrills because its strength is seemingly beyond anger. In her poem "In Distrust of Merit," written in the midst of World War II, Moore also contemplates the glory of inner restraint during war:

> In snow, some on crags, some in quicksands,
>   Little by little, much by much, they
> are fighting fighting fighting that where
>   there was death there may
> be life. "When a man is prey to anger,
> he is moved by outside things; when he holds
>   his ground in patience, patience
>   patience, that is action or
>   beauty," the soldier's defense
>   and hardest armor for
> the fight.[5]

Moore means to be paradoxical in extolling the bravery of *not* acting, but her paradox was a thoroughly familiar one to many generations of Americans. Just think of the classic cowboy movie.

The plots of hundreds of these movies turn on the action of a man who would prefer not to fight. He was, once upon a time, a sheriff, a marshal, or a gunslinger, but he has vowed not to draw a gun again. He is the retired Sheriff Will Kane in *High Noon* (1952); Sheriff Washington Dimsdale in *Destry Rides Again* (1939); the outlaw Quirt Evans in *Angel and the Badman* (1947); the retired gunfighter in *Shane* (1953). And he is Alejandro de la Vega in *The Legend of Zoro* (2005).

He is provoked, but resists. He may try peaceable alternatives before he is finally pushed too far—by opponents who
have, all along, been reveling in their easy anger. In the key
scene, we see him go to *that* drawer, the one where he put
away his gun (and all that it symbolizes). And he goes into
action one last time, perhaps over the tearful remonstrations
of his girlfriend or wife.

In a 1958 episode, "Bloody Hands," of the TV Western
Gunsmoke, Marshal Matt Dillon has quit his job, sickened at
having to shoot down some outlaws. He goes fishing with
Miss Kitty, but his ex-sidekick Chester arrives with the news
of a gunslinger loose in Dodge City. The marshal inevitably
answers the call.

Reluctant anger; anger as a last resort; anger that we
know will be deadly and will give him no pleasure—that's the
kind of anger that, until just yesterday, Americans imagined
as heroic. The justified wrath of the slow-to-anger man may
be just a story, but it is a story that informed the moral judgment of many generations of Americans and that many still
find powerful. I take particular interest in the turning point
of the story, where the hero retrieves a part of himself that he
had put away, presumably forever.

Self without God

In 1963, the U.S. Supreme Court decided in favor of a single
mother from Baltimore named Madalyn Murray O'Hair, who
had brought a suit seeking to outlaw prayers in public
schools. This was to be the signal accomplishment of Mrs.
O'Hair's career as America's best-known militant atheist. The
Court agreed with her that the First Amendment clause that
prohibits the government's "establishment of religion" must
be read as requiring that the children of atheists be spared
the sights and sounds of other children praying in public
schools.

Mrs. O'Hair's ambitions, however, extended still further.
She founded American Atheists, Inc. and several other atheist organizations, and she launched new public campaigns. In

1971, for example, she brought a suit to forbid astronauts from making religious statements in space, and in 1975 she collected 27,000 signatures in a campaign to stop Apollo-Soyuz astronauts from praying or reading the Bible. After that, Mrs. O'Hair gradually faded from the scene, although in the years that followed, her name could still provoke anger among the devout.

O'Hair might well be called a prophet of New Anger. According to her biographer, Bryan Le Beau, before her Supreme Court case O'Hair had been a member of the Socialist Labor Party, which she quit in favor of the Socialist Workers Party. In 1959, after being expelled from a master's degree program at Howard University, she applied for citizenship in the Soviet Union. In the summer of 1960 she traveled to Paris and spent a month petitioning the Soviet embassy there to help her in her quest. They turned her down. Her diaries record her deep discontent and sense of being "trapped."

This was the context in which O'Hair discovered her vocation. In the spring of 1960, she had enrolled her son William in a junior high in the Baltimore Public Schools and was outraged to learn that William, along with the rest of his class, was required to recite the Lord's Prayer. She challenged the school counselor about it and got even more infuriated when the counselor defended the prayer as in keeping with American traditions. O'Hair took no action at the time, but during the trip to Paris that summer, William goaded her to stand up for her beliefs. When they returned to Baltimore in the fall, O'Hair launched her campaign.

From the start, O'Hair combined legal tactics with vehement expressions of outrage. Anger became central to her public performances. As her new career took off, she indulged more and more in scabrous attacks on Christianity that often provoked hate mail, which she would then use to further publicize her campaign. Having learned that anger produced more anger and that both produced publicity, O'Hair devised ever more flamboyant ways to express her sheer disgust not with religion in general, but with Christianity specifically.

In October 1977, for example, she barged into a bingo game in a Catholic church in Austin, according to one witness, "grabbing bingo cards, pushing and shoving people." Immediately afterward, she filed an $11 million suit against the governor of Texas and other public figures for failing to enforce antigambling laws. She told a reporter that she believed her abrasive behavior was the only way to fight for her cause ("I'm going to teach Austin a lesson"), and she saw some vindication in the heated responses she elicited: "All of their threats, all of their vilification, all their hatred, they have to wrestle with that."[6]

On this last point, O'Hair was surely right. She had found a way to infect her traditionalist opposition with her own rage. Anger performed at the right pitch of aggressive offensiveness proved its power to shatter the composure of ordinary people who typically relied on the inertia of their beliefs and were ill equipped to deal with a foul-mouthed provocateur. O'Hair had become the self-styled Angry Victim. What sort of "self" did she possess and what sort did she promote? The clearest answers are that she was aggressively angry, assiduous in seeking grievances, and tiresomely eager in her pursuit of both notoriety and financial support. She sought and found supporters from among people who were bitter over their disappointments and caustic toward their communities. Atheism as pronounced by O'Hair was a doctrine not of private unbelief, but of public dissent and disparagement of the assumptions that informed everyday life for most Americans.

William Murray, whose required schoolroom recitation of the Lord's Prayer provided the spark that launched his mother's crusade, announced his conversion to Christianity in 1980, on Mother's Day. He went on to write several books, including *Let Us Pray: A Plea for Prayers in Our Schools* (1995).

Militant atheism remains a rather eccentric pastime in the United States, but its sunnier cousin, mainstream secularism, is thriving. And mainstream secularism actually owes quite a bit to cousin O'Hair, who did much to establish the culture-war premise that religion has no legitimate place in the nation's public life. In 2001, two professors of political science, Louis Bolce and Gerald De Maio, examined the alignments between religion and politics in the United States and concluded that:

> The media mistakenly frames cultural conflict since the 1970s as entirely the result of fundamentalist revanchism. In so doing, the media ignores the growing influence of secularists in the Democratic Party and obfuscates how their worldview is just as powerful a determinant of social attitudes and voting behavior as is a religiously traditionalist outlook.

Bolce and De Maio argue that secularists have become one of the "front line" groups in the culture wars, on the side of the *progressivists*—those who "embrace a humanistic ethic drawn from reason, science, and personal experience." A secular worldview, of course, has been available to Western intellectuals for centuries, but it had no real political salience until recently, as Bolce and De Maio observe:

> Secularists first appeared as a political force within a major party at the 1972 Democratic National Convention. Prior to then, neither party contained many secularists nor showed many signs of moral or cultural progressivism. Moreover, prior to the late 1960s, there was something of a tacit commitment among elites in both parties to the traditional Judeo-Christian teachings regarding authority, sexual mores, and the family. This consensus was shattered in 1972 when the Democratic Party was captured by a faction whose cultural reform agenda was perceived by many (both inside and outside the convention) as antagonistic to traditional religious values. The political scientist Geoffrey Layman has defined this block, the largest in the party, as "secularists"— that is, self-identified agnostics, atheists, and persons who never or seldom attend religious services. Over a third of white delegates fit this description, a remarkable figure considering that...only about 5 percent of the population in 1972 could be described as secularists.

Examining data on more recent voter behavior, Bolce and De Maio find that in the 1990s, "persons who intensely dislike fundamentalist Christians have found a partisan home in the Democratic Party." Clinton took 80 percent of this vote in both 1992 and 1996, and Gore captured 70 percent of it in 2000.[7]

The "secularist" block, it is clear, does not consist of people blandly indifferent to God or to organized religion. Rather, it consists of people who have ranged themselves on the side of Madalyn Murray O'Hair's trenchant hostility to Christians and to the presence of religious references, no matter how anodyne, in public life.

Democrats are, of course, not all secularists, and they are aware of the political danger of being seen as fervently supportive of the secularist aversion to religious expression. As the columnist John Leo recently pointed out, the 2004 Democratic National Convention was bedizened with religious affirmations aimed at lulling churchgoing viewers into a comfortable illusion. But, said Leo, "Even semi-alert people who follow politics with one eye shut" know that "the Democrats are morphing into a secular, or non-believing party."[8]

Thus we come back to the familiar cultural chasm between left and right in America—a chasm for which party politics is only a rough approximation. The left—or the progressivists, as Bolce and De Maio prefer to say—is increasingly defined by its adherence to an ideal of radical self-discovery.[9] Human autonomy, from this perspective, consists of the freedom to move beyond the constraints of family, state, economic competition, and traditional authority in even its most attenuated form. The self, forced to live under those constraints, is *alienated* from its true nature and either capitulates to its oppression or sinks into misery. Meanwhile, the right clings to a version of traditional wisdom in which men and women discover their rightful places by exercising judgment in accord with laws that reflect both the hard-won experience of earlier generations and—for most conservatives—God's will. But the division between left and right is not a simple parting of the ways. Just as the Democratic Party felt the need to deploy traditional-sounding religious self-representation at its 2004 national convention, the right reciprocates by appropriating whenever it can the rhetoric of radical self-discovery. And the rhetoric of radical self-discovery, no matter who uses it, is New Anger.

Circuitry

The prophets of New Anger in the 1950s and 1960s were not all, like O'Hair, avatars of self-resentful bitterness. Some, to the contrary, struck their own mystic chords and came to reevaluate as a way of dissenting from what they felt was the confining complacency of American life.

The sense of self promoted by the gurus of self-actualization and advertised by the lifestyles of rock stars in this period was plainly part of the repudiation of the older ethic of self-control. The new attitude had no room for the sacrifices of personal longing for the sake of one's family; it tossed aside old injunctions against the selfishness of leading one's life only for one's own sake; and it substituted a new goal for a life well lived: authenticity. The new attitude was antimaterialist at least to the extent of inveighing against people whose sense of identity was wrapped up in material wealth. That sentiment showed up frequently in popular songs such as Red Hayes and Jack Rhodes' "Satisfied Mind," covered by The Byrds and by Joan Baez among others:

> Then suddenly it happened, I lost every dime,
> But I'm richer by far with a satisfied mind.

The self, according to this view, was not to be defined by the things that a person acquired, but by some deeper quality or essence.

Before this newfangled self could win the hearts of popular musicians, however, it had to be conjured by someone. Conventionally, it is ascribed to the Beat poets and avant-garde writers of the 1950s, and if we need a specific date, Allen Ginsberg's reading of his poem "Howl" at the Six Gallery in San Francisco on October 13, 1955, will do. The event, arranged by fellow Beat poet Michael McClure ("Peyote Poem") and hosted by Jack Kerouac, who offered a rhythmic accompaniment by slapping a bottle of wine, galvanized the audience. "Howl" doesn't offer much as poetry, but continues to mesmerize a certain kind of undergraduate. The line "I saw the best minds of my generation destroyed by madness, starving hysterical naked" might be a more familiar opening to contemporary students than anything by Shakespeare or Keats. Dwaipayan Banerjee, "undergraduate student," recently posted his essay "Allen Ginsberg's *Howl*: Genius or Incoherence?" on the Web. Genius, of course, says Mr. Banerjee:

> The spontaneity in form [in "Howl"] is reflective of the honesty in content. For Ginsberg, and this is true of most beat poets, there is no distance between the poet and the poem. The poem is almost always an honest and direct expression of the poet's defiant preoccupation with his self.[10]

The opinion of the undergraduate student, Dwaipayan Banerjee, is much more interesting in its way than that of any established literary critic, for Mr. Banerjee provides the Beat mythology with no trace of complicating second and third thoughts.

A seasoned critic would hardly be caught saying that Ginsberg's stage radicalism and elaborate posing were simple "honesty" or that "the poet and the poem" had no distance between them. And Ginsberg's "defiant preoccupation with his self" in the poem is thick with stock imagery rolled out for a particular audience:

> Moloch! Solitude! Filth! Ugliness! Ashcans and unobtainable dollars!

The "honest and direct expression" of the self that Mr. Banerjee sees in this poem is surely nowhere in the vicinity of lines like this. Even so, Mr. Banerjee captures what we need to know about the Beat contribution to the newly emerging "self" of the 1960s. "Howl" does indeed give us "defiant preoccupation with his self," posed as fearless honesty, liberation from conventions, and a new kind of instant authenticity. It is a poem that only at the most superficial level asks the listener to think or reflect. Instead it invites the listener to *feel*—and the key feeling for this communion is outrage.

It is too much to say that Ginsberg invented this particular sense of self, but he did play a key role in proselytizing it. For example, in December 1960, he met Timothy Leary, then a forty-year-old Harvard faculty member. Leary recruited Ginsberg to the "Harvard Psilocybin Project" to experiment with hallucinogenic mushrooms. Leary later introduced Ginsberg to LSD, and Ginsberg, building on his Beat reputation as an exponent of a new kind of consciousness, became the nation's leading advocate of using LSD to open the mind to higher levels of awareness. Leary, in turn, played off Ginsberg's reputation. At the trial of the "Chicago Eight," Leary was called as a defense witness and cited Ginsberg:

> *Mr. Kunstler:* Now, with reference to the founding of the Youth International Party, which we will refer to as Yippie, can you state what was said by the people attending there with reference to the founding of this party?
>
> *Mr. Leary:* Well, Julius Lester said that the current parties are not responsive to the needs of black people, particularly young black people. Allen Ginsberg said that the Democrat and Republican Parties are not responsive to the creative youth and to college students and high school students who expect more from society. Abbie Hoffman, as I remember, was particularly eloquent in describing the need for new political tactics and techniques.[11]

But Leary especially drew on Ginsberg's enthusiasm in building his eccentric "Eight Circuit Model of Consciousness." The eight circuits take us from basic biology ("the bio-survival circuit") through emotions, dexterity, social life, into the druggy domains of the neurosomatic, neuroelectric, neurogenetic, and neuroatomic circuits.

The acid insights inspired by LSD guru Timothy Leary are evidently very large—larger, say, than anything that might be contained in an average self-storage locker; but he belongs in this story as one who exemplifies the invention of a new kind of self. Leary, of course, still has his devotees. New Age theorist Robert A. Wilson (1932–), for example, championed Leary, and Wilson's own pronouncements on Leary are now quoted with awed respect on hundreds of websites. Here is Wilson, from 1977, quoted by "Paul," March 4, 2004:

> It is no accident that the pot-head generally refers to his neu-
> ral state as "high" or "spaced-out." The transcendence of
> gravitational, digital, linear, either-or, Aristotelian, Newton-
> ian, Euclidean, planetary orientations (circuits I–IV) is, in
> evolutionary perspective, part of our neurological prepara-
> tion for the inevitable migration off our home planet, now
> beginning....
>
> This Einsteinian, relativistic contelligence (consciousness-
> intelligence) recognizes, for instance, that the Euclidean,
> Newtonian and Aristotelian reality-maps are just three
> among billions of possible programs or models for experi-
> ence. I turned this [neuroelectric] circuit on with Peyote, LSD
> and Crowley's "magick" metaprograms....
>
> The evolutionary function of the sixth [neuroelectric] cir-
> cuit is to enable us to communicate at Einsteinian relativities
> and neuro-electric accelerations, not using third circuit
> laryngeal-manual symbols but directly via feedback, tele-
> pathy and computer link-up. Neuro-electric signals will
> increasingly replace "speech" (hominid grunts) after space
> migration....
>
> Space Migration plus Increased Intelligence plus Life
> Extension means expansion of humanity into all space-time.
> SM + I^2 + LE = infinity.[12]

It's useful to be reminded where this leads. On February 9, 1997, some of Timothy Leary's ashes were launched infinity-wards into space in a rocket, in what is perhaps the most flamboyant act of self-storage in recent times.

Ginsberg and Leary somehow do not register in our his-torical memory as angry people. Ginsberg perhaps figures mostly as an early out-of-the-closet advocate of gay love and Eastern mysticism, and Leary as the nutty Harvard professor who lost himself in LSD. But if they had softer edges than O'Hair, they nonetheless, like her, offered radical rejections of traditional American culture. And looked at seriously, they based those rejections on an anger at the repressive qualities of American society. With Ginsberg ("Moloch! Filth!") this seems fairly clear. With Leary, we have to push some of the beatific cobwebs aside to glimpse his consternation with a world that just wasn't ready for chemically enhanced neuro-atomic circuits. Both inspired followers to seek their true selves over the edge of the horizon, in a place where the difference between waking and dreaming disappears. They offered two of the possible paths to narcissistic self-absorption and to the personality that rages against others because of its own emptiness.

Self-Census

Ginsberg, the son of radical parents, indulged in politically radical postures, but he could hardly be called a proponent of a regimented socialist society. Leary likewise danced on the fringe of sixties radicalism, but his message was: "Turn on, tune in, drop out." O'Hair was the only one of the three to attempt to lead an organized social movement and the only one to employ the courts to advance her agenda. She grew up in a working-class Pittsburgh family without any unusual political interests, but in time her militant atheism was frequently combined with support for radical-left causes.

O'Hair's project was parallel to the counterculture but not really part of it. She was too sterile and too mean to appeal to the consciousness-expanding crowd. Her message, in fact, was consciousness-contracting. She sneered at the intuitions of the divine that inform the lives of many, even most people, while Ginsberg and Leary drew from all manner of religious traditions in a solipsistic profusion of God-identities.

O'Hair played her part in the dismantling of traditional American values, but her great frustration was that Americans yawned at her message. No one much cared anymore about atheist manifestos. Her movement had become simply another tiny island of crankdom that could be swallowed in the vast sea of tolerance. Not believing in God was no longer shocking; and in a way, belief had become an intellectually more interesting form of dissent from the cultural status quo. The American sense of self turned out, after all, to be defined by spiritual longing, even if the social patterns that once gave that longing practical definition had been badly eroded. In the end, O'Hair and her supporters could rouse very little anger in others, although they still cultivated their own resentful sense of being outsiders who were unfairly pushed around by American laws and customs.

O'Hair's real legacy is the intense anger among secularists on the left (and some on the right) at the prospect of having religious views "forced" on the public. Driving these emotions is the fusion of the personal-searching self that Ginsberg and Leary helped to define—the quester for whom spiritual want can be answered only by an expansive, unlimited self—and the antagonistic, liberated self who has escaped once and for all the old claims of family, community, and church, except to the extent that these are lifestyle choices. The personality that is ripest for today's New Anger takes something from all three of these radical dissenters: O'Hair's angry repudiation of public piety; Ginsberg's self-congratulatory sense of himself as anger artist; and Leary's contempt for conventional boundaries.

New Anger takes its basic coordinates from the social dislocations these three figures represent. O'Hair, Ginsberg, and Leary are peripheral figures in the larger historical drama of the last half-century, but they symbolize (and in part instigated) the dissolution in American culture of an ideal of the adult as measured, self-controlled, wary of expressing too much, too soon, and respectful of authority. Americans were by no means unfamiliar with men and women who fell short of the ideal, or with outlaws and renegades who repudiated it. But the core and normative American personality was shored up by a mindful religious piety, commitment to parents and children, and respect for public institutions. The sense of self that gave meaning to these commitments was, however, far more vulnerable than anyone at the time realized. A new sense of self, one that was fueled by anger at the repressive and self-limiting aspects of all that piety, commitment, and respect, was gathering steam—and vehemence.

The sense of self that these developments, taken together, implied was *powerful, free,* and *large.* It was powerful in that those who embraced the new outlook took license to do things (drugs, casual sex, protest) that were previously available only to those willing to move outside dominant social norms. It was free in the sense that the new counter-cultural participants in these forms of expressive behavior insisted that the experience be interpreted as liberation from rather than violation of the norms. And it was large in the sense that participants saw their behavior as part of a trans-formation of the whole society, and possibly the whole world. The counterculture aimed at "revolution," a word that evoked much more than the mere "regime change" of which we speak today.

Cultural change, however, rarely stays within its intended course. The counterculture inflated the *sense of self* for its own participants, but it also transformed the sense of self for those who lived outside it. On the other side of the "generation gap," people whose sense of individuality had been defined in great part by how well they lived up to their commitment to their children found that the rules had changed. A self in which being a "good mother" and a "good father" meant a lot of self-sacrifice and a large commitment to a stable, prosperous nation was faced with children who, to varying degrees, shrugged off the importance of these sacrifices and commitments. Some of the more articulate chil-dren explicitly repudiated their parents' sense of self; many others simply acted out a pattern that implicitly diminished what their parents had achieved. This slow-moving crisis pro-voked endless arguments and family anger, but it inevitably also undermined the older sense of self, which could not be sustained without the validation of the next generation.

What then happened to the parents? Their sense of self shifted in various ways. Some became fellow travelers of the counterculture. But many others shifted to a new identity that at first seemed hard to define. Nixon, running for presi-dent in 1968, offered one rubric in appealing to "the silent majority." But within the seeming silence of this generation, a large cultural change was under way. People were assimi-lating the premises of the counterculture and turning them to new uses. If marriage, family, and personal responsibility on the *old* terms were discredited values, could they be sustained on some new basis? Out of this ferment came a series of outwardly traditional but inwardly quite new conceptions of the self.

The Inchoate Anger of Unbounded Self

People enticed to pursue liberated consciousness face certain practical problems. One possibility is to reject *in toto* traditional aspirations for a secure home and family in favor of efforts to "follow your bliss." Follow it where? "Follow your bliss," which sounds much like a distillation of Ginsberg, Leary, and the whole New Age movement, is actually the command of Joseph Campbell, a professor of mythology who retired from Sarah Lawrence College in 1972. Campbell's 1949 book, *The Hero with a Thousand Faces,* anticipated the countercultural fascination with individuals who dare to transgress the world's boundaries in their search for the ultimate. But his real celebrity came in 1988, a year after his death, when he was featured on PBS in six hour-long conversations with Bill Moyers. "Follow your bliss" suddenly entered the lexicon and *The Hero with a Thousand Faces* came out of retirement for sixteen weeks on the bestseller list.[13]

Nothing could sound less angry than "Follow your bliss," which makes it a good window into how the vaguely upbeat prescriptions of expressive individualism actually connect with the angri-culture. As Campbell surged to posthumous popularity, old acquaintances and colleagues emerged to say that the man was not quite as majestic as he seemed in Moyers' interviews. The critic Brenden Gill attacked him with a broadside in the *New York Review of Books,* saying that Campbell was an anti-Semite, a racist, and a political reactionary. He had once joked to Gill that "the moon would be a good place to put the Jews." Another colleague, Carol Wallace Orr, recollected Campbell's "vexation" that blacks were being admitted to Sarah Lawrence College. And another colleague, Roy Finch, called Campbell "a cryptofascist" who blamed "western decadence" on Christians, Communists, liberals, and Jews. "Follow your bliss," said Gill, was Campbell's way of advising people to reject "fellow feeling or social responsibility." But Moyers defended Campbell as "transforming the very idea of the hero." The bliss, said Moyers, was "discovering that you are your own hero and that you are going on your own journey irrespective of the price and the sacrifice."

Despite the attacks, Campbell's stock continued to rise. Some saw "Follow your bliss" as an empty banality. The TV critic Walter Goodman compared it to Norman Vincent Peale's advice to think positively. Others noted the irony of Campbell, "a lifelong conservative bordering on the reactionary," becoming a hero to people who were attempting to shrug off conventionality. And an education professor at Boston College, William Kilpatrick, dismissed "Follow your bliss" as a version of the "Do your own thing" assault on character education.

Thus, though Campbell's three-word slogan doesn't sound angry, it somehow had the dark magic to elicit anger in others who appeared alarmed that too many people were being tempted by totemic vision quests at the expense, variously, of fighting for social justice or cultivating moral virtues. The critics, left and right, caught the scent of Campbell's wide-open relativism. A letter to the editor in the *San Francisco Chronicle* perhaps best illustrates what the phrase really meant to many of the people who adopted it. Michael Spurek opined:

> This world is great for the same reason it sucks. One person's happiness is another's misery. Whoever you are, whatever you believe, just keep it up and "follow your bliss." As long as you are doing what you want, to the best of your ability, then you are a success. If you are a cop, be the best cop you can. If you are a crook, be the best crook you can.... The world is great, just the way it is.

Spurek's strange counsel of ambitious quiescence is presented in the voice of know-it-all cynicism rather than anger, but the personality that is primed for New Anger seems not far away. After all, we are presented with a person whose reason for writing a letter to the editor is to declare his emotional stance to the world. He offers no real point other than the spectacle of his own sarcastic nonjudgment. A person who believes the world sucks, however amused he may be with the situation, is only a hair's breadth from anger.

In following their bliss, it turns out that few people are satisfied to entertain a totally private and inward quest for authenticity. The quester typically wants to be recognized as such and to that end dons the outward symbols of his pilgrimage. Certainly Ginsberg and Leary were not content to achieve their revelations in secret. On the contrary, they flamboyantly publicized their views. Richard Howard, a poet and admiring critic of Ginsberg, mentions the "devotion [Ginsberg] wishes to inspire in us."[14] The new questing self ostensibly sought profound inner experience, but ostentatiously advertised what he was up to. In the legends of Percival and Galahad, by contrast, the hero pursues his quest for the Grail with a pure heart, free of any eagerness that the world should know.

We "wrap ourselves in images," to borrow a phrase from the anthropologist Alfred Gell—images that declare *to other people* who we are. But as soon as the quester after a new, authentic self and a satisfied mind dresses the part, he has returned to the world of outward possessions. In truth, the human condition seems to impose an absolute prohibition against total dispossession. If we radically reduce our accouterments to a single pair of ripped jeans and a T-shirt, the jeans and the T-shirt themselves fill up with symbolic significance. The self never exists as a pure metaphysical entity, but constantly shapes itself to external, material forms.

And the search for a deeper inner self faces one more confounding problem: the boundlessness of the enterprise. The old, conventional answers to the question "Who am I?" were often compact but powerful: I am a father; I am a mother; I am a law-abiding citizen; I am a steady worker; I am a believer in God. The appeal of those answers for generations of Americans was that they were woven together with the particularities of an individual life. *My* self was the self that struggled, with more or less success, to live up to a set of well-defined social expectations.

New Anger was, in its first incarnation, simply an explosive negation of all those expectations. If the responsible individual had been one who kept his discontents in check out of regard for others, the new rebels of the 1950s and 1960s would shred their own respectability and proclaim themselves liberated from its trammels. New Anger today, fifty years or so later, looks different, partly because the world at which the prophets of New Anger railed has vanished. But New Anger today also differs in having its own self-generated context. We have political movements deeply shaped by New Anger. We have New Anger music. We have curricula designed to ensure that little girls will become little grrrls. We have self-help for adults aimed at getting people to the exact right pitch of anger. In short, we have the angri-culture, and it is now part of the establishment. Perhaps most importantly, we have developed and cultivated personalities that find some of their most important gratifications in expressing anger. New Anger has its own sense of self, albeit a preening, Godzilla-sized sense of self.

The sociologist Morris Janowitz, who in 1978 attempted a synthesis of developments in America over the preceding half-century, took note of the increasing unwillingness of Americans to accept and live with discomfort in personal relationships; our "willingness to externalize private attitudes"; our frequent search for psychological treatment (which he termed "psychological consumerism"); and our "enlarged self-indulgence," sexual permissiveness, and hedonism. Permissiveness, he observed, had long been indulged by the wealthy but had recently become "democratized."[15]

Janowitz's summary sounds perfectly accurate as far as it goes, but he misses entirely the motivational glue that holds these elements together. A new kind of American was emerging, one whose "self" is intolerant of others and outraged if they infringe on one's "personal space." The new self has poured itself out in monologue, partly because its sense of its own existence depends, Ancient Mariner–like, in perpetually retelling its story. Nothing is too "private" for this self to tell others, because this new self has few if any inner zones protected by modesty or shame. Telling others its feelings is proof that it has feelings. Short of telling, it feels mostly emptiness. Counseling in the form of psychological consumerism is one of its ways of transforming its narrative into a project to be worked on, rather than a life to be lived. And all the self-indulgence, sexual and otherwise, is the activity of a self that cannot acknowledge legitimate bounds, because to do so would be to compromise the entire self-image.

This empty-souled but spiritually ambitious creature of unending appetites is the modal personality in which New Anger finds its abode. New Anger is both its basic stance toward the myriad frustrations of its appetites and its cry of despair at a world that looks at it—and shrugs.

To seek an authentic self in the sense that dawned in the late 1950s was to embark on a private expedition without a clear destination. Such a search proves psychologically intolerable for most people. The boundlessness has to be reduced, either by restoring the old conventional answers (e.g. "I discovered what being a father really means") or adopting new conventions (e.g. "I was raised a Catholic, but now I'm Buddhist"). Moreover, the unbounded self is a ghostlike figure that passes through walls and strictures in an endless search for something solid against which it can prove its own existence. New Anger is the desperately intense effort of these ghosts to feel real.

Salvation

Around 1970, a new industry was born in the United States: mini-warehouses that provided "self-storage" for people who needed a little more room for their worldly possessions. The first self-storage facilities were low-tech and rural. They combined cheap real estate, low-cost construction, and a pattern of ownership by small-scale entrepreneurs. The idea, however, caught fire. Self-storage is now a large industry. The Self Storage Association has some 2,300 company members representing over 6,000 facilities.[16] Some of this storage is motivated by the very practical needs of Americans moving from one city to another, but there is more to it than just this. As it happens, Americans like to store stuff.

"Self-storage is sort of a profile of all Americans from the homeless to the super-wealthy and everyone in between," says Tom Litton, owner of Litton Property Management in Lodi, California.[17] Interviewed in a public radio program on self-storage, Litton resisted the repeated invitation of the host to dwell on the "dark side" of self-storage and instead emphasized the democratic spirit of the enterprise. Self-storage managers, Litton said, are a gregarious bunch who enjoy getting to know their customers.

But undoubtedly self-storage does have some shadows. It involves, as the radio host Dick Gordon put it, people packing "lives and identities in boxes until they can be unpacked again." Often that occurs after a funeral. Sandra Bell, one of the owners of Top Hat, a high-end self-storage business in Austin, Texas, told the *Austin Chronicle,* "Anytime someone stores something, there's something stressful going on in their life." The most common: "Lots of divorces," which turns out to be an occupational hazard for people who own self-storage businesses.[18] One spouse puts stuff in storage while the other is at work, and "Then I have the other spouse in here ranting and raving, saying, 'You have my hunting gear.'"

Self-storage certainly isn't always prompted by distress. Some people are pack rats; some are remodeling; some are house hunting. But somehow the self-storage locker has a slightly dissolute air. It evokes lives that have been fractured; secret disorders; and an inordinate longing to hold on to the husks of days gone by. Maybe self-storage is, as some would have it, testimony to the American frenzy of consumption in the last half-century, but that view cannot explain the actual contents of what many people store—collections of keepsakes, paraphernalia of outlived hobbies, and never-to-be-repaired pieces of broken furniture. Self-storage is often surprisingly literal: people store away their outworn past selves, embodied in their material remnants.

The self-storage industry in the United States rose roughly at the same time as American culture was abandoning its long-held ideals of personal self-restraint. I doubt that there is a simple and direct connection between these two developments, but consumer tastes come from somewhere. For hundreds of years, Americans had stored their excess belongings in trunks, attics, basements, and garages. Then in the space of a few years, thousands of Americans—then hundreds of thousands more—began renting commercial storage units. Why?

Possibly because a lot of adults who in yesteryear would have been married and living in a house were now living alone in little apartments. But the industry indicates that's only a fraction of the market.

People no doubt have lots of reasons to rent self-storage spaces, but one particular—though large—segment of the self-stored public throws an interesting light on how American character changed in response to the cultural dislocations of the 1960s. This segment is exemplified by a caller to that same public radio program, a man who identified himself as Peter from Marblehead, Massachusetts.

> *Peter:* This is a story of a devilish invention, self-storage. I've had several previous lives and they are all in a room in Salem. And I spend about $4,000 a year maintaining my previous lives.
> *Dick Gordon:* What's in there, Peter?
> *Peter:* Well, there is a lot of ephemera: photographs, 10 mm films, 8 mm films, papers, books...
> *Dick Gordon:* Tell me, why is it you have that stuff in storage?
> *Peter:* It seems like every box has a gem in it, a little nugget somewhere where I could throw out 80 percent of the box but then I find the lost paper, the lost letter, the lost address—the connection to the past.

What self-storage did for Peter from Marblehead is to create the opportunity for hoarding at a distance. Some people find this meets a psychological need. They can distance themselves from objects that represent bygone epochs of their lives without reaching an irrevocable decision to throw them away. Self-storage differs from the attic or garage as a more radical exile, and self-storage also appeals because it seems to offer the owner of the objects (and the memories they represent) efficient control over them. They no longer crowd in on everyday life, but the owner can retrieve them at will. And in holding open this possibility, the self-storage units whisper the possibility of retrieving the former selves that the objects represent.

Peter is by no means alone in responding to these whispers. On the same radio program, Eugene Halton, professor of sociology and American studies at the University of Notre Dame and co-author of *The Meaning of Things: Domestic Symbols and the Self*, emphasized how often the items people put in self-storage are of little material value but deep personal significance:[19]

> [I]n doing interviews with people about their special possessions, I experience something similar where people begin to tell you much more about themselves than if you asked them directly about themselves, because it was as if they were talking about just inanimate objects, about things, when really they are talking about these mirrors of their selves. I happened to get a call this morning on my way here from an auctioneer I know, and I said, "Do you ever go to self-storage places for auction sources?" He said he's done that over the years a number of times and his description was, "There is a lot of useless crap there. I don't know why people put it there."

Halton went on to explain that the items tended to represent not any old period in a person's life, but particular times when one version of the self gave way to another:

> People have their reasons [for storing "useless crap"]. They have memories locked into these things. If you just look at it without knowing the histories of things, it is hard to see that. There are incredible biographies of things that people have with them as well and not only symbols of identity: crisis figures, symbols of transition they have gone through.

Peter from Marblehead thus seems to have lots of company. Self-storage entrepreneurs, academic observers, and auction-

eers are familiar with the phenomenon, even if it strikes
some of them as puzzling. People who rent self-storage for
their mementoes often reach a point where they fail to keep
up payments; the storage company then auctions the property. Many auctioneers shun this task because, like Professor
Halton's friend, they find all too frequently that the contents of storage lockers are worth little; but some auctioneers
specialize in self-storage defaults, and this offers some clues
to the self-storage world.

California Storage Auction News, for example, reports that
among the 2,900-plus storage facilities in that state, about
800 in any given month will have an auction for abandoned
property.[20] Even with about 9,600 auctions a year, the association estimates that about $3 million changes hands—or
about $312.50 per auction. Self Storage California says the
average lot sells for less than $300, an amount equal to about
two or three months of rent for the space. These figures offer
some empirical evidence of the Peter-from-Marblehead syndrome. A lot of people appear willing to spend an amount
of money to store things that is far in excess of the resale
value of those things. The stored objects are usually *replace-
able* (if they are valued for their practical uses) at a fraction of
what it costs to keep them. Frugality is not the dominant
motive. Clearly, much of what goes into self-storage is kept
because of what it means.

So why are many contemporary Americans unwilling
to let go of the bric-a-brac of earlier episodes of their lives?
And is this anything new? Haven't Americans always been
eager to hold on to little pieces of the past?

First, self-storage *is* new in the sense that some ordinary
Americans once filled up attics, basements, and garages with
keepsakes, but very few took the step of renting warehouse
space. The mini-warehouses and such facilities that sprung
up around 1970 had no real precedent for ordinary Americans except for safe deposit boxes in banks. And, yes,
Americans of earlier generations were often eager to keep—
and display—family heirlooms. But self-storage is something
else. Instead of maintaining a collection of prized objects that

are kept to be passed along to another generation, self-storage appears much more frequently to be a matter of maintaining a horde of things that have *private* significance—things that speak to the question "Who was I?" rather than the question "Who are we?"

The self-storage industry was an incidental effect of the cultural watershed of the 1960s, but an illuminating one. Houses are, for Americans, a root metaphor for the self, and what we put in or take out of them speaks pretty clearly to our overall sense of ourselves.[21] In that light, the adult who is psychologically unable either to integrate the past with the present or to discard it altogether seems destined for internal conflict.

This conflict between who we once were and who we are (or aspire to be) now is, of course, nothing new. The ex-sheriff who kept his guns in a locked drawer was storing an aspect of himself that he couldn't throw away altogether. But just as we should distinguish between ordinary anger and New Anger, we should also distinguish between the ordinary impulse to hold on to some pieces of an outworn, former self and the distinctly contemporary phenomenon of *self-storage*—a phenomenon that goes beyond renting a locker for excess furniture.

Indeed, a few people have taken the idea of self-storage another step. In 1962, Robert Ettinger published *The Prospect of Immortality,* extolling the idea that people might be frozen at death to be revived many years later when medical technology would be up to the task. Several companies took up the challenge, only to go bankrupt in the 1970s. But the cryonics movement lives on. A company called Alcor in Scottsdale, Arizona, stores the frozen corpses of over one hundred would-be immortalists. Many of these self-cicles were rich, and the movement seems especially to attract the wealthy, who, naturally, wish to be wealthy again when they are eventually thawed and revived. It is a large enough business that a new branch of estate law has sprung up to offer "personal revival trusts." The idea is to leave all or a portion of one's estate to one's self, to be claimed when one is

reanimated. More than twenty states permit this arrangement. Some of the wealthy prospects for cryonic storage are
calculating that, with compound interest, they might one
day command even greater wealth. An Arizona resort opera-
tor, David Pizer, told the *Wall Street Journal* that he could
wake up in one hundred years as "the richest man in the
world." Well, only if he wakes up first and pulls the plugs on
the other frozen plutocrats.[22]

The prospect of cryonics is fraught with complications.
Could a life insurance company recover its payout if a dead
policyholder returns alive? What if the living great-grand-
children do not care to bring great-grandpa back?
Fortunately, lawyers and estate experts are giving careful forethought to these matters. Wachovia Trust Company, for
example, offers such services. In December 2005, experts
gathered in Florida for the First Annual Colloquium on the
Law of Transhuman Persons—"transhuman persons" being
the Leary-esque term for dead people who go on acting as
though they were alive.

Self-storage—whether of the kind indulged by Peter of
Marblehead with his collection of "previous lives" or the
kind that David Pizer looks forward to—takes us some distance from the histrionics of New Anger. But New Anger
thrives, above all, because we have undergone a profound
change in how we regard our inner selves. Many of us find it
very difficult to grow beyond and integrate past experience in
the present. We want to "have it all"—literally. Surely the
wiser thing to do is to relinquish what we no longer need—
and who we no longer are. The insistence on "having it all,"
I take it, is one deep source of anger, since no matter how
hard we try, we can't.

A change of this sort is not easily measured or even
characterized, since it is by nature a change in tacit assumptions and attitudes. But such changes aren't altogether
invisible either. They show up most prominently in the sensibility of novels and movies, in the music we create, and in
self-help books. Sociologists look for external correlates of
the inner change. Robert Putnam's brilliant analysis of the
decline of civic participation in American life, *Bowling Alone*

(2000), captures one aspect of our psychological sea change: how we have been pulled apart from one another. Self-storage offers itself as a metaphor for another aspect of that sea change: how we now seek to defy our temporal limits and aggrandize the self, as though we were each an Egyptian pharaoh stocking our tomb for eternity.

By the end of the 1960s, some people began to store away their obsolete but undiscarded selves because they found themselves with an unusual problem. The mechanisms by which people had traditionally integrated the parts of their lives had broken down and a new emphasis on self-exploration had unsettled the country without pointing to any specific destination. Some people—distinctly a small minority—thrived in a milieu where the self dissolved and reformed, in a kaleidoscope of personae. The kaleidoscopic self has worked for people as varied as Bob Dylan, Richard Nixon, and—more recently—Madonna. But most people still longed for a more stable self, a recognizable "me" at the center of "my story." Larger-than-life performers and politicians could shift masks with no danger of misplacing that core identity. Ordinary people attempting to make sense of new freedoms often faced a tougher challenge. Self-exploration could well lead to rootless alienation and an impoverished sense of identity.

The movement toward greater emotional openness and expressivity in the 1960s was praised by many of its apostles as promoting a stronger and healthier sense of self among overly repressed Americans. It offered freedom to do and say much that was previously off-limits, but also to *feel* a lot of impulses that earlier generations had denied themselves. But opening the American character to these feelings does not, from the perspective of four decades later, appear to have been an especially enriching experience. We have, instead, accumulated our collection of outworn selves that we no longer want but can't bear to give up.

Phantoms

A lot of the people putting things in storage today are

divorced. Many others are widowed, and still others are the adult children of parents who have died. In the United States 75 or 100 years ago, people in such circumstances usually had other family members close by. Households were broken up as people faced life crises or death, but the material possessions typically cycled into the households of other family members. Of course, that happens today too, but less so. Families in America are physically dispersed and family ties have attenuated.

Because the immediate family is still a vivid reality for most Americans, we often have a hard time recognizing the thinning out of kinship commitments. But to anthropologists looking at Americans in a global context, or to historians comparing recent decades to a century past, the looseness of the claims of kinship in contemporary America is dramatic and extreme. Except for the United States, Canada, Western Europe, Australia, and New Zealand, family remains the matrix in which most people find their primary identities— and their primary obligations to other people. The Taita in Kenya, casting out anger against fellow kinsmen by spitting out mouthfuls of sugarcane beer or water, exemplify one aspect of what kinship means everywhere: a context in which the individual must reconcile to the needs of the family and the larger circle of kin. Failure to do so often means death— not because the family will execute a renegade, though that happens too, but because family solidarity is an individual's only reliable defense in a dangerous world. Thus, though the individual may find family demands onerous and frustrating at times, he or she bears with them.

The West in general and the United States in particular have gone remarkably far in breaking free of this oppressive side of family life. We have, in a sense, torn down our family trees and chopped them up to fuel the engines of expressive individualism. Where families once constrained our choices, we now largely make our own on matters such as whether and whom to marry, where to live, and how to earn a living, as well as the vast range of "lifestyle" options over which the individual has nearly absolute control.

Our sense of individual freedom, in other words, is in large measure an escape from the inevitable restrictions of the traditional family. American expressive individualism—whether we take the Ginsberg, Leary, or O'Hair version—takes its first punch at the family, and continues to flail against its imaginary father and mother figures long after they themselves have set sail on their Carnival world cruises. The personality type that emerged in the children who grew up from the 1960s through the 1990s was one in which the family, reduced to unprecedented weakness, had to be imagined nonetheless as powerful and oppressive. For without such an opponent, the individual lacked a crucial means of defining himself—or especially herself. The remnants of family authority had to be reassembled again and again for the sake of repudiating them.

This I take to be the center of the Angry Leftist: a person so desperate to repudiate an oppressive authority that he is driven to imagine one where none can be found. New Anger can and does get directed at real people, but its actual targets are phantoms. The angri-culture consists of an imaginary war perpetually fought against a faceless enemy who is everywhere because he is nowhere.

In a recent essay, "Eminem Is Right," Mary Eberstadt emphasizes a related point: that the extreme anger on display in a lot of the music popular among adolescents arises from the children of divorce.[23] She writes, "If yesterday's rock was the music of abandon, today's is the music of abandonment." In support she cites hits such as Papa Roach's "Broken Home," on that band's 2000 album *Infest*. The lyrics include:

> I know my mother loves me
> But does my father even care?

Blink-182 had a top-forty hit in 2001 with "Stay Together for the Kids," which expresses a child's desperate longing for an intact family. On the singer Pink's top-ten album in 2002, *Missundaztood*, her song "Family Portrait" consists of a child begging her father not to leave.

The actual parents of Pink, who grew up as Alecia

Moore, separated when she was nine, but "Family Portrait" is a good place to pause for a reminder that art is not life. Pink actually had a warm if imperfect relationship with both her parents when she was growing up. Her first album is dedicated "to my daddy, my hero, my glue, my mentor," and she adds, "Mommy, thank you for loving me even when it was hard." She lived with her father for a period and told an interviewer, "he was an angry man but the greatest life teacher; he gave me opinions to rebel about. My anger had a direction as he made me aware of politics, government, aware of being a survivor."[24] After the song came out, Pink played up her early family life as a "personal World War III," but her parents objected to this story and she soon began to express regret that she had depicted them so negatively. She also realized what she had inadvertently done to herself. "After songs like *Family Portrait,* everyone thought I was really damaged. But I'm just writing about this stuff. I'm okay—really." What "okay—really" seemed to mean, however, was that Pink switched from the tone of introspective suffering to the more triumphant "to hell with you songs."[25]

Eberstadt piles up the examples of contemporary songs about the consequences of fathers who abandon their children. Many of these songs are written and performed by the children of divorce, but most of them are not angry in the way that I have been describing. They are very angry, but they are not histrionically angry. Rather, they are broken, forlorn, wistful, traumatized, and profoundly hopeless. The music of parental abandonment seems to be filled more with the New Self-Pity than with New Anger. Self-pity and anger are close cousins generally, and are typically combined in New Anger, where they urge on each other's emotional claims. So we might well ask why the music of Good Charlotte, Korn, Everclear, Linkin Park, Blink-182, Slip-Knot, Nickelback, Papa Roach, and Disturbed (all bands that Eberstadt discusses) is *not* angry in the New Anger mode?

Eberstadt provides what I think is the right answer, which she quotes from the music journalist William Shaw's essay "Why Are America's Rock Bands So Goddamned Angry?"

> This is the sound of one generation reproaching another—
> only this time, it's the scorned, world-weary children telling
> off their narcissistic, irresponsible parents. [Divorce] could be
> rock's ideal subject matter. These are songs about the chasm
> in understanding between parents—who routinely don't
> comprehend the grief their children are feeling—and chil-
> dren who don't know why their parents have torn up their
> world.[26]

In other words, the music of abandonment is a kind of anger
music, but it is the mournful inner anger of the generation
that has grown up suffering the consequences of its parents'
self-indulgent New Anger. The family cycle never ends, even
when the family is broken on the altar of self-empowering
free expression of grievance.

Absentee fathers and parental abandonment can and
often do spark New Anger too. Our emotions are seldom so
sealed off from one another that we feel and express only one
kind of anger. Some of the mournfully angry bands sing
grandiose New Anger songs too, and Eberstadt's exploration
of the music of abandonment also turns to singers who are
almost exclusively voices of New Anger: the rappers, the late
Tupac Shakur, Jay-Z (who raps to his absent father, "Fuck
you very much / You showed me the worst kind of pain"),
and Eminem.

If New Anger is, as I have argued, the culmination of a
two- or three-generation transformation in the American
family—from a place where mothers and fathers work to provide children with inward mastery and self-control of
emotion, to a place where children are encouraged to express
themselves with a minimum of either external or internal
control—we can expect that at some point a kind of emotional bewilderment will emerge, in which a fair number of
people won't even have the tropes of New Anger to shape
their inchoate selves. I suspect that the mournful, self-lacer-
ated anger of Papa Roach and such bands is what this
bewilderment sounds like.

It's what happens when New Anger's expansiveness
becomes so diffuse that it loses even the certainty of self.

That's because the sense of authenticity promised by the gurus of anger indispensably requires a contrast to a world that it can repudiate as inauthentic—or *phony,* as Holden Caulfield called it in one of the foundational visions of New Anger, J. D. Salinger's 1951 novel, *Catcher in the Rye.* Hence so much of the rhetoric of New Anger consists of characterizing the foe as a liar, a hypocrite, or the agent of a conspiracy. The terms of opprobrium carry the implied message: I'm authentic; you're not.

This is true wherever New Anger breaks out. Much of the fury on the right against Clinton focused on his lying. When country music turns its angry attention to the cultural elites, the core accusation is that those elites are phonies. But the theme is surely at its most intense in Bush-hatred, which revels in the conceit that Bush was "selected" in his first term, not elected, and therefore remains a phony president. The lavish attention given to his family history likewise fuels the sense that he is a creature of the old, discredited, and phony system of family loyalties, rather than the new, approved, and authentic system of credentialed elites. "He only got into Yale because his dad pulled strings," say the members of this elite, expressing their own greatest vanity: that *they* got into college based on their individual brilliance and creative individuality.

Before the rise of New Anger, when the family still sought to ensure that children learned how to exercise emotional self-control, the task of learning how to head off anger was not always easy to accomplish. The satisfactions that came from knowing you were the master of your temper were hard won and real. The individual who had cause to feel anger but put it aside gained the esteem not only of family members but also of a larger community. Self-control was a crucial part of the ethos of family life. Or, rather, it still *is* a crucial part of family life even if we de-emphasize and neglect it. We have merely forced it underground, where it takes the form of counseling people to express particular kinds of discontent in carefully crafted, unthreatening ways. Many of the self-help books—*Anger Is a Choice; You Can't Say That to*

Me; When Anger Hurts; Our Inner World of Rage; and so on—essentially repackage what the Taita practice: figure out why you are angry, find a controlled environment to present your grievance in a nonconfrontational manner, state it forthrightly, and let it go.

Of course, the "let it go" part is never easy and is all the less so when we have other counselors telling us (*Make Anger Your Ally; The Anger Advantage*), "don't let go of your anger. Rather, use it to dominate your relationships and overcome those who would keep you down."

The principle that brings the Taita to *cast out* anger, however, is universal. A *family* endures only if its members abide by some implicit limits on their anger toward each other. Bickering, unhappiness, and estrangement are not modern inventions. What's modern is our conceit that we can purchase relief from these ills by expressing rather than controlling our anger. That conceit leads to more broken marriages and more children raised by single parents—but we are hardly ready to abandon the family. What we want is a way to combine the ideal of expressive individualism with our longing for the satisfactions of family life. The trouble is that the two not only are a poor fit, but are opposed at a deep level. Expressive individualism is an ideology that arose in rebellion against the traditional family's very real curbs on individual freedom. The search for a compromise that will allow us to have it both ways has not yet produced an answer that commands widespread cultural assent. Free-form expression of emotion just doesn't fit very well with the inherent needs of men and women for each other or with the dependency of infants and children.

The new individualism has never quite figured out what to do with itself. It searches constantly for some purpose beyond mere day-to-day existence, and it continues to exalt such searching as its own reward. But humans are not really designed for such aimlessness. Many end up hungering for what they no longer have: a thriving ideal of the family not shattered by our newfound loathing of hierarchy, sexual division of labor, and the obligations of kinship. This unappeasable hunger is the quality now built into the American character. It is why we are so angry.

Living Large

In August 1995, Madalyn Murray O'Hair, then seventy-six years old, attended an atheist convention in Denver and immediately afterward dropped from sight. In October, Dan Barker, an executive of the Freedom from Religion Foundation, told a *Rocky Mountain News* reporter that he could not say where she was. "Maybe she's creating a mystery. Maybe she died. And maybe she's on vacation."

By December, word had leaked that the IRS was seeking $750,000 in back taxes from O'Hair and her son and granddaughter, who had also disappeared. The son, Jon Murray, was president of American Atheists, and the granddaughter, Robin Murray-O'Hair, was the executive secretary.[27] The IRS had investigated claims that the family had received a large unreported income from American Atheists, Inc. and purchased a Mercedes, a Porsche, a house in Austin, and maid services with it. But the IRS had been close to settling the case, and it wasn't clear that the three would abscond just to avoid taxes.

The mystery lingered as the months turned godlessly into years. Followers recalled O'Hair writing in 1986 of her determination not to let "religionists" have the opportunity to "get their filthy paws on my corpse." She added, "I don't want any damn Christer praying over the body or even putting hands on it." Had she fled to avoid that awful fate? *Vanity Fair* reported sightings of her in Auckland, New Zealand. Had she taken her money with her?

As it happened, no. In January 2001, the FBI, digging on a Texas ranch, uncovered what turned out to be the remains of O'Hair, her son, and her granddaughter. The real story had started to become clear in June 1998 with an anonymous tip. By 1999, police had worked out most of the story. An Austin ex-con and former employee of American Atheists,

Inc., David Roland Waters, along with two accomplices, Gary Paul Karr and Danny Raymond Fry, had kidnapped the O'Hairs in August 1995, held them for a month to extract a $600,000 ransom from them, and then killed them. Waters and Karr then killed Fry as well, to avoid having to divide the ransom three ways. Karr was convicted of extortion in 2000 and sentenced to life. Waters was convicted in 2001 on a charge of conspiracy in a plea-bargain that gave him a twenty-year sentence in exchange for showing where O'Hair and the others were buried.

O'Hair, who worried about her dead body falling into the hands of "Christers," miscalculated. Her body was left in the hands of her killers, led by one of her own followers who had turned his fury in her direction. After strangling her, the three conspirators took her—where else?—to a self-storage locker, where they cut her corpse into pieces, which they then buried on a ranch outside Austin. This grotesque episode, however, doesn't quite finish the story. The killers had also converted the ransom for O'Hair, her son, and granddaughter into $500,000 in gold coins, which they stashed in a self-storage unit. A few days later, some petty thieves jimmied the lock and were astonished at their good luck. Madalyn Murray O'Hair, converted to cold coin, spent the next two years supporting a gambling spree.

Anger does not seem, on the whole, to be a good basis for a career or a life. Even the muffled anger of the self-explorers who follow their bliss but carry a big stick seems to lead for many to a long-term desolation. In creating a new self free of the trammels of traditional roles in the family, traditional demands of church and community, and traditional satisfactions of self-control, we have created an American type who, unless he is angry, feels he is nothing at all.

EIGHT

COOLING OFF

Some autumn afternoon when the later flowers are luxuriating in the golden light, look for a bumblebee drowsy with his harvest—and stroke him gently with your index finger. He won't sting or even take flight. Whether weary with his work or just replete with the season, he seems not to mind the light touch. Best not to try this with a hornet.

Culture has its seasons too, but they are much less predictable than the ripening of the marigolds. When exactly will a golf player look at his "Don't play mad...PLAY ANGRY" golf cap and feel embarrassed to wear it?

Playing angry might, after all, lose its luster. The epitome of anger in sports, John McEnroe, in 2004 began to host a cable television interview show with a comedic touch. This is the man who as recently as 2000 turned on a fan at a Champions Senior Tennis Tournament in Central Park and spat out, "What the fuck do you care, asshole?" The spectator had merely called out "C-mon, Mac, not already!" after McEnroe charged the net and began to quarrel with the referee about a lines call in the opening minute of the match.

And if cultural critics such as Alan Wolfe are to be believed, the angri-culture is an illusion anyway. According to Wolfe, the American political elites are just continuing their centuries'-old grudge matches, which for ordinary Americans hold about as much interest as New Zealand cricket scores. Wolfe and other social scientists who claim to see a broad cultural consensus beneath the apparent political polarization rely a lot on opinion surveys. I don't doubt that these surveys capture something, but culture is lived experience that loses much of its texture when reduced to answers on a questionnaire.

That someone like John McEnroe could emerge not only as a champion in his sport in the early 1980s but also as the object of a kind of dark and enduring public admiration speaks more clearly than any opinion survey about anger's new position in the culture at large. On his way to winning seven Grand Slam tournaments and seventy-seven singles titles, McEnroe screamed obscenities at umpires, opponents, fans, and even himself. Sportswriter Larry Platt offered an assessment of McEnroe's behavior:

> Behind the blowups was a self-loathing narcissism ("I'm so disgusting, you shouldn't watch. Everybody leave!" he screamed between points during the '81 Wimbledon tournament) and a class resentment in reaction to tennis' pretension. He would rail against the sport's "phonies and elitists," earning him antihero status.[1]

McEnroe's ex-wife, Tatum O'Neal, explained that he actually thrived on the animosity of the crowd and saw each victory as beating not just his opponent but also the officials and the spectators. But Platt also observed that while McEnroe can be "smart and funny" as a commentator, he is never far from the angry darkness that he displayed on the court.

McEnroe's contempt for the people who share an interest in his sport (and who provided him with fame and fortune) is echoed in the words and behavior of the Alpine skiing champion Bode Miller. What does Miller have to be angry about? Almost everything. In November 2005 he told a *Newsweek* reporter: "A lot of the people involved with the U.S. [Olympic] Ski Team—the people I'm representing—are unbelievable assholes. Rich, cocky, wicked, conceited, super-right-wing Republicans." Miller, who was the 2004–2005 World Cup champion and a silver medalist in the Alpine combined event at the 2002 Olympics in Salt Lake City, is recognized as one of the world's greatest skiers. He is exceptional for competing at the top level in both downhill speed events and slalom events. But he is also notorious for mouthing off.

After threatening to quit the U.S. Ski Team in 2005, Miller decided to stay, but in December he denounced the sport's ban on performance-enhancing drugs. Then he got into a furious argument with ski officials by refusing to allow them to measure his boots, as required by racing regulations. In January 2006, he appeared on *60 Minutes* declaring—unapologetically—that he had skied World Cup events drunk or hung-over ("If you have ever tried to ski when you are wasted, it's not easy"). At first, he angrily disparaged CBS for airing the interview. "I told them the story to test their integrity," he claimed. "...If they were interested in doing the right thing, or doing what they should be doing in terms of painting a role model for kids, they would have left that stuff out."[2] But after an Alpine avalanche of criticism, Miller offered a tepid apology, regretting the "pain and confusion" he might have caused friends and family. The next day he proceeded to a World Cup event in Lauberhorn, Switzerland, where he picked a hair-splitting argument over whether he had illegally "straddled a gate" or merely "stepped on it." That evening he failed to show up for a public ceremony, which cost him his place in the next day's downhill event.

Miller sneers not only at racing officials but also at reporters, sponsors, fans, and even his own ghostwriter, as when he told one reporter that he had never read his own "autobiography," *Bode: Go Fast, Be Good, Have Fun*. He loathes the idea that as an Olympic icon he will be "used" to prop up a capitalist society. As for fans, "I don't know you, so don't fucking come up and give me high-fives and say 'sign this.'"[3]

Whence Bode Miller's anger? What has the world done to him except celebrate his accomplishments?

Miller was raised in rural New Hampshire in a family commune by "hippie" parents who, as a longtime acquaintance of his put it, gave him "unbridled freedom": "He was home-schooled by adults who lived by many of the idealistic values of the 1960s. He had few rules imposed upon him."[4] In other words, Bode Miller is the epitome of the Newly Angry generation, whose parents valued emotional expressivity and "honesty" over self-control, and who raised their children not to have any of the lingering hang-ups that they carried from *their* childhoods.

Miller's candor is the characteristic most remarked by reporters. "He hates the media, yet almost never ducks a direct question," says Chris Dufresne, a writer for the *Los Angeles Times*. "He's foulmouthed and combative, and he's stubbornly, refreshingly honest," says Devin Gordon in *Newsweek*. "Miller is stubborn and appears to thrive on arguing with authority," says Nathaniel Vinton, a writer for the *New York Times*.[5] These comments are only a step short of gushing admiration for Miller as a performer of New Anger. That comes next. "Can someone be petulant *and* engaging?" asks Dufresne, who adds, "You don't converse with Miller as much as you joust." *Newsweek*'s Gordon calls Miller "the scrappy, backwater, regular dude" and "an expert insurrectionist."

A readiness to "play angry" or perhaps the inability to play any other way is not confined to sports. A reporter for *Newsday* recently interviewed several writers of mystery novels who mix "social issues" with tracking down villains. Jessica Speart, whose recent book *Blue Twilight* features Special Agent Rachel Porter of the U.S. Fish and Wildlife Service, says, "I want to write about something that really fuels me, that makes me angry." She is not alone in choosing the anger muse for inspiration. Carl Hiaasen, author of *Skinny Dip,* featuring a villainous biologist who aids the polluters of the Everglades, says that he picks his topics on the basis of "whatever happens to be ticking me off."[6]

As with writers, so with some critics. John Leonard recently reviewed a collection of literary criticism aptly titled *Hatchet Jobs,* by Dale Peck, a frequent critic for the *New Republic*. Leonard describes Peck as falling down "on the head of the pedestrian author like a piano or safe. He is his own blunt instrument." Peck seems to devote himself to finding fresh ways to deride the authors he reviews. He describes one novel as "the doughy center of a half-baked cake," and another as "watery oatmeal." But Leonard—the reviewer of the reviewer—does not exactly restrain his own anger. He says of Peck's book:

> This isn't criticism. It isn't even performance art. It's thugee. However entertaining in small doses—we are none of us immune to malice, envy, schadenfreude, a prurient snuffle and sucker punch—as a steady diet it's worse for readers, writers and reviewers than self-abuse; it causes the kind of tone-deaf, colorblind, nerve-damaged and gum-sore literary journalism that screams "Look at me!"[7]

Writers who are moved by social injustice and critics who admire their own malice are certainly nothing new. What makes these writers sound so up-to-the-minute is not their anger per se, but their self-conscious cultivation of it as a source of inspiration. The rule seems to be: Play angry or don't play at all. Leonard ends his review with a call for civility in the form of a jibe against the "preening scribblers"— "GET OVER YOURSELF," which is not very far from McEnroe's "I'm so disgusting, you shouldn't watch. Everybody leave!" Or Bode Miller lamenting his celebrity: "I am, for sure, much more of a dick now than I used to be."

Leonard's review was titled "Smash-Mouth Criticism." Originally the adjective was used in football. In 1986, the Houston Oilers coach Jerry Glanville called his game "smash-mouth football," and explained: "We want ours [our players] to be the ones you wouldn't let your kids play with, the meanest guy on the block."[8] But by the late 1980s, newspaper columnists began to write of "smash-mouth politics" too, and the angri-culture gained a versatile term for an ostentatiously aggressive style—a performed anger that announced a willingness to transgress whatever rules normally restrained people. In 1994, a band in San Jose, California, named itself Smash Mouth, claiming inspiration from Chicago Bears coach Mike Ditka's use of the term to mean a "no mercy style" of play. Smash Mouth's mixture of "rock, ska, punk, and well, just about everything else" has kept the band popular. In 2001, Dana Milbank, a *Washington Post* reporter, published his account of the 2000 presidential campaign: *Smashmouth: Two Years in the Gutter with Al Gore and George W. Bush*. The season of smash-mouth politics seems a good deal longer than any football game.

But performed anger always has a gamelike quality and the performers tend to expect that, as in any other game, it will wrap up at the end and everyone will go home. When the Dixie Chicks ran afoul of country music fans for their anti-Bush comments in March 2003, they were surprised that anyone would be upset, and indignant that some radio stations launched a boycott. Shannen Coffin, a Washington lawyer, recently referred to this reaction as "Amendment One-and-a-Half," which is the imaginary right of boorish celebrities to say what they want "without any repercussions."[9] At a concert at the Las Vegas Aladdin Casino on July 17, 2004, Linda Ronstadt praised Michael Moore's film *Fahrenheit 9/11* and was roundly booed by members of the audience, some of whom tossed cocktails in the air. Moore, among others, later complained that the treatment of Ronstadt was "un-American." But members of a crowd responding to a performer's angry opinions with angry opinions of their own provide a timely reminder of the real nature of anger. The shining moment of empowered clarity may well be followed by the showering moment of frozen daiquiris.[10]

In any case, whether we look to actual sports, the arts, or entertainment, "playing angry" seems to remain in fashion. "Tennis has missed McEnroe," wrote a newspaper reviewer of his 2002 book, *You Can't Be Serious*. Since his retirement, no one has captured "fans' imaginations."[11] But lots of people have perpetuated his style of contempt for sportsmanship. New Anger admires that willingness to step over the line, and unbridled rage commands deference from fainter souls who only fantasize about turning loose all of their pent-up resentments.

Spectators at sports events have always gotten angry, but it is possible that New Anger has added a sinister twist to this old anger. Colleges and universities, for example, are now faced with fans who attempt to rattle the players on rival teams with personalized insults. The *Chronicle of Higher Education* reported a basketball game at the University of Kentucky in spring 2004 where Kentucky students taunted the University of Florida forward Matt Walsh with chants of "Matt is gay" and signs that "insulted his girlfriend, a *Playboy* magazine Playmate." A University of Iowa basketball player who had pleaded guilty to an assault charge met jeers of "Rapist!" at an Iowa State University game. And at games across the country, student spectators now freely chant and display obscenities. None of this can be explained as an increase in the emotional engagement of the students. Rather, the students accurately sense that the standards for acting out "team spirit" have shifted. Personal taunting, lewdness, and obscenity are now "part of the game," even if college officials don't like it.[12] Riots after championship victories have become so common that police in most American cities prepare for them as routine events.

What accounts for this change in atmosphere? Several U.S. Supreme Court decisions since 1970 have expanded the zone of First Amendment free speech, but the deeper reason for the increase in brazen insults and obscenities is the feeling among the students that these kinds of taunts are perfectly good ways to express enthusiasm and, if possible, to unnerve the other team. These are students who have come of age in the angri-culture and know implicitly that anger can be a tool of intimidation and that rhetorical excess is proof of one's cleverness and sincerity. They are a long way from "Go team!" College sports fans' new style of anti-cheering is akin to the heavy metal music played at many professional sports games: they project power by being loud, fast, and ugly.

The angry fan, of course, isn't confined to the arena, or even to sports as we usually think of them. Bruce Tan, writing in the UCLA student newspaper, the *Daily Bruin,* reported his reaction to watching the National Spelling Bee Championship on ESPN:

"A-U-T-O-C-H-T-H-O-N-O-U-S," he recited. Collapsing to my
knees, I flung my *Merriam-Webster* dictionary at the television in anger. I was rooting for the underdog of the spelling
bee, Akshay Buddiga.... I continued to curse at the television
as Tidmarsh went through his celebration dance.[13]

The champion, David Tidmarsh, incidentally, spelled
"sophrosyne" correctly on his way to victory. It is an old-
fashioned word for temperance, self-control, and prudence.
Sophrosyne is the determination not to have a bee in one's
mouth.

The angri-culture doesn't look as if it's about to fade out.
It has become too much a part of our inner lives—our hopes
and our dreams—and too fluid a medium of expression to
recede like the career of yesterday's sports antihero, smash-
mouth catchphrase, or political pique. The music we listen to
changes constantly, but even as angry subgenres like punk
and grunge fade away, anger reappears in new voices and
new styles. Perhaps today's anger clothing and body pierc-
ing will be gone in a few years, but I would wager that the
emotional couture that comes along next will include a full
line of New Anger spleen. This angry moment won't last forever, but it isn't leaving soon.

Happy Bunny

I know what some New Anger smells like. It smells like bubblegum.

I made this discovery recently. Every time I opened a
particular file drawer, the odor of bubblegum wafted out.
Picking through the files, I couldn't find a source, except that
the odor seemed strongest in the vicinity of my photocopy of
"On Anger" by Seneca. The Stoic philosopher says that ora-
tors do poorly when they are actually angry, but may stir an
audience when they pretend to be angry. But Seneca, as far as
I know, did not chew Bubbalicious. My notes on Aristotle,
who says in his *Ethics* that anger undermines our ability to
choose wisely, were nearby, along with Heraclitus' chilling
fragment that personifies anger as a kind of suicide bomber

who achieves his purpose at the expense of his own life. But they were no fans of Bazooka Joe.

As the scent grew stronger, I looked again and finally found the source. It was an item I had picked up on eBay and had somehow lost among the ancient philosophers: my Happy Bunny air freshener.

A novelty company called C & D Visionary, Inc. in North Hollywood, California, sells a variety of licensed paraphernalia—"stickers, patches, keychains, air fresheners, & more"—including the "It's Happy Bunny" products designed by Jim Benton. Happy Bunny is essentially one joke replayed in dozens of variations: a cutesy bunny rabbit as from a greeting card with an insulting caption: "You smell." "Hi loser." "You suck." C & D Visionary, Inc. offers other items in this spirit, such as its "Just Plain Mean" line, which depicts a smiling little girl in a frock trampling flowers, kicking people, and biting the tail of a cat. But what stands out as the distillation of this little province of self-amused disaffection is the Happy Bunny caption, "Your anger makes me happy." And the powerful chemical scent of bubblegum in the air freshener diffuses even through its cellophane wrapper.

Provoking other people for the sake of enjoying their anger is, I suppose, older than Seneca or even Heraclitus. It is one way playground bullies torment their victims, but playground bully demographics seemed an unlikely market for scented air fresheners. Who actually purchases this particular taunt and the other Happy Bunny products? Judging from Internet chat groups, the buyers are people like Elle, who enjoys seeing people snicker at her Happy Bunny "You're ugly and that's sad" button; Christy, Jen, Denis, Susan ("I'm a Kiss my a** happy bunny"), Maria, Lauren ("My whole room is Happy Bunny"), K-Lynn, Ashley ("Happy Bunny is the world's most awesome thing!"), Zinda, Chistina, Megan, and a whole lot more tween girls. A woman blogger adds this more articulate explanation:

> For those who have had enough of the unrelenting preciousness, It's Happy Bunny is the perfect foil. The deceptively cute rabbit, a little mascot of nastiness, appears on mugs,

T-shirts, stickers, toilet paper, and other items. Our favorites? The *Give Me Your Lunch Money* lunch box, *I Hate You So Bad* socks, the *I Hate Everything* air freshener, the *School Prepares You for the Real World Which Also Sucks* pen, and offensive lip glosses and mints.[14]

It's Happy Bunny is adolescent cynicism for girls who are not grrrls but are still at odds with their own attraction to plush toys and the softer images of juvenile femininity. The mildly disguised rudeness of Happy Bunny appears to these young women as hysterically funny and gives them their own distinct foothold in angri-culture.

Insta-Anger

There are many more ways in which Americans "play angry." Perhaps the venue that offers the greatest scope for putting on the masks of anger is the Internet, which is justly famous for heated debates that turn into personal attacks in the blink of a cursor. The Internet has made it easier to insult people by e-mail from the safety of anonymity. It allows people to post vituperative comments on Amazon.com and other commercial sites that depend on customer feedback. And it can be used to organize sudden and large-scale smear campaigns. I'll let these growling dogs lie, but one use of the Internet that seems especially prone to New Anger deserves a closer look: the Web log, or blog. A blog is a website diary that can be updated almost instantaneously and linked to other websites. The best blogs are well written and provide very timely and often witty commentary on breaking news. Many blogs vividly capture the personality of their creators. Some are topically focused.

For example, *discriminations.us* is a blog, maintained by a father and daughter, John and Jessie Rosenberg, that follows daily news about racial and ethnic discrimination in the United States. *Number 2 Pencil* (kimberlyswygert.com) is a teacher's blog on "testing and education reform." Another lively blog on education is *joannejacobs.com. The Mudville Gazette* (mudvillegazette.com) is a military blog by "an American warrior and his wife who stands by him." *Steve Miller's Culture Watch* at indegayforum.org is a blog that tracks stories about gay issues in the mainstream press. *SmartChristian.com* is a blog that follows "missional activism to Christians worldwide." *The Volokh Conspiracy* (volokh.com) offers a libertarian-conservative commentary on legal issues.

Almost any topic in which more than a handful of people have an interest has at least one blog and probably several. Bloggers pay attention to one another and frequently provide links to other sites. Go to Hugh Hewitt's conservative commentary blog (hughhewitt.com), and you can link to other political blogs, such as *Little Green Footballs* (which deals with national security), *Lileks,* or *Powerline;* or to a list of religious blogs grouped as "Godblogging"; or to a list of military blogs under the heading "Milblogs." Go to *Eschaton,* a left-wing blog by "Atrios" (the nom de guerre of Philadelphia economist Duncan Black), and you can link to other blogs on that side of the political spectrum, including *Pendagon, Daily Kos, TBogg,* and Josh Marshall's *Talking Points Memo.*

The more successful bloggers attract advertisers who "blogroll" them; others solicit donations or go it alone. Some sites, such as *Blogniscient,* provide a kind of *Reader's Digest* of blogs, linking the top blogs of the day on the political right and the left, as well as in science, sports, entertainment, and business.

Blogging has achieved such popularity that some readers may view this explanation as akin to explaining the principle of the safety match or the revolving door. But in fact, only a small fraction of the American public reads blogs. Estimates vary, but in May 2005, Carl Bailik in the *Wall Street Journal* came up with an approximate 3.5 million active blog sites; between 350,000 and 900,000 new postings per day; and possibly as many as 32 million American adults reading blogs. That number strikes some observers as too high, but even if true, it is only 10.6 percent of the American population. A truly popular site like *Little Green Footballs*—then ranked seventh in number of daily visitors—drew some 87,000 visitors a day.[15] *Little Green Footballs* as of January 2006 had slipped to around 81,800 visitors a day (and to fifteenth place among most-visited blogs). We know this because of another site, *the truth laid bear* (truthlaidbear.com), which provides traffic rankings for blogs.

Like a lot of cultural phenomena, however, the importance of blogs goes way beyond the number or the percent of active participants. Blogs have become key to how public information is shared and political opinions are shaped in our society. Blogging has drastically reduced the power of newspapers and television to determine what is newsworthy and what views will be heard. It changed the dynamics of the 2004 presidential election for both major parties, and it appears likely to change permanently the way in which political elites in the United States attempt to rally popular support.

Blogging made high-profile appearances at the Democratic and Republican national conventions in 2004, and it got somewhat dressed up for both occasions. Blogging, especially blogging about the news, is often a much more biting—and angry—form of exchange than print-based opinion journalism or online journals.

Bloggers who follow the news often specialize in providing quick, highly skeptical responses to official versions of events and to mainstream newspaper accounts. As Christopher Conkey put it in the *Wall Street Journal,* bloggers "relentlessly skewer" the mainstream press "for what they call overplaying or underplaying stories, bias and other perceived errors."[16]

Blogging had only a few practitioners until Pyra Labs in San Francisco released a free Web application for blogging in 1999. By February 2003, blogger.com, which offers a free blog-hosting service, had over a million registered users. A Pew Internet survey that year found 4 percent of Americans relying on blogs for news and opinions. Perseus Development Corporation in Braintree, Massachusetts, estimated that by summer 2004, some 4.12 million blogs had been created, although about half were defunct. Perseus also projected that by 2005, over 10 million blogs would exist.

About 10 percent of bloggers update their blogs daily, and about 93 percent of current blogs are the work of people under age thirty.[17]

A great many of these blogs deal with narrow or eccentric interests ("microblogs") or offer, as the British journalist David Rowan puts it, "tedious journals dedicated to observations about the writer's cat," appropriately known as "kittyblogs." But the blogosphere really turns on the axis of political bloggers, perhaps the most famous of whom is Glenn Reynolds. At a time when Reynolds' *Instapundit* was averaging about 75,000 individual visits a day, Linda Seebach, a reporter for the *Rocky Mountain News,* noted that he had "a larger circulation than about 90 percent of daily newspapers."[18] By January 2006, *Instapundit* was up to 137,742 visits per day. Reynolds' comments are often sardonic but seldom angry. He has a light and deft touch and a keen eye for interesting comments on other sites. His art lies in making short, perceptive remarks that never devolve into ponderous essays, and he seems to wear his celebrity in good spirit. If we are looking for anger in the blogosphere, *Instapundit* isn't the right destination—except that Reynolds is frequently the target of sniping comments from bloggers on the left.

Noah Millman, the author of *Gideon's Blog,* wrote to me that Glenn Reynolds and Andrew Sullivan (whose blog, the *Daily Dish,* advocates "gay rights as well as conservatism") "do a lot of ridiculing of opponents, some of it facile, some of it ad hominem," but he too thinks that "angry" is the wrong adjective. Millman is not especially a fan of either blog. He characterizes Reynolds' and Sullivan's styles as "lazy and generally unenlightening. But angry? Contemptuous is better, maybe." And he ventures a generalization: "Yes, I think bloggers are overly contemptuous of political opponents."

Millman, however, strongly defends the spirit of blogging. He is drawn to the "more reflective and quirky writers in the blogosphere," and his own blog, begun in the wake of 9/11, exhibits sensibilities closer to Mr. Pickwick than to Mt. Vesuvius. He is "not sure [blogging] contributes to an angry culture," he says in response to a question from me, nor even that "the critical takedown of an opponent" that is "the classic blogosphere form" is best viewed as an expression of anger.

Millman's distinction between anger and contempt is helpful. Since he sent these comments to me in 2004, I would say that Sullivan has more clearly moved into a quadrant of the angri-culture, while Reynolds has more and more become an advocate for civility, although it is civility with a curt edge. In a recent *Washington Post* online discussion, Reynolds expressed his weariness with the screamers:

> My own sense is that it's very hard to preserve civility—or even a good ratio of interestingness to flaming—on sites that have high traffic without a fair degree of moderation. There's some sort of a threshold after which things tend to break down into USENET-style flamewars, which some people like, but which I'm tired of. I find the comments on Atrios, Kos, or for that matter Little Green Footballs, to be tiresome.[19]

Sullivan, a onetime supporter of President Bush who turned against him largely because of Bush's opposition to gay marriage, has acquired an often-venomous tone, though his blog still ranks (January 2006) as the 24th most visited.

The other main conservative blogs (*Powerline, Little Green Footballs, Michelle Malkin, The Corner, Hugh Hewitt*) tend toward testy with occasional outcries of anger, but not the blow-a-fuse anger of John McEnroe, nor the biographical anger of rap singers and self-empowering feminists, nor the boiling rage of the Deaniacs—though they too were a blog-based phenomenon.

Perhaps the dominant form of political blogging in general (left and right) is a sassy, hyperarticulate belittling of one's opponents. The blogger's rhetorical stance is one of self-confident control over the facts and sneering disregard for the intelligence and honesty of those he criticizes. Bloggers who work in this vein can and do moderate their tone, but when they take hold of a topic that riles them, the moderation vanishes.

As the *Wall Street Journal* writer John Fund observes, "Blogs attract high-profile readers in media and politics," and thus can prove unexpectedly influential. Fund cites the 2002 flurry of blogging about the racial remarks by Senator Trent Lott[20] that led to his resignation as Senate majority leader; bloggers' attention to the efforts by Lieutenant-Governor Bustamante of California to circumvent campaign finance laws in the 2003 gubernatorial race, which threw his candidacy into a tailspin; and Howard Dean's *Blog for America,* which attracted 100,000 visitors a day at its peak. Bloggers, according to Fund, also managed to get under the skin of Randell Beck, editor of the *Sioux Falls Argus Leader,* which had the habit of offering uncritical support to Senator Tom Daschle. Beck denounced bloggers for "their nutty opinions," which, he lamented, play "a pivotal role in creating the polarized climate that dominates debate on nearly every national issue.... If Hitler were alive today, he'd have his own blog."

Millman or Beck: who is closer to the truth? Are blogs peripheral to the angri-culture or one of its underlying sources? I don't know of a sure way to answer this question, but I suspect that blogs play a pretty substantial role in crystallizing communities of opinion in the United States. As many observers have pointed out, blogging circumvents the old custodians of acceptable opinion. In the debate about gay marriage, the *New York Times* long declined even to mention— let alone cover—the secular arguments and scholarly studies that focused on how same-sex registered partnerships in Scandinavia and gay marriage in the Netherlands had helped to dampen the interest of young heterosexuals in getting married. Other newspapers followed suit, with the result that the only way most Americans could even know about this significant part of the debate was through exchanges on the Internet, highlighted by the bloggers, including the pro–gay marriage Andrew Sullivan. Without a doubt, the *Drudge Report,* a portal, played a crucial role in galvanizing opposition to President Clinton in the year before his impeachment. The veterans who, in August 2004, attacked Senator Kerry's Vietnam record likewise relied heavily on blogging to back up their claims. As the blogger Dean Esmay put it:

What's been most stunning about the Vets' story, however, is
not their allegations, but the fact that this group has been
able to completely bypass the mainstream media. Even more
stunning, when Kerry-friendly newspapers have launched
attacks on them, they have been able to attack back, answering charges, pointing out where they feel they've been
misquoted or misrepresented, and answering their accusers
point-by-point—and they have not had to rely on sympa-
thetic reporters and editors to get their message out. Just a
web page, and a host of citizen journalists (i.e. "webloggers")
to point their message out.[21]

Esmay smiles in satisfaction that "the *New York Times*, the
Washington Post, the *Los Angeles Times*, and the *Boston Globe* are
no longer the arbiters of what's important and what's not; of
whose criticisms of our politicians will be heard and whose will
be ignored. The Internet has detected the mainstream media as
a form of censorship and simply routed around them."

This particular power of bloggers became unmistakable
in September 2004, when Dan Rather aired a report on CBS
News based on four documents that allegedly showed that
George W. Bush had used political pressure to win release
from his National Guard duties in August 1973. By the next
morning—September 9—four bloggers, including John Hin-
deraker at *Powerline* and Bill Ardolina at the *INDC Journal*
blog, were busy examining the documents and serving as collection points for the efforts of hundreds of others who
doubted the documents' authenticity. Charles Johnson, who
is the man behind *Little Green Footballs,* delivered the coup de
grâce to the CBS story with a careful analysis of typefaces.
CBS initially stonewalled, and a former CBS vice president,
Jonathan Klein, declared on *The O'Reilly Factor* on FOX: "You
couldn't have a starker contrast between the multiple layers
of checks and balances [at *60 Minutes*] and a guy sitting in his
living room in his pajamas writing."

Klein's sneer at the bloggers came back to haunt CBS.
The guys in the pajamas had the story right, and it had taken
them only hours to unmask a fraud that CBS, for all its
resources, hadn't seen through. The network attempted to
ease its way out of the situation. Dan Rather headed into

retirement. Mary Mapes, the CBS News producer who had obtained the fraudulent documents, was fired, and other CBS executives resigned. CBS News apologized to its viewers.

The moral of the story: the mainstream media, like CBS, could no longer trust that they defined the news. The sleepy men in pajamas toiling away in the blogosphere could and would hold people like Dan Rather accountable for factitious stories.

Blogging works for both the left and the right by connecting people to discussions that capture their imaginations. Blogs draw attention to real and sometimes important information, but more importantly they put that information in the context of emotionalized opposition. The best example of this is the form of skeptical analysis called *fisking*, named after Robert Fisk, a reporter for the left-wing British newspaper *The Independent*. In the late 1990s, some of Fisk's British critics began to speak satirically of *fisking* in reference to Fisk's habit of leaving out of his stories information that didn't support his anti-U.S., anti-Israel biases. But the word took on an entirely new meaning to American bloggers after Fisk was beaten and stoned by Afghan refugees in Pakistan in early December 2001.

Fisk immediately wrote a story about the assault, blaming it on American air strikes in Afghanistan, which he said had angered the refugees (from the Taliban!), who were also outraged by what they had seen on television of "the Mazar-i-Sharif massacres," meaning the American assault on the Taliban prison and fort. All in all, Fisk decided that stoning a random Westerner wasn't a bad idea, even if it happened to be himself. Even as stones were smashing "to my face and head" and blood obscured his sight, "even then, I understood. I couldn't blame them for what they were doing."[22]

Fisk's attempt to justify his stoning as a spontaneous anti-Bush protest caught the eye of Andrew Sullivan, who in his blog, the *Daily Dish*, took Fisk's account apart as a "classic piece of leftist pathology." Quoting several sentences from Fisk at a time, Sullivan inserted his own ripostes. Here are two examples:

> *Fisk:* "I couldn't blame them for what they were doing. In fact, if I were the Afghan refugees of Kila Abdullah, close to the Afghan-Pakistan border, I would have done just the same to Robert Fisk. Or any other Westerner I could find."
>
> *Sullivan:* "What does this mean, you might well ask? What it means is that someone—anyone—is either innocent or guilty purely by racial or cultural association. An average Westerner is to be taken as an emblem of an entire culture and treated as such."
>
> *Fisk:* "Goddamit, I said and tried to bang my fist on my side until I realized it was bleeding from a big gash on the wrist—the mark of the tooth I had just knocked out of a man's jaw, a man who was truly innocent of any crime except that of being the victim of the world."
>
> *Sullivan:* "No, Mr. Fisk, that man who attacked you was not truly innocent of any crime. You were. He was not the victim of the world. You were the victim of a thieving, violent mob. For those who believe that the left-wing intelligentsia is capable of critical thought or even a modification of their ideology in the face of evidence, this incident is a wonderful example of why it won't happen."[23]

Sullivan was far from the first to adopt this procedure of dissecting a story and answering its points *ad seriatim*, but his demolition of Fisk's pretentious exculpation of his Afghan assailants gave bloggers their new word. As Linda Seebach put it, *fisking* is "line by line exegesis of idiocy," named after "journalist Robert Fisk, who often deserves it."

Fisking is now a widely practiced technique. Done well, it can be a tight and illuminating form of argument. Or, as is all too often the case, it can amount to a blur of tangential points, nitpicking corrections, and snide comments. Done well or poorly, it is still a little like setting upon a journalist with a pile of rocks. The object of *fisking* is, for the moment, entirely under the control of a hostile party who can tear his prose limb from limb—and make jokes about it as he goes along.

The targets of this kind of blogging may well deserve their fates, but it is still a mean business. And like other forms of the proud maliciousness around us, it both draws its warrant from the angri-culture and extends the possibilities of performative malice.

But blogging has one more dimension that breathes even more fire into the angri-culture. The heavily visited left-wing *Eschaton* blog by Atrios is notorious for its angry and often obscene language. Atrios recently stepped back and, in one of his calmer moments, explained, "Why We Say 'Fuck' a Lot." He said he is driven to it by sheer frustration:

> The problem really is that no matter how many times we try to kill right wing horseshit (or as Media Matters delicately calls it, "conservative misinformation") it keeps coming back to haunt us. It infects the media bloodstream. We politely ask for corrections. They don't happen. We start screaming for corrections. They still don't happen. Eventually some half-assed weaselly blame-the-uncivil-critics statement is released. We scream louder. And, then, the horeshit pops up again on CNN.... Major newspaper has big megaphone. Readers generally have no megaphone. Journalists have responsibilities and these ethics I keep hearing about, including the responsibility not to be as factfree as they keep claiming blogs are. When you explain, calmly and repeatedly, that 2+2=4 and they keep denying it you get a little mad. Civil behavior isn't about restraining from insults or obscenities, it's about behaving like a fucking decent human being.

The German word *Rechthaberei,* which refers to the attitude "I'm right and everyone else is wrong," may describe part of what gives Atrios and bloggers like him their distinct flavor of mad rationality. If at first you fail to convince your adversary, why then, what could be more rational than to have a screaming fit? The comments by Atrios resonated with other Angry Left bloggers, including "Wally" at *Wally Whateley's House of Horrors,* who added:

> Once again, when you force a huge chunk of the population to be voiceless and powerless, when you ignore their concerns and lie almost constantly, you can expect those people to get angrier and angrier and angrier. The issue shouldn't be "Why do those uncouth liberals say swears?" but "Why is the fucking media so goddamn fucking awful?"

The most heavily trafficked blog of all is the *Daily Kos* (dailykos.com), written and managed by Markos Moulitsas Zuniga. As of January 2006, the *Daily Kos* was receiving over

642,000 visits per day. Most of the site consists of "open threads," in which "Kos" presents a short essay and then invites visitors to post their own views in response. The *Daily Kos* has become a magnet for the Angry Left, in which a seemingly endless parade of I-hate-America, I-despise-Bush, liberals-are-too-wimpy & we-need-to-turn-up-the-heat diatribes roll out hour after hour. The *Daily Kos* is the Internet furnace in which New Anger is continuously forged.

It is tempting to dismiss it as the extreme fringe of the political left, except that Moulitsas has achieved mainstream respectability. Recently John Kerry guest-blogged on the site, and, as the *Washington Monthly* puts it, Moulitsas is now treated by the Democratic establishment as the avenue to "the party's young, liberal, professional grassroots.... [He] has become so well incorporated into the party machinery that the Democratic Congressional Campaign Committee uses him to recruit candidates."[24] He gets regular calls from Senate Democratic leader Harry Reid.

Moulitsas speaks about himself in a manner very similar to the self-loathing statements of John McEnroe and Bode Miller: "Everybody says I'm an asshole, and they're right, I am." At times, he seems truly intent on proving that he has no sense of civility or shame. Perhaps most famously, when four American contractors were murdered, burned, and dismembered in Fallujah in June 2003, and a mob dragged their corpses through the street, Moulitsas commented, "I feel nothing.... Screw them." Asked in the *Washington Monthly* interview how he sees the matter now, "His mouth stretched into a smile: 'Vindicated,' he said."

Long-time-listener-first-time-caller

If blogging is the hot new medium where the left's anger is most conspicuous, talk radio is the hot old medium where the right's anger far and away dominates. It does so, first, because conservative talk shows vastly outnumber liberal and leftist talk shows; and second, because many of the conservative talk shows are, in essence, forums for airing conservative complaints about liberal government programs, leftist ideology, and what conservatives see as their exclusion from mainstream culture.

The Internet is open to anyone who cares to create a blog. The entry costs are minimal and, if a blog fails to attract readers, it is up to the blogger whether to continue the effort. Radio, however, *has* to attract an audience to survive. And this, according to William G. Mayer, a professor of political science at Northeastern University, explains why most talk radio stations are conservative. He argues in a recent article that survey data consistently show that conservatives outnumber liberals in the general population. Mayer reviewed 134 distinct surveys conducted between January 2002 and August 2003 by ten different polling organizations, and all of them showed large conservative majorities in the United States. The average margin of conservatives to liberals was 1.8 to 1.[25] Thus a medium that depends on attracting a mass audience has, according to Mayer, a built-in tendency to focus on programs that appeal to conservatives.

Why then do the major television networks, with the exception of FOX, all gravitate to the liberal/left side of the political spectrum? Mayer offers no explanation of this, but he does take the "perceived" liberal domination of television and other mass media as the spur that drives conservatives to talk radio. Because conservatives believe that the mainstream media are biased against them, they have turned, for over twenty-five years, to radio as a source of political community. The spur is strong. One survey found that 68 percent of Republicans in 1996 viewed the mainstream media as having a bias in favor of the Democrats. Only 7 percent of Democrats believed the opposite: that the mainstream media favor Republicans. As Mayer put it, "Liberals...do not need talk radio: They have Dan Rather, Peter Jennings, and Tom Brokaw—not to mention NPR."

Well, scratch Rather and Jennings. Liberals still have CBS, ABC, NBC, NPR, the *New York Times,* the *Washington Post,* and so on.

Nonetheless, the political left has long envied conservative domination of talk radio and has sought to establish its own popular radio programs. One after another, these attempts have failed due to low ratings. John Hightower, Mario Cuomo, Gary Hart, and Alan Dershowitz each had a short-lived radio talk program that was promoted at first as the liberal answer to Rush Limbaugh, but then fizzled. The newest attempt, Air America, launched in March 2004, is still on the air but has so far failed to attract the hoped-for mass audience.

Why? Well, perhaps Mayer is right that the *potential* mass audience just doesn't exist, and such audience as might exist is less motivated to tune in, since liberal views are already on the air over on NPR and the TV networks—and now on the blogs. But Mayer has one more illuminating suggestion. He wonders if the left's reliance on identity politics to build its base of support undermines the effort to build a mass audience for a single radio network. *Diversity* may be a successful rallying cry for conventions, but emphasizing the particularity of a category of people tends to foster insular tastes:

> Take blacks as an example. On paper at least, blacks ought to be a key constituency for liberal talk radio. On most issues, they are perhaps the most consistently liberal group in America.... But will blacks actually listen to a liberal talk station on a regular basis? Some will, of course. But others will probably spend most of their radio time listening to a more explicitly black-oriented station on another part of the dial— a station that will probably have its own black-hosted talk show, along with music, sports, and religious programming.

As with African Americans, so with other reliably Democratic constituencies.

The conservative domination of talk radio is not just a matter of a few outstanding figures such as Rush Limbaugh, Sean Hannity, and Laura Schlessinger, who command huge audiences. Their audiences are vastly bigger than those of any blogger. Limbaugh draws an average of 14.5 million (spring 2003 figures); Hannity, 11.75 million; Schlessinger, 8.5 million. Talk radio is also a medium that has grown from about 75 shows in 1980 to about 1,400 in 2004, when Mayer was writing. A 2002 Gallup survey found that 22 percent of Americans listen to talk radio every day, and 61 percent listen at least occasionally.

Mayer attempted to classify radio programs as conservative, liberal, moderate, and nonideological: "Of the top twenty-eight talk radio programs in Spring 2003, eleven—including four of the top five—were hosted by outspoken, undisguised conservatives." And the conservative domination continued down the list. Mayer found that there are some liberal talk shows that prosper, but they are typically small-audience local broadcasts.

Mayer's analysis gives a pretty compelling explanation of why conservatives dominate talk shows, but not why conservative talk shows tend to be angry. Talk radio often seems to be a magnet for traditionally minded folk to sound off about their grievances against liberal government programs, leftist or progressive ideologies, and whatever is playing at the moment in movie theaters. Often it seems as if the people Nixon called "the silent majority," upon hearing that label, decided to devote the rest of their lives to correcting the misimpression.

But the anger on display on conservative talk radio often fits the category of New Anger—or at least a subdivision of New Anger that would prefer to be old anger but can't quite recover the old restraint. It is New Anger with a guilty conscience. Unlike the bloggers, especially the people who post their screeds to the *Daily Kos* and such Angry Left sites, many of the callers on talk radio don't want to pronounce anathemas on their enemies or demonstrate their own innate superiority. But many indeed are eager to sound off against the left, and the hosts of some of these programs encourage that kind of histrionics.

I trust that the reader can fill in his own examples. My experience as a guest on over a hundred call-in radio programs is that the anger of those callers who appeared to be angry had an oddly tentative quality, as if they were seeking permission and hoping for a small nod of approval. The conservative hosts of these programs usually began segments with a small provocation. I had written a book, *Diversity*, in which I dissented from the campus orthodoxy on the topic. Many of the talk radio hosts asked for examples of how I had been ill treated because of the book. But I encountered no such ill treatment on my own campus and only some self-defeating rudeness on a few others. The most agile hosts quickly shifted to asking about ideas rather than grievances. A few, however, having been denied the bloody shirt, didn't seem to know what to do next.

I also found that the talk show hosts dearly hope that a guest will say something that will light up the phones. They know that one small segment of their audience consists of liberals who listen to get annoyed, and they treasure the moment when one of these listeners calls to dispute a point. During a commercial break, one host in Utah was delighted to tell me that I had prompted a call from "Tom," an argumentative lefty who could be relied on to stir up conservative callers. As it happened, he did.

Anger is fuel to these exchanges, but most talk radio burns at moderate heat: more like a bonfire of fall leaves than the acetylene torch of Internet *fisking* or other such blog-based takedowns. Partly this is the nature of the medium. Radio has to sustain the attention or at least a sliver of the attention of its listeners continuously. Mere fury can't sustain that level of interest. The Internet, by contrast, allows people to set their own pace, scroll past the epithets, linger there among the damned, or seek still hotter circles of the Inferno. Excesses of anger among the blogs are little monuments to *self* that we can admire or ignore as we please—a more difficult task with radio, but not impossible.

Some conservative talk radio does venture into the territory of hard rant, but that is territory more commonly occupied by "shock jocks" such as Howard Stern (now on the subscriber-only satellite radio network Sirius; 7.75 million listeners) and Don Imus (2.75 million listeners). Stern's angry performances were an on-and-off matter of his disputes with the Federal Communications Commission over his broadcast of obscenities. When it served his purposes, he mounted strenuous defenses of the First Amendment, before retreating to his stock mixture of potty jokes and interviews with porn actresses and exotic dancers.

Imus has a different niche. He is notorious for "flamboyant outrageousness," as Buzz Bissinger put it in a recent profile in *Vanity Fair.*[26] Over his forty-plus-year career, however, he moved away from annoying stunts like calling up "a local McDonald's posing as a sergeant to something called the International Guard" and ordering "1,200 hamburgers for his soldiers." By the early 1990s, he had beaten back alcoholism and a cocaine habit, retired some of the shock-jock persona, and begun to play for political influence. Bissinger says the pundits credit him with "a pivotal role in guest Bill Clinton's victory in the New York presidential primary." His guests these days include mainstream figures such as Tim Russert, Andrea Mitchell, and Senators Joe Biden and John McCain.

Imus nonetheless maintains his reputation for on-air cruelty and gratuitous nastiness toward people he doesn't like. On November 12, 2004, he referred to Palestinians during an on-air conversation with his sports anchor, Sid Rosenberg:

Imus: They're [Palestinians] eating dirt and that fat pig wife [Suha Arafat] of his is living in Paris.

Rosenberg: They're all brainwashed, though. That's what it is. And they're stupid to begin with, but they're brainwashed now. Stinking animals. They ought to drop the bomb right there, kill 'em all right now.

Bernard McGuirk (producer): You can just imagine standing there.

Rosenberg: Oh, the stench!

Imus: Well, the problem is that we have Andrea [Mitchell, NBC News chief foreign affairs correspondent] there. We don't want anything to happen to her.

Rosenberg: Oh, she's got to get out. Just warn Andrea, get out, and then drop the bomb, kill everybody.[27]

This provoked a complaint by the Canadian Radio-television and Telecommunications Commission, though seemingly the FCC took it in stride.[28]

Imus has also made a hobby of sorts out of picking on

individuals to whom he has taken some kind of personal dislike. Nothing much more than that seemed to lie behind his
attack on the MSNBC newsreader Contessa Brewer on April
29, 2005: "That skank has to spend three hours with makeup
in the morning.... That's why they have those big double-
doors there at MSNBC, you know, so they can get her fat ass
in makeup."[29]

Insults of this sort are, presumably, meant as a kind of
humor. A clever insult is indeed recognized as one vein of
American humor, and we have had a whole genre of stand-up
comedians (Don Rickles, Andrew Dice Clay, Dennis Miller,
et al.) whose act consists of dexterous insults and denunciations that go right up to the line of what an audience will
accept. But Imus's insults, like his attack on Brewer, are a
crude approximation of this technique. They seem instead
to convey genuine disgust and to contain malicious pleasure,
which puts Imus, I think, pretty squarely in the camp of the
Newly Angry. It is the show-off anger of a man too weary
with life to care what he says, but still enamored with himself. As Bissinger puts it, he brandishes his mean-spiritedness
"at the expense of others for a moment's amusement."

Stern and Imus provide anger as part of their radio personae, but it is only now and then political anger. Stern has
attempted to link himself to Bush-hatred in recent years;
Imus finds his political favorites on the basis of his own
whims. New Anger, being primarily a performance, can perform on behalf of politics, but it is always more "about me"
than about some vision of the public good.

The most successful hosts, such as Limbaugh, are masters of comic tone and timing. Limbaugh tells stories and
reads from articles with exactly the right pauses and intona-
tions to suggest a much richer picture than the words alone
convey. The words themselves are sometimes as provocative
as Imus's. He spoke at one point of American Indians, for
example, as "meaner to themselves than anybody was ever
mean to them. The people were savages. It's true, they damn
well were.... These people were out there destroying timber,
they were out there conquering and killing each other, scalp-

ing people." This is, of course the tone of the debunker, rather than that of seething anger, but it is clearly intended as much to needle those who dwell on the injustices of Euro-American conquest as it is to offer a counter-reading of history. It worked: Jose Barreiro, among others, rose to attack Limbaugh for his "Bigotshtick," as he titled a 1995 essay on Limbaugh's attitude toward Native Americans.[30]

Limbaugh possesses what even most of his critics admit is virtuosity as a speaker. He is, of course, despised by the left—but more as a purveyor of bigotry and an expert at cheap shots than as someone who himself is angry. The left-ist humorist Al Franken's bestselling *Rush Limbaugh Is a Big Fat Idiot, and Other Observations* (1997) has itself a New Anger quality, with a title that aims to say more about the audacity of the author than the substance of his criticisms.

Molly Ivins preceded Franken to the task in 1995 with an article, "Lyin' Bully," in the far-left magazine *Mother Jones*. Ivins began with a lament for what Limbaugh had done to the nation's civility: "One of the things that concerns a lot of Americans lately is the increase in plain old nastiness in our political discussion. It comes from a number of sources, but Rush Limbaugh is a major carrier."[31] In the spirit of overcoming that nastiness, Ivins gently reproved him: "I object because he consistently targets dead people, little girls, and the homeless—none of whom are in a particularly good position to answer back."

Sarcastic comedians trading barbs across the political divide in America, however, is pretty much business as usual, and need not detain us further. In a way, both Ivins and Limbaugh belong to a past which, though it could be rambunctiously offensive, is nothing like what we have now.

Daylight

The emotional ambiance of a society is, like daylight, both obvious and difficult to describe. This book has been an attempt to capture the changing light over America as we have moved from a society that generally disapproved of anger to a society in which anger is freely displayed and socially rewarded.

While working on the preceding chapters during the summer of 2004, I sometimes found myself walking home after dark while the Red Sox were battling out the American League season at Fenway Park. From a few blocks away, the ball park was a silent crater of brilliant white light. But if a Sox batter hit one, Fenway erupted in a roar of approval that made the stream of light seem an expression of joy. The roar—and the joy—might last a second or two and end in a moan (a fly caught in the outfield), or might suddenly jump in intensity or sustain itself until it died out in a few last cheers.

The cheers said a lot about the mood of the crowd, but weren't a very good way to tell the score. Likewise, it is fairly easy to see that America has become a place where anger is commonly and openly expressed, but very difficult to say what the exact consequences of this are. Does it contribute to the high rate of divorce? Does it swell our flood of lawsuits? Is it a factor in violent crime? Or is anger just a fact unto itself, like the blood-red sunset or a slate-gray afternoon?

I suspect that a society awash in anger is also drenched in real-world consequences of fatherless children, frivolous litigation, needless automobile accidents, and rage that escalates to violence. But this book has not been about that suspicion. Rather, I have tried to look at our abundant anger for what it is, to discern its distinctive qualities and to figure out the shifts that have made expressing anger seem not only acceptable but, to many, attractive.

These shifts, I have argued, are mainly cultural, in the anthropological sense of involving shared ideas and assumptions. We have not suddenly become more prone to anger than our forebears; we have only become less interested in repressing the anger that is an inevitable part of human nature. Nor have we suddenly found ourselves in a social world that has massively escalated the aggravations and obstacles that provide the occasions for anger. In practical terms, our lives are probably much less crossed by adversity and stress than generations past. We have merely opened ourselves to a greater possibility of railing against the innumerable annoyances of existence.

In 1849 a New England clergyman named John Mitchell (1794–1870) published a memoir, *My Mother, or Recollections of Maternal Influence,* in which he attempted to sift from his childhood the most enduring moral lessons. Among these was his mother's self-control:

> She never lost her temper with us. I have heard her say that she was naturally quick, and somewhat violent, in her resentments, but that the feeling of anger was so painful to her that she set herself to correct it; and such was the self-control she early acquired, by God's assistance, that, from the time of her professing religion, I presume no one ever saw the least appearance of anger in her, under whatever provocation. Such self-command is a great matter in the governing of children.

Mitchell, of course, may have idealized his mother's success, but the ideals themselves are perfectly clear—and worlds away from the expressive individualism that predominates today.

The picture that Mitchell paints of his mother, however, is more than a parade of pious generalities. The family endures smallpox, impoverishment, and discord. But smaller incidents perhaps reveal a great deal more about the ordinary emotional dynamics of the house. Once, as a child, Mitchell lost his temper at a maid who had crowded his tiny room with an extra piece of furniture. "Who keeps putting that plaguy chair between the bed and my trunk?" His mother ironically commands the maid not to "inconvenience" her son; at which point he:

> felt ashamed, went and restored the chair to its place, reflecting once for all, that there were others besides [myself] whose convenience was to be regarded, and the comfort of all, are to be promoted by each member, though at some sacrifice of individual convenience.

On another occasion, Mitchell, his older brother, and a visiting cousin sit in the yard watching the bees one summer afternoon and are taken with the idea of overturning one of the hives. They think the bees will fly away and they will then be able to help themselves to the honey. Mitchell pushes the hive over and the bees swarm out: "It was we that flew away, and not the bees." His mother rushes out and sets the hive aright without getting stung, but expresses no anger at the three boys, whom she trusts to draw their own conclusions. Mitchell adds:

> Do you know that bees have a special antipathy to some people, and will sting them almost unprovoked, while others can do any thing with them with impunity. She was one of their favorites, as they were hers.

Mitchell's book, which was printed in a few thousand copies and then seemingly forgotten, sums up the older tradition of suppressing anger. His mother (who is never named; he published the memoir anonymously) is presented as devout but "nothing novel or extraordinary," and suggests that "the wisdom and experience of those in the ordinary walks of life" are most likely to help others. He thus offers the memoir to a young woman to aid her "in the discharge of your own responsible duties as a mother."[32]

The attitude toward anger that Mitchell portrays as ordinary at the beginning of the nineteenth century remains alive in America to this day—but only in sectarian communities and isolated families here and there. It is not the attitude at play in *The Family Guy, South Park, American Pie,* or many another TV sitcom or magazine article, satirical or serious, that purports to represent typical American life. For mainstream America, anger has been thoroughly repackaged, repriced, and sold at volume discount. Mrs. Mitchell may have found the feeling of anger "painful." Today, more find that feeling empowering.

The consequence of our revaluation of anger is plain: we have to live in a culture in which many of the people around us act out their sense of entitled rage; their belief that they cannot be authentically themselves unless they feel their anger *and* give it voice; and their idea that their vision of the world can be brought to pass by sheer assertion of wrath. To live in a culture like this is to endure a lot of unnecessary noise and vexation. Very little of the rage, the verbal vehemence, and nasty attitudinizing means anything important. The people who succumb to it diminish themselves and often corrode their relations with family and friends. Contrary to one of the cultural premises behind New Anger, it is not empowering in any longer-term sense. A short-term tyranny may be gratifying in one's relationships, but like any other tyranny, it leads nowhere.

The same is true of anger on the larger political stage. New Anger inhabits not just the individual lives of millions of Americans, but the collective lives of our parties and ideological coalitions. The angri-culture grew in the last half-century far more from the cultural ambitions of progressives on the left than from those of traditionalists on the right. And New Anger at the moment is most conspicuous on the left, in the forms of Bush-hating, secularist aversion to religious expression, and the depiction of cultural opponents as backward and stupid. But cultural forces, once unleashed, seldom remain confined to the original partisans, and New Anger has found a home among traditionalists as well, including Clinton-haters, parts of the right-to-life movement, and some conservative bloggers.

I don't, however, want to conjure a false symmetry between the anger of the left and that of the right. At the moment, the left is far and away angrier. Markos Moulitsas speaks for many who believe it should get even angrier. He represents, as his *Washington Monthly* interviewer put it, "an unending belief in the triumphal capacities of the right kind of theatrics." He is not alone. Byron York's book *The Vast Left Wing Conspiracy* (2005) offers a gallery of political figures animated by such theatrical anger, among them Zack Exley (creator of the website AngryDems.org, originator of bumper stickers with slogans such as "GW Bush, Not a Crackhead Anymore," and a key employee of MoveOn.org during the last presidential election) and Mark Crispin Miller, a professor of "media ecology" at New York University who managed to convince a fair number of Democrats that President Bush intended, upon reelection, to establish an Old Testament theocracy in the United States, complete with the stoning of adulterers and heretics.

Some Americans have always been prey to outlandish conspiracy theories, but it is hard to think of a time in our history when conspiracy theory, stewed with livid anger, has become so central to a major political party. New Anger is by no means a monopoly of the political left, but the political right in the United States has not permitted its angriest and most ungrounded figures to have anywhere near the influence that the left has accorded its *Daily Kos* and MoveOn.org partisans.

When the satisfactions of expressing anger become a motive that outweighs the plain disadvantages of venting one's dissatisfactions, we are in the territory of New Anger— our distinctive cultural form of an old emotion. New Anger prefers to boil rather than simmer; to count to one rather than to ten; and to preen itself on its cleverness. New Anger does not regret that it has brushed aside Old Caution; rather it views that shrug as a magnificent display of strength. New Anger sees political division as an opportunity, not a failure. It simultaneously feeds the left's sense of righteous indignation and the right's sense of being unable, despite all its political gains, to stop the vulgarization of American culture and the erosion of American values. Its counsel makes both left and right act foolishly. But follies committed out of New Anger never worry the Newly Angry, who exculpate themselves by returning to the fight less in sorrow than in even more intense anger.

The grievances of the Newly Angry are often vague and elastic. Appease one and it will expand to include more. New Anger feels liberating; it is exhibitionist and theatrical, even as it lodges deep claims to authenticity. Is theatricality consistent with authenticity? No matter. Somewhere in New Anger is a thirst for revenge, and it takes an unseemly delight in the prospect. Michael Datcher, writing in *San Francisco*

Focus in 1992 in response to the Rodney King riots, presented a letter he had written to a friend on April 29, thirteen minutes after the judge had read the not-guilty verdict for the police officers accused of unlawfully beating King. Datcher wrote:

> I know there will be riots in the streets of L.A. tonight. I know people will die tonight. I want them to be white people, Kevin. I want white people to die, and experience injustice. To experience the land of equality like we experience it.[33]

New Anger consists not just in Datcher's *feeling* these things or even in his saying them in the heat of the moment to his friend. Rather, New Anger is most fully visible in his choosing to keep that letter and to publish it months later, and then to republish it years afterward in a collection of African American statements on "self-discovery."

Some selves, once discovered, should appall us. That they no longer do is a reason to worry.

RUN! RUN! RUN!

The *Florida Sun Sentinel* recently reported that the long-anticipated invasion of Africanized honeybees has reached the Sunshine State. In 2005, killer bees swarmed meter readers in St. Lucia County. They have killed two dogs and a horse, and have been found from Palm Beach to Disney World. They generally attack their victims by stinging the nostrils and mouth. Jerry Hayes, assistant chief of apiary inspection, however, is taking it in stride. Though the bees have killed over a thousand people since they buzzed out of a Brazilian lab in 1957, Florida already has so many exotic dangers that one more makes little difference. "We live in a state that has fire ants that actually kill people," says Hayes, who also mentions scorpions, spiders, and boa constrictors.

I am not so reassured. One of my neighbors in Vermont hauls his bees to Florida each winter. In the summer, he keeps them in a rusted-out minivan with holes in the side—a step he took after bears raided his hives once too often. I would just as soon that he leave all the Africanized honeybees down in Florida to keep company with the fire ants.

The trouble is that angry bees are pretty hard to avoid. The best advice that Arizona officials have come up with after several years of dealing with these bees is: "RUN! RUN! RUN!"[34]

ACKNOWLEDGMENTS

My thanks to Peter Collier, my former editor, first for indulging my interest in this topic at a time when it may not have seemed too promising, and second for his critical finesse in marking up successive drafts. My thanks also to my current editor, Roger Kimball, who astutely guided the text to its final form.

I am grateful to Jamie Gass and Keith Whitaker for their close reading of numerous drafts and their good counsel. Jamie was especially helpful with early American and colonial politics. Keith kept me mindful of older and larger philosophical debates about the passions.

I am indebted to Stanley Kurtz for his sustained interest in the manuscript. The main arguments of *A Bee in the Mouth* were shaped by many years of discussion between us on the nature of America's culture war and the best ways for social scientists to analyze and account for the emotional dispositions that are characteristic of social groups. Stanley also brought to my attention important articles and incidents that may otherwise have escaped my notice.

Some of the texture of the book derives from Joanne Evans, who kept a keen eye on the press and on the Web for anger stories, considerably extending the reach of my own search for luminous details.

My former colleague Professor Charles Lindholm of the Boston University Anthropology Department also read an early version of the manuscript and offered a helpful critique from the perspective of psychological anthropology. My dear friend and sage guide Edwin Delattre read portions of the manuscript and offered very helpful advice on anger in relation to the concept of the self. I am grateful to Paul Henderson, research and program director of the Maxim Institute in New Zealand. Some parts of the argument crystallized while I was fly-fishing with Paul. Stan Oakes, president of The King's College, read an early draft of the book and helped me sharpen my analysis of the selfishness of uncontrolled anger. I am also grateful for Stan's encouragement.

I am indebted to Benjamin Wood for his help on several parts of the "Anger Music" chapter. I am also indebted to "Methuselah," a young rap enthusiast who prefers not to be identified by his real name. Methuselah's assistance was invaluable in the section on the Wu-Tang Clan.

To Ingrid Wood, my thanks for the extraordinary care with which she read and critiqued the manuscript. Ingrid's imaginative annexes to the original argument prompted me to explore several key areas I had not at first reckoned with. I am also grateful to Ingrid for the "Furious George" photograph that appears on the dust jacket.

NOTES

Preface

1. Chris Rodkey, "Ben & Jerry's Co-Founder Inflamed by Bush," *Seattle Post-Intelligencer,* July 20, 2004.

2. Adam Nagourney, "Calling Senator Clinton 'Angry,' G.O.P. Chairman Attacks," *New York Times,* February 6, 2006, p. A16.
    Margaret Carlson, "Republicans' 'Angry Hillary' Ploy Won't Work," *Bloomberg.com,* February 9, 2006.

3. Beth Fouhy, "GOP's 'Anger' Strategy Has Dems Defensive," Associated Press, February 8, 2006.

4. Kim Ode, "We'll Be Gone, But Memories—and Records—Will Linger On," *Minneapolis Star Tribune,* January 5, 2003, p. E2.
    "Man Is Killed by Bee; Victim Staggers into City Street and Collapses," *Herald* (Glasgow), August 15, 1997, p. 7.
    Jane Van Der Voort, "Her Special Sister" (review of *My Sister from the Black Lagoon*), *Toronto Sun,* January 16, 2000, p. C8.
    Rita Zekas, "Candyman 2: Just a Hive of Activity," *Toronto Star,* January 27, 1995, p. C2.

5. Ambrose, *Offices,* Chapter 5.

6. "A Brief History of St. Ambrose Parish," http://www.geocities.com/ambrose_parish/history.html

7. See, for example, Carol Tavris, *Anger: The Misunderstood Emotion* (1982; New York: Touchstone Books, 1989), pp. 101–27.
    Glenn R. Schiraldi and Melissa Hallmark Kerr, *The Anger Management Sourcebook* (New York: McGraw Hill, 2002), pp. 277–83.
    Matthew McKay, Peter D. Rogers, Judith McKay, *When Anger Hurts: Quieting the Storm Within* (Oakland, California: New Harbinger Publications, 1989), pp. 28–31.
    Kristin Nelson, "Feeing Angry? Good for You!" Women's

Bioethics Project, November 30, 2005, http://womensbioethics. blogspot.com/2005/11/feeling-angry-good-for-you.html

Chapter One: Angri-Culture

[1] "Postal Worker Charged in Death of Postmaster," *New York Times*, December 3, 1983, p. A8.

Karl Vick, "Violence at Work Tied to Loss of Esteem," *St. Petersburg Times*, December 17, 1993, p. A1.

On January 30, 2006, a former postal worker named Jennifer San Marco went to the mail processing plant in Santa Barbara where she had previously worked. There she shot and killed six workers and then committed suicide. Police later found that she had also shot and killed a neighbor before going on her rampage. "Postal Killer Acted Irrational Years before Attack," Associated Press, February 1, 2006; Randal C. Archibold, "Death Toll Climbs to 8 in California Postal Plant Rampage," *New York Times*, February 2, 2006, p. A16.

[2] The physiological effects of anger are complex and sometimes contradictory. Anger, for example, can make people feel "hot" or "cold" depending on which of two hormones, epinephrine (adrenaline) or norepinephrine, is driving the body's responses. Both hormones are secreted by our adrenal glands. Norepinephrine and adrenaline have some overlapping and some distinct effects. Norepinephrine, triggered by anger, for example constricts blood vessels, while adrenaline, triggered by fear, dilates them. The truly angry person therefore blanches, while the truly fearful person flushes. Norepinephrine produces bradycardia, which is an abnormal slowing of the heartbeat, while adrenaline produces tachycardia, which is an abnormal acceleration of the heart beat. The truly angry person therefore slows down; the truly fearful person gets jumpy. Both hormones raise systolic blood pressure, but norepinephrine also increases diastolic pressure, while adrenaline lowers it. Adrenaline causes bronchodilation: we can take in more air. Norepinephrine has no effect on respiration. Both hormones dilate the pupils, increase sweating, and reduce gut motility.

The subjective experience of feeling angry, however, doesn't necessarily correlate with the exact physiological effects of norepinephrine. This is probably because anger and fear are so often mixed up with each other and it is often easier to be conscious of and admit anger than fear.

The physiological study of anger is usually traced to G. Stanley Hall, who in 1894 examined the self-reports of 2,184 volunteers. Carol Tavris provides a helpful and duly skeptical summary of Hall's work and other physiological studies in *Anger:*

The Misunderstood Emotion (1982; New York: Simon & Schuster, 1989), pp. 70–100.

3 Kate Ledogar, "Living the Fairy Tale," *Weekly Dig,* vol. 6, no. 19 (May 12, 2004), p. 26.

4 The word "culture" has as many definitions as a plum tree has plums. In 1952, two anthropologists, Alfred Kroeber and Clyde Kluckhohn, cataloged dozens of the technical definitions in use among anthropologists and divided them into six categories (descriptive, historical, normative, psychological, structural, and genetic). Since then, matters have only gotten worse for anyone hoping for a generally agreed-on meaning for such a widely used term. My own view is that we can live with a word that lacks precision but usefully designates a broadly recognizable reality. Calling something a "rock" is also imprecise; but it distinguishes adequately between hard lumps of minerals and garden hoses, mud puddles, and daffodils. In this book, when I use the word "culture," I generally refer to the assemblage of ideas, assumptions, attitudes, and motivations that people who form some kind of community *share* in common. Culture in this sense of shared assumptions does not preclude conflict. It merely sets the frame of assumptions within which conflict occurs. In emphasizing shared assumptions, I depart from those definitions of culture that include behavior per se. Human actions in my view reflect and are informed by "culture," but they are not culture itself. The concept of culture, in my view, is maximally useful in drawing distinctions between the realm of shared assumptions and other frameworks that impinge on life within a community, such as social organization, law, the economy, and the institutional arrangements that constitute the family, education, religion, the military, and so on. Culture can and does affect these other arrangements, but it is recognizable as a distinct and separate force. The "culture of law enforcement" is not the organization of the police force or the act of enforcing laws. The word "culture," moreover, draws our attention to the larger, encompassing frameworks that overarch communities. It is more useful to speak of the "culture of the Midwest" than the culture of Muncie, Indiana; and more useful still to speak of the culture of America than the culture of the Midwest. This last point is, however, much in dispute by "multiculturalists," who emphasize divisions and differences within a broader community rather than its shared assumptions. Alfred Kroeber and Clyde Kluckhohn, *Culture: A Critical Review of Concepts and Definitions,* Papers of the Peabody Museum, vol. 47, no. 1 (Cambridge, Mass.: Harvard University Press, 1952).

5 "TO [Truthout] Interview with Howard Dean," May 22, 2003.

William Rivers Pitt interviewed Dean. The interview is posted at: http://www.truthout.org/docs_03/052203A.shtml

[6] Interview on WOAI, a San Antonio radio station, December 5, 2005. Dean said, "We ought to have a redeployment to Afghanistan of 20,000 troops. We don't have enough troops to do the job there and it's a place where we are welcome." The radio station provided a partial transcript and a full recording at: http://www.woai.com/news/local/story.aspx?content_id=C36A8 7B9-63A0-4CDE-AA91-B41571AFD3AF

[7] For example, Jan Frel, who claims to have worked on Dean's campaign in Vermont, responded to his call for 20,000 additional troops in Afghanistan by denouncing him on the leftist blog *Alternet* as an "imperial Democrat." See: http://www. alternet.org/bloggers/frel/29142/

[8] Edward Kennedy, "On Wiretapping, Bush Isn't Listening to the Constitution," *Boston Globe,* December 22, 2005, p. A19.
Jonathan Saltzman, "UMass Teacher Blasts Colleagues on Hoax Story," *Boston Globe,* December 29, 2005, p. B3.

Chapter Two: Pollyanna Meets Tar-Baby

[1] Quoted in James R. Mellow, *Nathaniel Hawthorne in His Times* (Boston: Houghton Mifflin, 1980), pp. 551–52. According to Mellow, "Hawthorne confessed that he was not one of Brown's admirers; he described the abolitionist, in fact, as a 'blood-stained fanatic.' Nor could he believe that Brown's death had 'made the Gallows as venerable as the Cross'—which was, reportedly, Emerson's view. 'Nobody was ever more justly hanged,' Hawthorne countered." Mellow also quotes Hawthorne on the topic of Brown's execution: "Any common-sensible man, looking at the matter unsentimentally, must have felt a certain intellectual satisfaction in seeing [Brown] hanged, if it were only in requital of his preposterous miscalculation of possibilities."

[2] Joel Chandler Harris, *The Complete Tales of Uncle Remus,* compiled by Richard Chase (1955; Boston: Houghton Mifflin, 1983), pp. 8–9.

[3] Dashiell Hammett, *The Maltese Falcon* (1929; San Francisco: North Point Press, 1987), p. 271.

[4] Jonathan Welsh, "Why Cars Got Angry," *Wall Street Journal,* March 10, 2006, p. W1.

[5] The speech was widely reported, but for a comment on Senator Clinton's phrase "you know what I'm talkin' about" see Mark Goldblatt, "You Go Girl! A Missing Consonant and the Race Card," *National Review Online,* January 27, 2006.

[6] Christopher Lasch, *The Culture of Narcissism: American Life in the Age of Diminished Expectations* (New York: Norton, 1978).

[7] Norah Burch, "Rant and Rage. Harvard Fired Me after Reading My Online Diary; I Didn't Really Want to Bomb the Campus, But There's a Reason I Wrote That in My Blog," *Boston Globe*, June 27, 2004, Magazine, p. 7.

[8] Burch quotes herself as having written the words "I'm two nasty e-mails...," but the *Harvard Crimson* quoted her blog with a slightly different phrasing:

> "Work is aggravating me," she wrote in an April 28 entry on the publicly accessible journal, the contents of which have since been taken offline. "I am one shade lighter than homicidal today. I am two snotty e-mails from professors away from bombing the entire Harvard campus."

Leon Neyfakh, "Online Weblog Leads to Firing," *Harvard Crimson*, May 26, 2004.

I am not sure what to make of Burch's gentle suppression of the phrase, "I am one shade lighter than homicidal today," or why she apparently shifted "snotty" to "nasty" in her retelling of the incident.

[9] Mark W. Davis, "Shoot to Sell: Knopf's Tangos with Presidential Assassination," *National Review Online*, July 15, 2004, http://www.nationalreview.com/comment/davis200407150818.asp

[10] Carol Zisowitz Stearns and Peter N. Stearns, *Anger: The Struggle for Emotional Control in America's History* (Chicago: University of Chicago Press, 1986).

[11] Ibid. On the periodization of American anger, pp. 10–11, 36–109, 241; on the etymology of the word "tantrum," p. 29.

[12] Ibid., p. 238.

[13] Ibid., p. 9.

[14] Ibid., p. 11.

[15] Ibid., p. 239.

[16] Quotation from ibid., p. 202. The Rubin quotation is originally from the *Ladies' Home Journal*, November 1975, p. 32; the Popenoe quotation is also from the *Ladies' Home Journal*, June 1975, p. 18. The Stearnses claim that such permissiveness failed to shake the older consensus that anger is dangerous and best kept in check.

[17] Harriet Lerner, *The Dance of Anger: A Woman's Guide to Changing Patterns of Intimate Relationships* (1985; New York: HarperCollins, 1997).

Reneau Z. Peurifoy, *Anger: Taming the Beast* (New York: Kodansha International, 1999).

Redford Williams, *Anger Kills* (1993; New York: HarperCollins, 1994).

Suzette Elgin, *You Can't Say That to Me: Stopping the Pain of Verbal Abuse* (New York: John Wiley & Sons, 1995).

18 Theodore Rubin, *The Angry Book* (New York: Simon & Schuster, 1998).

Stephen Diamond, *Anger, Madness, and the Daimonic: The Psychological Genesis of Violence, Evil, and Creativity* (Albany: State University of New York Press, 1999).

Neil Nehring, *Popular Music, Gender, and Postmodernism: Anger Is Energy* (Thousand Oaks, California: Sage Publications, 1997).

Neil Clark Warren, *Make Anger Your Ally* (Wheaton, Illinois: Tyndale House Publishers, 1990).

19 Daniel Goleman, *Emotional Intelligence: Why It Can Matter More Than IQ* (1995; New York: Bantam Books, 1997.) pp. 56–65.

20 Tom Lutz, *Crying: The Natural and Cultural History of Tears* (New York: W. W. Norton & Company, 1999), p. 300.

21 Sian Griffiths and Jennifer Wallace, eds., *Consuming Passions: Food in the Age of Anxiety* (Manchester, U.K.: Manchester University Press, 1998).

Sari Locker, *Mindblowing Sex in the Real World: Hot Tips for Doing It in the Age of Anxiety* (New York: HarperPerennial Library, 1995).

David Anderegg, *Worried All the Time: Rediscovering the Joy of Parenthood in an Age of Anxiety* (New York: Free Press, 2004).

22 Carol Tavris, *Anger: The Misunderstood Emotion* (1982; New York: Touchstone Books, 1982), p. 108.

23 Philip Rieff, *The Triumph of the Therapeutic* (New York: Harper & Row, 1966).

24 Bernard Weinraub, "Amid Protests, Elia Kazan Receives His Oscar," *New York Times,* March 22, 1999, p. E3.

Michelle Caruso, "Kazan Draws Applause, Protest for Special Honor," *New York Daily News,* March 22, 1999, p. 4.

Jerry Schwartz, "Kazan Honor Stirs Firestorm in Film World," *Atlanta Journal and Constitution,* March 22, 1999, p. 1C.

Benedict Nightingale, "Legacy of a Hollywood Witchhunt," *The Times* (London), March 4, 1999.

25 Thomas Oliphant, "Honoring a Dishonorable Man," *Boston Globe,* March 2, 1999, p. A15.

David Aaronovitch, "An Oscar That Reminds Us of a Cowardly, Shameful Little Episode," *Independent* (London), March 23, 1999, p. 3.

Chapter Three: Self-Government

1 "Wasp Attack Spreads German Traffic Jam," Reuters, August 17, 2004.

2 Lizette Alvarez, "A Word to Finns: 'For Your Own Good, Blow Your Top,'" *New York Times,* March 11, 2004, p. A4.

3 David Edelstein, "Marlon Brando: The Largest Actor of Them All," obituary, *Slate,* http://www.slate.com, July 2, 2004.

4 See, for example, Maruška Svašek, "Introduction: Emotions in Anthropology," in *Mixed Emotions: Anthropological Studies of Feeling,* ed. Kay Milton and Maruška Svašek (New York: Berg, 2005), p. 6.

5 A *trait* is a longstanding component of an individual's personality, e.g. "Tulip is a generally angry person." A *state* refers to the short-term experience of an actual emotion, e.g. "Tulip was furious when Land's End delivered the wrong color sweater."

For accounts of emotions as traits, see:

Carroll E. Izard and Brian P. Ackerman, "Motivational, Organizational, and Regulatory Functions of Discrete Emotions," in *Handbook of Emotions,* ed. Michael Lewis and Jeannette M. Haviland-Jones, 2nd ed. (New York: Guilford Press, 2000), pp. 253–64.

Carroll E. Izard, *The Psychology of Emotions* (New York: Plenum Press, 1991).

Jeannette M. Haviland-Jones and Patricia Kahlbaugh, "Emotion and Identity," in *Handbook of Emotions,* ed. Lewis and Haviland-Jones, pp. 293–305.

For an account of emotions as states, see:

Michael Lewis, "The Emergence of Human Emotions," in *Handbook of Emotions,* ed. Lewis and Haviland-Jones, pp. 265–80.

The trait/state distinction, however, doesn't seem to offer a very useful way to decipher New Anger, which involves both well-developed psychological dispositions *and* transitory episodes of extreme excitement, and is thus both *trait* and *state.* Moreover, New Anger involves a third quality, which is neither *trait* nor *state,* but a repertoire of symbols, acts, clichés, gestures, words, and expressions that together constitute an external world—the angri-culture—which individuals, regardless of their personalities or their momentary feelings, must negotiate.

Psychologists who specialize in the study of emotion will find that in this book I have bypassed most of the current theoretical controversies in the field about the nature of emotion. My analysis of New Anger in America is closer in spirit to the anthropological study of emotion; see e.g. C. Lutz and G. M. White, "The Anthropology of Emotions," *Annual Review of Anthropology,* vol. 15 (1986), pp. 405–36; but here too I have attempted to steer clear of academic debates and technical issues.

6 Melville's source for Moredock's life was James Hall, *Sketches of*

History, Life, and Manners in the West (1835). Hall complained that Moredock was omitted from a recently published account of the early history of Illinois, and it is Hall's vindication of Moredock that Melville puts in the mouth of a callow flimflam man.

[7] Sherman Alexie, *Indian Killer* (1996; New York: Warner Books, 1998), pp. 419–20.

[8] See, for example, Marsha Stewart and H. Khalif Khaliah, *O. J. Simpson's Double Jeopardy: Revenge Lynching* (Hampton, Va.: U.B. & U.S. Communications Systems, 1997).

[9] X. J. Kennedy, ed., *Tygers of Wrath: Poems of Hate, Anger, and Invective* (Athens, Georgia: University of Georgia Press, 1981).

[10] Kenneth Baker, ed., *I Have No Gun but I Can Spit: An Anthology of Satirical and Abusive Verse* (Boston: Faber & Faber, 1991).
William Cole, *I'm Mad at You: Verses* (E. Rutherford, New Jersey: Price Stern Sloan Publishers, 1978).
Jacqueline Sweeney, *Poems about Anger by American Children* (New York: Benchmark Press, 2002).

[11] Not that the ancient Greeks were immune to the temptations of histrionic anger. The poems of the early Greek poet Semonides of Amorgos provide an example of anger raptly enjoying itself.

[12] Richard Brookhiser, *Founding Father: Rediscovering George Washington* (New York: Simon & Schuster, 1996), p. 116.
Richard Norton Smith, "The Surprising George Washington," *Prologue Magazine,* U.S. National Archives and Records Administration, vol. 26, no. 1 (Spring 1994).

[13] Brookhiser, *Founding Father,* pp. 115–17.

[14] David Hackett Fischer, *Washington's Crossing* (New York: Oxford University Press, 2004), pp. 232–33.

[15] Peter Sanders, "Anger Management," *Daily Breeze* (Torrance, California), February 29, 2004.

[16] Ibid.; Anna Gorman, "Treating Anger for Profit," *Los Angeles Times,* October 12, 2001, p. B1.

Chapter Four: Wackadoo Politics
[1] Theodoric, "Heroic Bee Stops Man from Singing Crappy Song," http://www.mrcranky.com/movies/dirtyprettythings/138.html
Associated Press, "Bee Causes Man to Crash Car," *Ottawa Citizen,* September 19, 2003, p. A14.

[2] Alan Wolfe, "The New Pamphleteers," *New York Times Book Review,* July 11, 2004, p. 12.

[3] Curtis Brown, letter to the editor, *Boston Globe,* July 27, 2004, p. A14.

4 Jeanne Stapleton, letter to the editor, *Boston Globe,* July 23, 2004, p. A20.

5 Gary S. Lightfall, letter to the editor, *Rocky Mountain News,* July 20, 2004, p. A32.

6 H. L. Mencken, diary entry, April 15, 1945, quoted in *The Assassin's Cloak: An Anthology of the World's Greatest Diarists,* ed. Irene and Alan Taylor (Edinburgh: Canongate Books, 2000), pp. 195–96.

7 William Safire, "Of Wrongs and Rights," *New York Times,* January 14, 2004, p. 7.

8 Sandy Grady, "As Our Founding Fathers Spin in Their Graves," *Milwaukee Journal Sentinel,* January 17, 1997.

9 David Tell, "The Lincoln Bedroom Caper," *Weekly Standard,* March 10, 1997, p. 11.

10 Mary McGrory, "Comic-in-Chief," *Washington Post,* May 4, 1997, p. C1.

11 Mary McGrory, "It Didn't Happen, But Clinton's Sorry," *St. Louis Post-Dispatch,* June 6, 1977, p. C13.

12 Sandy Grady, "Grubby White House Glad-Handing," *Buffalo News,* October 21, 1997, p. B3.

13 Robert H. Bork, "Should He Be Impeached?" *American Spectator,* December 1997.

14 William Kristol, "Clinton's Fate," *Weekly Standard,* May 4, 1988, p. 22.

15 Joe Fitzgerald, "The Starr Report," *Boston Herald,* September 12, 1998, p. 9.

16 George Will, "Sorry Only for Getting Caught," *Chicago Sun-Times,* September 19, 1998, p. 19.

17 David Tell, "A Crooked President," *Weekly Standard,* November 9, 1998, p. 7.

18 A. M. Rosenthal, "On Cleansing America," *New York Times,* December 11, 1998, p. A35.

19 David Tell, "Impeach—Now More Than Ever," *Weekly Standard,* December 14, 1998, p. 7.

20 Jeff Jacoby, "Rape? Sounds Like Our Bill," *Boston Globe,* March 1, 1999.

21 Andrew Sullivan, "Outsiders Could Yet Be President," *Sunday Times* (London), November 21, 1999.

22 Tim Wise, "Working for the Man Every Night and Day," *LiP Magazine,* July 22, 2004, http://www.alternet.org/story/19294. Tim Wise is "race and ethnicity editor" for *LiP Magazine,* which further identifies him as "among the most prominent antiracist writers and activists in the US, and has been called the 'foremost white antiracist intellectual in the nation.'"

23 Terry Collins, "NAACP's Bond Urges Macalester Audience to Be Involved," *Minneapolis Star Tribune,* March 13, 2001, p. A6.
Gordon Russell, "Convention Opens with Blast on Bush," *New Orleans Times-Picayune,* July 9, 2001, p. 1
Jeff Jacoby, "Smears, Slanders from the Left," *Boston Globe,* December 23, 2001, p. D7.

24 David L. Greene and Michael Dresser, "Bush: Ties with NAACP Leaders 'Nonexistent,'" *Newsday,* July 11, 2004.
Kelly Brewington, "NAACP Leader Castigates Bush; President Faulted on Iraq, Civil Rights, 2000 Election," *Baltimore Sun,* July 12, 2004.

25 Rod Paige, "Naked Partisans," *Wall Street Journal,* July 15, 2004, p. A10.

26 John McWhorter, "NAACP Hasn't Advanced Anything in a Long Time," *Los Angeles Times,* July 15, 2004, p. B13.

27 Brian C. Anderson, "Illiberal Liberalism," *City Journal,* Spring 2001, pp. 42–53.

28 Gore's speech to the NAACP in July 1998 was widely reported but the full text of it was not. For his comparison of opponents of affirmative action to the racist killers in Virginia see Jeff Jacoby, "Poisonous Rhetoric from a Would-Be President," *Boston Globe,* July 23, 1998, p. A19.

29 Ramesh Ponnuru, "The Case against Bush Hatred," *New Republic,* September 29, 2003, pp. 24–26.

30 Leon Festinger, Henry Reicken, and Stanley Schachter, *When Prophecy Fails: A Social and Psychological Study of a Modern Group That Predicted the Destruction of the World* (New York: Harper & Row, 1956).

31 Bill Lambrecht, "Clinton Using Foes' Attacks to Solidify Role," *St. Louis Post-Dispatch,* March 13, 1992, p. A1.

32 Robert L. Bartley, "Angry Democrats: Lost Birthright," *Wall Street Journal,* September 22, 2003, p. A19.

33 Charles Krauthammer, "We're Experiencing a Serious Outbreak of Bush Derangement Syndrome," *Pittsburgh Post-Gazette,* December 6, 2003, p. A14.

34 John Dickerson, Karen Tumulty, and James Poniewozik, "The Love Him, Hate Him President," *Time,* December 1, 2003, p. 28.

35 Geoffrey Nunberg, "Anger Management: Using the Other Guy's Vitriol to Win Votes," *New York Times,* December 28, 2003, Week in Review, p. 6.

36 Mark Simon, "Anti-Bush Ad Contest Proves Popular Online," *San Francisco Chronicle,* January 13, 2004, p. A1.

37 "Voter Anger Alone Can't Capture the White House," *USA Today,* March 3, 2004, p. A12.

[38] Stephen Miller, "Anger Mismanagement," *Wall Street Journal,* March 19, 2004, p. W13.

[39] "Rage Is All the Rage," *Los Angeles Times,* May 2, 2004, p. 4.

[40] James Taranto, "Guilty Gore Goes Gaga," *OpinionJournal (Wall Street Journal),* May 27, 2004, www.opionionjournal.com/best/?id=110005134
Maureen Dowd, "Marquis de Bush?" *New York Times,* May 27, 2004.

[41] Quoted by Dowd but also reported by Conor O'Cleary, "Gore Demands Resignations over Iraq," *Irish Times,* May 27, 2004, p. 15; and the subject of an editorial, Shadow Boxing: Gore Embarresses Kerry Advisors, but Kerry Turns Off Democrats," *Pittsburgh Post-Gazette,* May 28, 2004, p. A17.

[42] John Tierney, "A Nation Divided? Who Says?" *New York Times,* June 13, 2004, p. A1.

[43] James Q. Wilson, "How Divided Are We?" *Commentary,* February 2006, pp. 15–21.

[44] Alan Wolfe, "She Just Doesn't Understand," *New Republic,* December 12, 1994.

[45] Alan Wolfe, "Idiot Time," *New Republic,* July 8 & 15, 2002.

[46] James Taranto of the *Wall Street Journal's OpinionJournal,* July 2, 2004, noticed this example of an advocate of civility turning, in quick succession, to surliness:

> "The combination of attack campaigns and media sensationalism has debased American politics and destroyed all traces of civility in public life.... Editorial writers and columnists may decry the decline of civility. Yet they rarely ask if their own behavior has contributed to and shaped the vicious partisanship that afflicts American life." (Andrew Greeley, "Sensationalism Destroys Civility," *Chicago Sun-Times,* July 2, 2004.)

> "[President Bush] is not another Hitler. Yet there is a certain parallelism. They have in common a demagogic appeal to the worst side of a country's heritage in a crisis. Bush is doubtless sincere in his vision of what is best for America. So too was Hitler." (Andrew Greeley, "Is U.S. Like Germany of the '30s?" *Chicago Sun-Times,* June 11, 2004.)

> The newspaper columnist William Raspberry likewise traces this particular dramatic arc. In 1999, inveighing against those who temporized with violent demonstrators at the protests against the World Trade Organization in Seattle, Raspberry counseled against being "understanding" toward those who push protest past ethical bounds:

> "Because understanding unacceptable behavior encour-

ages unacceptable behavior, and the result is the destruction
of civility, trust and even conversation that could help
build community and help us solve our problems....

"Well, what's the harm in a little rhetorical overkill?...

"Said [Robert] Theobald, outrageous rhetoric can pave the
way for outrageous behavior and make it seem not so outrageous after all."

William Raspberry, "Extremism: Don't 'Understand,'" *Denver Post,* December 3, 1999, p. B11.

The importance of civility is a key theme in Raspberry's writings: "But courtesy and civility ought to apply in all aspects of
our lives." (William Raspberry, "What Happened to 'Free Exercise?'" *Denver Post,* September 7, 2000, p. B11.) But somehow,
when it came to the applause he heard for Michael Moore's anti-
Bush propaganda film, *Fahrenheit 9/11,* Raspberry discovered in
himself an unexpected readiness to "understand" extremism
and dispense with civility:

"They applauded, I suspect, for much the same reason so
many members of the black Christian middle-class applaud
the harangues of Black Muslim minister Louis Farrakhan.
Some of his facts may be wrong and some of his connections
strained, but his *attitude* is right. What's more, he'll say in
plain language what nice, educated people cannot bring themselves to say: *The man is a devil.*"

William Raspberry, "Fiery Hatchet Job," *Washington Post,* June
28, 2004. I am grateful to Mr. Taranto for pointing out this
example, too.

47 Michael Novak, "Hatred or Hope?" *National Review Online,* July
23, 2004.

48 William J. Bennett, "The Fire This Time," *National Review Online,*
July 23, 2004.

49 Jeff Jacoby, "Bush-Haters Do Kerry No Favors," *Boston Globe,* July
25, 2004, p. E11.

50 Curtis Brown, letter to the editor, *Boston Globe,* July 27, 2004,
p. A14.

51 Gary Alan Fine, "Ire to the Chief," *Washington Post,* August 6,
2004, p. A19.

52 E. J. Dionne, *Stand Up Fight Back: Republican Toughs, Democratic
Wimps, and the Politics of Revenge* (New York: Simon & Schuster,
2004), p. 104.

53 "So Democrats Really Are Smarter," *Economist,* May 15, 2004,
p. 26, http://www.vdare.com/sailer/brown_debate.htm; http://
www.isteve.com/Web_Exclusives_Archive-May2004.
htm#38115.6465670139

54 Clif Garboden, "Screw You, America: Sometimes the Fish in the Barrel Deserve to Die," ALTWeeklies.com, November 17, 2004, http://www.indyweek.com/durham/current/mews/html

55 Byron York, *The Vast Left Wing Conspiracy: The Untold Story of How Democratic Operatives, Eccentric Billionaires, Liberal Activists, and Assorted Celebrities Tried to Bring Down a President—and Why They'll Try Harder Next Time* (New York: Crown Forum, 2005). Jacob Laksin, "Look Back at Anger," *OpinionJournal* (*Wall Street Journal*), April 5, 2005, http://www.opinionjournal.com/la/ ?id=110006516

56 Cathy Young, "Poisoned Politics," Boston.com, December 26, 2005.

57 "Bush Bashing Part of Berkeley Holiday Spirit," Yahoo.com, December 24, 2005.

58 Dahlia Lithwick, "Please Don't Feed the Federalists," *Slate,* January 13, 2006, http://www.slate.com/id/2134287/

Chapter Five: Anger Music

1 William Zinsser, *Easy to Remember: The Great American Songwriters and Their Songs* (Jaffrey, New Hampshire: David R. Godine, Publisher, 2000), pp. 145–48. Robert Gottlieb and Robert Kimball, eds., *Reading Lyrics* (New York: Pantheon Books, 2000).

2 "Wu-Tang Slang": http://zeeh.fpn.hu/_dwad_/frameset.php? path=http://zeeh.fpn.hu/zeeh/slang.html, which in turn credits WuTangWorld.com. The term "Cuban Linx" refers not to an exotic feline but to a type of gold chain that Raekwon is seen wearing on the cover of an album.

3 The transcription of the last line follows the rendering of my informant "Methuselah." The lyrics to "C.R.E.A.M." have not been published by the Wu-Tang Clan, and the most popular transcription on the Web renders the line, "Ch-chick-POW! Move from the fate now." Methuselah suggests that the Tec-9 is here serving as a starting gun for a horse race, with the Wu-Tang Clan on their debut album bursting forth.

4 "Methuselah," personal communication, July 23, 2004.

5 I've culled this list from "The Rapper Deathstyle," Way of Life Literature, Port Huron, Michigan, July 15, 2004, http://www.wayoflife.org/fbns/rapper-deathstyle.html+Rapper+Deathstyle+Baptist&hl=en

6 All Dylan lyrics quoted from *Bob Dylan: Lyrics, 1962–1985* (New York: Alfred A. Knopf, 1990).

7 Amazon.com editorial review, copyright 1994, Reed Business Information, Inc.

 8 Bart Niedzialkowski, Punkrockreviews.com, posted August 23, 2003.

 9 DragStrip Riot Band page, www.soundclick.com/bands/page-music.cfm?bandID=20867

10 "Jimi Hendrix," www.classicbands.com/Hendrix.html

11 Michael Campbell and James Brody, *Rock and Roll: An Introduction* (Belmont, California: Wadsworth Group, 1999), pp. 216–19.

12 Jim Fusilli, "That's Good Enough for Me: Cookie Monsters of Death-Metal Music," *OpinionJournal (Wall Street Journal)*, www.opinionjournal.com, February 1, 2006.

13 Anonymous, "Grunge," http://puggy.symonds.net/~prahladv/grunge.php

14 Jamie Allen, "Smells Like Teen Spirit," www.Salon.com, April 15, 2002.

15 The others in the top ten were: (1) Phil Ochs, "I Ain't Marchin' Anymore"; (2) The Beatles, "Taxman"; (3) Pat Benetar, "Invincible"; (4) The Who, "Won't Get Fooled Again"; (5) Barry McGuire, "Eve of Destruction"; (6) Pete Seeger, "Waist Deep in the Big Muddy"; (7) Suzanne Vega, "Widow's Walk"; (10) Public Enemy, "Black Steel/Hour of Chaos." The list was created on July 26, 2002, and had accumulated 507 votes by August 7, 2004. http://www.wanderlist.com/angrysongs. The list is puzzling. Some of these songs do not express much anger or offer anything more than superficial comment on it, but 507 people seem to think otherwise.

16 Stanley Kurtz, "Love Your Country," *National Review*, October 14, 2002.

17 Steve Morse, "He's Not Afraid to Speak Out for His County," *Boston Globe*, July 23, 2004, p. C1.

18 Stanley Kurtz, "Those 9/11 Songs," *National Review Online*, August 27, 2002.

19 Kevin M. Cherry, "Taking Springsteen Seriously," *National Review Online*, July 30, 2003.

20 Jeff Leeds, "Rock Stars Announce a Swing-State Tour," *New York Times*, August 5, 2004, p. A17.

21 Bruce Springsteen, "Chords for Change," *New York Times*, August 5, 2004, p. A23.

22 Betty Clarke, "The Dixie Chicks," *Guardian*, March 12, 2003, p. 28.

23 Paul Krugman, "Channels of Influence," *New York Times*, March 25, 2003, p. 17.

24 Jim Patterson, "Montgomery-Gentry Revives Outlaw Country Music," Associated Press, May 13, 1999.

Chapter Six: In the Bee Hive

1. Coco Henson Scales, "The Hostess Diaries: My Year at a Hot Spot," *New York Times,* July 11, 2004, Sec. 9, pp. 1, 6, 7.

2. Marcela Sanchez, "The Angry American," *Washington Post,* August 7, 2004, p. A21.

3. Grace Gredys Harris, *Casting out Anger: Religion among the Taita of Kenya* (New York: Cambridge University Press, 1978), pp. 25–26.

4. Fred R. Myers, "The Logic and Meaning of Anger among Pintupi Aborigines," *Man,* n.s., vol. 23, no. 4 (December 1988), pp. 589–610.

5. The comparative study of emotions in different cultures has precedents in anthropology going back to the nineteenth century, but the field has grown substantially since the 1970s. See C. Lutz and G. White, "The Anthropology of Emotions," *Annual Review of Anthropology,* vol. 15 (1986), pp. 405–36. The "universality" of emotions, including anger, is widely accepted by contemporary anthropologists who, however, dispute the degree to which the experience of emotional states is shaped by culture. Anthropologists are also divided on whether emotions are better viewed as internal states or as attributions that people make about each other's behavior. And, within anthropology, there are some sharp differences of opinion over whether to give primary emphasis to the biological side of emotions, such as hormones; the cultural definitions of anger; or the social rules that govern the expression of anger. I have sidestepped these debates to focus in this book on an ethnographic account of New Anger in America, but it should be clear that I regard emotions like anger as multidimensional. This book, however, focuses on the *cultural* transformation of the United States as we went from one way of regarding anger to another.

6. Carol Zisowitz Stearns and Peter N. Stearns' book, *Anger: The Struggle for Emotional Control in America's History* (Chicago: The University of Chicago Press, 1986), discussed in Chapter Two, provides a detailed account of these efforts.

7. Deborah Cox, Karin H. Bruckner, and Sally Stabb, *The Anger Advantage: The Surprising Benefits of Anger and How It Can Change a Woman's Life* (New York: Broadway Books, 2003), pp. 1, 5, 76–77, 280–81.

8. Neil Clark Warren, *Make Anger Your Ally,* 3rd ed. (Wheaton, Illinois: Tyndale House Publishers, 1990), p. 6.

9. Harriet Lerner, *The Dance of Anger: A Woman's Guide to Changing the Patterns of Intimate Relationships* (New York: HarperCollins, 1997), pp. 90, 102.

10. Francesca M. Cancian and Steven L. Gordon, "Changing Emo-

tion Norms in Marriage: Love and Anger in U.S. Women's Magazines since 1900," *Gender and Society,* vol. 2, no. 3 (September 1988), pp. 308–42. The chart is based on data in Table 1, p. 326.

[11] Clarissa Pinkola Estés, *Women Who Run with the Wolves: Myths and Stories of the Wild Woman Archetype* (New York: Ballantine Books, 1992), pp. 3, 346–50, 368–73.

[12] Cathi Hanauer, ed., *The Bitch in the House* (New York: William Morrow, 2002), pp. xi, xiv, xvi, 3–13, 23–44.

[13] Renee Graham, "Northampton Lesbian Festival," *Boston Globe,* July 14, 1995, p. 31.

[14] Pete Brady, "Grrrl Power," *Cannabis Culture,* November 1, 1999, http://www.cannabisculture.com/articles/76.html

[15] John Seabrook, "Odes to Spring: A Portfolio of the Season's Trends," *New Yorker,* March 19, 2001, p. 110.

[16] Cherie Turner, *Everything You Need to Know about the Riot Grrrl Movement: The Feminism of a New Generation* (New York: Rosen Publishing Group, 2001).

[17] Robin Morgan, "Letter to a Sister Underground," in *Sisterhood Is Powerful: An Anthology of Writings from the Women's Liberation Movement,* ed. Morgan (New York: Vintage, 1970).

[18] Joyce Brothers, "When Your Husband's Affection Cools," *Good Housekeeping,* May 1972.

[19] Marilyn French, *The Women's Room* (New York: Summit Books, 1977), ch. 14.

[20] "Pet Abuser Ordered to Take Class on Anger," *New York Times,* June 13, 2004, p. 28.

[21] Willard Gaylin, *The Rage Within: Anger in Modern Life,* 2nd ed. (1984; New York: Penguin Books, 1989), pp. 25, 190, 166, viii, xv, xiv, 138.

[22] John Ferling, *Adams vs. Jefferson: The Tumultuous Election of 1800* (New York: Oxford University Press, 2004), p. 106.

[23] Alan Bullock and Stephen Trombley, eds., *The Harper Dictionary of Modern Thought,* rev. ed. (New York: Harper & Row, 1988).

[24] Caroline Knapp, "Grace Notes: An Ode to Best Friends," *The Merry Recluse: A Life in Essays* (New York: Counterpoint, 2004), p. 41. (First published in *Siren Magazine,* 2000.)

[25] Garret Keizer, *The Enigma of Anger: Essays on a Sometimes Deadly Sin* (San Francisco: Jossey-Bass, 2002), pp. 50–51, 64, 71–74, 78, 99–100, 340, 346–47.

Chapter Seven: Self-Storage

[1] "Rock-Throwing Kids Anger 120,000 Bees," Reuters, CNN.com, August 16, 2004.

[2] Wolfgang Mieder, Stewart A. Kingsbury, and Kelsie B. Harder, *A*

Dictionary of American Proverbs (New York: Oxford University Press, 1992).

3   Stuart Berg Flexner, *I Hear America Talking* (New York: Simon & Schuster, 1976), p. 239.
    Stuart Berg Flexner, *Listening to America* (New York: Simon & Schuster, 1982), pp. 359–62.
    J. E. Lighter, *Random House Dictionary of American Slang,* 2 vols. (New York: Random House, 1994, 1997).

4   Herman Melville, *The Collected Poems of Herman Melville* (Chicago: Packard & Company, 1947), p. 80.

5   Marianne Moore, *The Poems of Marianne Moore,* ed. Grace Schulman (New York: Viking, 2004), p. 251.

6   Bryan F. Le Beau, *The Atheist: Madalyn Murray O'Hair* (New York: University Press, 2003), pp. 37–44, 255–56.

7   Louis Bolce and Gerald De Maio, "Our Secularist Democratic Party," *Public Interest,* no. 149 (Fall 2002).

8   John Leo, "Talk about Getting Religion!" *U.S. News & World Report,* August 9, 2004, p. 59.

9   They borrow this term from James Davison Hunter, who used it in his *Culture Wars: The Struggle to Define America* (New York: Basic Books, 1991).

10 Dwaipayan Banerjee, "Allen Ginsberg's *Howl:* Genius or Incoherence," http://www.literatureclassics.com/essays/989

11 Testimony of Timothy Leary on December 19, 1969, at the Chicago Seven trial (September 24, 1969–February 18, 1970). Transcript at: http://www.law.umkc.edu/faculty/projects/FTrials/Chicago7/Leary.html

12 Robert Anton Wilson, *Cosmic Trigger: The Final Secret of the Illuminati, Tunnel-Realities and Imprints* (1977; Tempe, Arizona: New Falcon Publications, 2002). Wilson's book has been reprinted seventeen times. These excerpts are from a December 28, 2005 website posting at http://lightandlife.wordpress.com/2005/12/28/the-eight-systems-of-consciousness/

13 Joseph Berger, "A Teacher of Legends Becomes One Himself," *New York Times,* December 10, 1988, p. 29.
    Joseph W. McPherson, "Fostering the Noble Life," *Washington Post,* November 1, 1992, p. R26.
    Michael S. Spurek, Letter to the Editor, *San Francisco Chronicle,* March 4, 1992, p. A14.
    Nancy Kilpatrick, "Joseph Campbell: The Man Behind the Myths," *Toronto Star,* December 28, 1991, p. W1.
    Richard Bernstein, "After Death, a Writer Is Accused of Anti-Semitism," *New York Times,* November 6, 1989, p. C17.

Walter Goodman, "Robert Bly Tells Moyers What's Wrong with Men," *New York Times,* January 10, 1990, p. C20.

[14] Richard Howard, *Alone with America,* enlarged ed. (New York: Atheneum, 1980), p. 180.

[15] Morris Janowitz, *The Last Half-Century: Societal Change and Politics in America* (Chicago: University of Chicago Press, 1978), p. 409.

[16] Self Storage Association webpage, http://www.selfstorage.org/newsite/about.cfm#who

[17] "Storing the Self," broadcast on the radio program *The Connection,* on WBUR, Boston, December 29, 2003; archived at: http://www.theconnection.org/shows/2003/12/20031229_a_main.asp

[18] Rob D'Amico, "What's in Store," *Austin Chronicle,* September 1, 2000.

[19] Mihaly Csikszentmihalyi and Eugene Rochberg-Halton, *The Meaning of Things: Domestic Symbols and the Self* (New York: Cambridge University Press, 1981).

[20] http://www.storageauctions.com/3.htm

[21] See, for example, Clare Cooper Marcus, *House As a Mirror of Self: Exploring the Deeper Meaning of Home* (Berkeley: Conari Press, 1995). Marcus writes as a Jungian and takes the metaphor of house for self as emotionally natural. She also notes the degree to which objects as well as places become invested with personal meaning. "Objects, like people, come in and out of our lives and awareness, not in some random, meaningless pattern ordained by Fate, but in a clearly patterned framework that sets the stage for greater and greater self-understanding" (p. 11). In my view, Marcus goes slightly astray in two ways. The heap of objects that reflect individual experience by no means necessarily leads to "greater and greater self-understanding." It can and often does lead to a more fractured and dis-integrated self: a collection of parts that fails to add up to a whole. Marcus also takes the equation of "house" and "self" as straightforward, but the house in many societies and probably in much of American history is better understood as an image of the family than of the "self." The house is also rich in other metaphoric possibilities. The eighteenth-century Iroquois conceived their tribal confederation in the image of a giant longhouse that stretched from Lake Erie to the Adirondacks. Houses—teepees—among the nineteenth-century Plains Indians were apt symbols of social groups that consisted of frequently shifting alliances. The American habit of thinking of a house as an expression of the owner's

inner world reflects a cultural preference for interpreting objects through the lens of individuality, rather than group affiliation.

22 Antonio Regalado, "A Cold Calculus Leads Cryonauts to Put Assets on Ice," *Wall Street Journal,* January 21, 2006, p. 1.

23 Mary Eberstadt, "Eminem Is Right," *Policy Review,* no. 128 (December 2004–Janaury 2005). See also: Mary Eberstadt, *Home Alone America* (New York: Sentinel Books, 2004).

24 Kate Spicer, "Shocking Pink," *Observer Magazine,* November 9, 2003, p. 36.

25 Jim Farber, "An Aggressive Streak of Pink," *New York Daily News,* November 9, 2003, p. 14.
Robert Webb, "Story of the Song, *Family Portrait,"* Independent (London), August 22, 2003, p. 15.

26 William Shaw, "Why Are America's Rock Bands So Goddamned Angry?" *Blender,* August 2002.

27 Robin Murray-O'Hair was the daughter of Madalyn's oldest son, William. Over William's objections, Madalyn adopted Robin as a "daughter" in 1974. News accounts often refer to her inter-changeably as Madalyn's daughter or granddaughter. Both terms are accurate.

Chapter Eight: Cooling Off

1 Larry Platt, "John McEnroe," www.Salon.com, July 11, 2000.

2 Quoted in Howard Kurtz, "After Bode Miller's Downhill Turn, Two Weeks on the Lift," *Washington Post,* January 23, 2006, p. C1.

3 Devin Gordon, "You Don't Know Bode," *Newsweek,* January 23, 2006, p. 40.

4 Tony Chamberlain, "Remarks Have Created Uphill Climb," *Boston Globe,* January 12, 2006, p. C11.

5 Chris Dufresne, "Winter Olympics: Different Slopes," *Los Angeles Times,* January 12, 2006, p. D1.
Nathaniel Vinton, "Miller Going to School to Clarify View," *New York Times,* January 25, 2006, p. D6.

6 Aileen Jacobson, *Newsday,* August 4, 2004, p. B2.

7 John Leonard, "Smash-Mouth Criticism," *New York Times Book Review,* July 18, 2004, p. 10.

8 "Bronco Claims Raider Tried to Blind Him," *Toronto Star,* September 12, 1986, p. F9.

9 Shannen W. Coffin, "Amendment 1 1/2," *National Review Online,* July 26, 2004.

10 "US Singer Linda Ronstadt Kicked Out of Casino for Praising Michael Moore," Agence France-Presse, July 20, 2004.

[11] Alex Lee, "After All These Years, John McEnroe Still Fascinates," *Daily Utah Chronicle,* July 17, 2002.

[12] Eric Hoover, "Crying Foul over Fans' Boorish Behavior," *Chronicle of Higher Education,* April 9, 2004, pp, 1, 35–37.

[13] Bruce Tran, "Blood, Sweat and Tears Spell Sports, Not Just a Bee," *Daily Bruin Online,* June 4, 2004, www.dailybruin.ucla.edu

[14] "Show Me the Bunny," www.dailycanndy.com, April 12, 2004.

[15] Carl Bailik, "Measuring the Impact of Blogs Requires More Than Counting," *Wall Street Journal,* May 26, 2005.

[16] Christopher Conkey, "Bloggers Enter Big-Media Tent," *Wall Street Journal,* July 27, 2004, p. A6.

[17] Chris Mooney, "How Blogging Changed Journalism—Almost," *Pittsburgh Post-Gazette,* February 2, 2003, p. F1.
James Hebert, "A Penny for Your Blogs," *San Diego Union-Tribune,* February 4, 2003, p. D1.
"Technology Briefs," *Seattle Times,* March 1, 2004, p. E3.
John Fund, "Beantown Becomes Blogtown," *OpinionJournal* (*Wall Street Journal*), www.opinionjournal.com, July 26, 2004.
L. A. Lorek, "Companies Get on Blog Bandwagon," *San Antonio Express-News,* August 8, 2004, p. L1.

[18] David Rowan, "Technobabble," *The Times* (London), August 26, 2003, p. 21.
Linda Seebach, "Why Blogging Is Important to Me, You and Democracy," *Rocky Mountain News,* November 16, 2002, p. B23.

[19] Jeff Jarvis, Jane Mansher, Jay Rosen, Glenn Reynolds, and Jim Brady, "Panel: Interactivity Ethics," *Washingtonpost.com,* January 25, 2006.

[20] On December 5, 2002, at a party celebrating Senator Strom Thurman's 100th birthday, Lott praised Thurmond's 1948 run for the presidency as a Dixiecrat. Lott said, "And if the rest of the country had followed our lead, we wouldn't have had all these problems over all these years, either."

[21] "Tsk Tsk," *Dean's World,* August 20, 2004, www.deanesmay.com/posts/1093004085.shtml

[22] Robert Fisk, "My Beating by Refugees Is a Symbol of the Hatred and Fury of This Filthy War," *Independent* (London), December 10, 2001, in www.counterpunch.org

[23] Andrew Sullivan, *The Daily Dish,* December 9, 1991, http://time.blogs.com/daily_dish/archives.html. Sullivan quoted from Robert Fisk's article, "If I Was an Afghan I Too Might Have Attacked Robert Fisk," *Counterpunch,* http://www.counterpunch.org/fiskbeaten.html. Sullivan's original critique appears no longer to be available, but portions of it are quoted at

http://fiskingcentral.typepad.com/fiskingcentral_opeds/2006/04 /firstly_i_have_.html

24 Benjamin Wallace-Wells, "Kos Call," *Washington Monthly,* January/February 2006.

25 William G. Mayer, "Why Talk Radio Is Conservative," *Public Interest,* no. 156 (Summer 2004).

26 Buzz Bissinger, "Don Imus's Last Stand," *Vanity Fair,* February 2006, pp. 150–53, 180–85.

27 "Imus Anchor on Palestinians," *Media Matters,* November 19, 2004.

28 Etan Vlessing, "Imus Slurs Are 'Abusive,' Canada Watchdog Says," Reuters Canada, January 30, 2006.

29 "Imus Attacks Contessa Brewer," *TVNewser,* May 1, 2005.

30 Jose Barreiro, "Bigotshtick: Rush Limbaugh on Indians," *Native Americas,* Fall 1995.

31 Molly Ivins, "Lyin' Bully," *Mother Jones,* May/June 1995.

32 John Mitchell [published anonymously], *My Mother: or, Recollections of Maternal Influence* (New York: William H. Hyde, 1849), pp. 155–56, 162–63, 179–80, iii–iv.

33 Michael Datcher, "The Fire This Time," reprinted in *Testimony: Young African-Americans on Self-Discovery and Black Identity,* ed. Natasha Tarpley (Boston: Beacon Press, 1995), pp. 24–25.

34 Robert P. King, "Killer Bees Join List of Hazards of Florida Living," *South Florida Sun-Sentinel,* January 28, 2006.

INDEX